CHRISTIAN ASCETICISM
AND
MODERN MAN

CHRISTIAN ASCETICISM
AND
MODERN MAN

Translated by Walter Mitchell and the Carisbrooke Dominicans

LONDON
BLACKFRIARS PUBLICATIONS
1955

First published in French by Les Éditions du Cerf under the title of 'l'Ascèse Chrétienne et l'Homme Contemporain'.

First published in English in 1955.

Nihil obstat: Joannes M. T. Barton, s.t.d., l.s.s.
Censor deputatus

Imprimatur: E. Morrogh Bernard
Vic. Gen.

Westmonasterii, die 6a Aprilis 1955

PRINTED IN GREAT BRITAIN
BY THE DITCHLING PRESS LIMITED, DITCHLING, SUSSEX.

CONTENTS

FOREWORD

CHRISTIAN asceticism and the man of today: such is the theme this book proposes to Catholics, clergy and laity alike, for their mature consideration. It will, I hope, be admitted that our sole motive in raising the question has been the wish to facilitate clarification in the intellectual sphere and realism in the moral, these being now explicitly recognised as essential if asceticism is to be adjusted to fit the needs of the times. Moreover, the reader will be able to judge for himself, as he reads the following pages, what sort of result has in fact followed our attempt to conduct the enquiry objectively and to avoid barren controversy, as is advisable when the subject is one on which feeling runs so high. It is, however, only to be expected that the mere fact of discussing in public one of the most controversial points of Catholic spirituality will probably seem to some a task difficult to accomplish with any degree of competence, praiseworthy though it may be in itself, while to others it will appear useless or even dangerous.

With regard to the difficulty of the undertaking, the fact that the book is not the work of a single writer, however well qualified, but results from the united efforts of doctors, psychologists, historians and theologians ought to go some way towards reassuring those who share such fears. The book consists of the substance of papers contributed by these specialists in their various fields to a conference organised on the subject by the promoters of *La Vie Spirituelle*.

The objection to the work on grounds of utility, i.e. the objection that there is no occasion for it, would seem to deserve a more detailed reply, since at bottom it amounts to questioning the validity of the problem itself. Here in the foreword it will be enough to point out that the chief aim of the various papers is not to work out a new form of asceticism down to the last detail, but to show why the question of overhauling the accepted forms may have to come up for consideration and to indicate the proper way of stating the problem. I will confine myself, then, here, to a few preliminary observations on the line of enquiry we have tried to follow, together with the scope and method of the investigations we have undertaken in our endeavour to bring out the implications of the basic idea.

The proposal to see whether the kind of asceticism practised by our forebears and ourselves is really within the power of men today springs from the desire that the Christianity we profess should be the thing it was meant to be. This obviously cannot imply doubt about the permanent value of the elements which enter into every variety of asceticism claiming the name of Christian. In other words, those who think there has been development in this field can no more call in question the truths that faith presents them with or the conclusions of reason working on the content of revelation or on the nature of man in the concrete—i.e. of man as a sinner—than those who maintain that all is still as it was.

This absolute standpoint is essential if we are to remain loyal to our faith. Nevertheless, it has still to be seen whether the application of these truths to asceticism does not involve the possibility that some degree of adjustment may prove necessary, inasmuch as human life is subject to history and so to becoming, with all that that implies in the way of change in individual and collective behaviour. Anyone doubting this need only read the surveys here assembled of the history of spirituality in the last nineteen centuries, and he will become convinced of its truth. Within due limits, the same can be said of asceticism as is seen to be true of the various forms in which the kingdom of God has been embodied. Just as Christianity is one, while the forms of Christian polity are many, so asceticism is one and is always essential to sanctity, but in the course of history the Spirit of God has provided different forms for it to take. Asceticism was viewed in one light in the patristic period, in another in the middle ages and, *a fortiori*, in yet another during the period that began with the Renaissance. The bearing of these considerations on the legitimacy of the present undertaking is evident. Yet it must be admitted that although they point the way, they can be of no assistance in getting at the heart of the problem. For that reason, an element of risk creeps in. We hope that the contrast of views to which it will give rise will prove a fruitful one.

The difficulties raised in the book and the solutions they call for can hardly receive adequate elucidation from the ascetic experiments of the past.

The reader may set his mind at rest: he will not find in the following pages the slightest pretension to assess the merits of value of the ascetic practices of the past in so far as they have been approved by the Church. History shows that people who have used those practices with due responsibility and prudence have achieved holiness and reached a remarkably high degree of union with God. It is none the less true, however, that Christians intent on perfection are beginning to feel uneasy in their minds and to have faint doubts about the efficacy or even the wisdom of certain means of penance, both of the material and of the psychological kinds, hitherto considered as fundamental to all forms of higher asceticism.

Some, it is to be supposed, will ascribe this doubt to the deleterious effects of the naturalistic environment in which we live. Far be it from me to deny the element of truth underlying so Christian a reaction. Between the sense of what is due to God, the sense of sin and the recognition of the need for the cross there is real solidarity, both in the sphere of faith and in the realm of morals, as history proves. Yet, however much this kind of objection may be prompted by religious considerations, it does not seem to exhaust the possibilities of the situation. The testimony of spiritual directors and those whose business it is to introduce clerical students to the life of the spirit could be adduced in support of this qualification. Cases are not unknown in which conscientious practice of the old type of asceticism has not resulted in spiritual freedom but only too often has made people unbalanced—which is of no use to anyone. These repeated failures have made some thinkers— people no less submissive to the Church for being attentive to reality—wonder whether such a phenomenon does not show the need for further study of the biopsychical conditioning of the moral aspect of asceticism, inasmuch as science reveals the probability that development has taken place in that sphere.

Leaving the Church to decide matters of which she alone is competent to judge, the present book is thus an attempt not to solve the question but merely to investigate it. Since in a field like this, all progress is conditioned first and foremost by theological method, the reader will see why before setting to work we first made a thorough survey of the faith accepted in the Church and serving as the basis of Christian life.

The first part is devoted to an account of the teaching of the gospels, the apostles and the fathers. An attempt is made in the next group of papers to give a fairly detailed analysis of the various experiments in asceticism, with their several guiding principles and particular practices, and to show in what light they have been regarded and how they have been used in the great religious families or schools of spirituality, from the fathers to the twentieth century. In the last resort, there is nothing so instructive as contact with the saints and revelation when the aim is to seek light and guidance as to what to throw out now and what to introduce in the future, if some sort of adjustment comes to seem essential. It would have been profitable to extend the survey, for purpose of comparison, to non-Catholic and non-Christian forms of experiment too. The most suggestive of these—the Hindoo, with which early Christian monasticism is supposed to have had connections—will, at any rate, be found here. Two studies of the theological aspect of asceticism then close this inspection of the material provided by tradition.

The defining of the exact part to be played by the different kinds of renunciation—all of which, we are told, should have as their principle and term our supernatural end (i.e. the love of God and the love of ourselves as God wants us to be) and should conduce to the life of virtue—is the rightful province of those who specialise in that science which ought to be coextensive with wisdom.

The synthesis thus effected by reason working in the light of faith and the history of the spiritual life will be of value for two reasons. One comes from the fact that we are here presented with a statement of the proper scale of values; the other is that we are given scientific illustration of the coefficient of relativity, which helps to determine even the function of asceticism itself. The purpose of P. Chenu's suggestions, which he bases on more sociological considerations, is to give some idea of the fossilised survivals that may attend upon this relativity and also of the new perspectives it may open up, in view of the inter-dependence of man and his environment in time and space. Once the reader has gained some acquaintance with these theological principles, he will be in a position to turn to the second part and follow an analysis of the new elements in asceticism.

As an undertaking of that kind necessarily involves know-ledge of things belonging to the anthropological order, it will be readily understood that we should have called in people who analyse such things professionally. Thus, we sought help exclusively from doctors practising as psychologists and from philosophers with special qualifications in physiology or psychiatry. The novelty of the question raised and the slow rate of progress in such complex fields as the interaction of the physical and the psychic, the influence of the unconscious on the conscious and, *a fortiori*, the effect of civilisation, mean that much critical analysis and observation will be needed before anything about them can be accepted as scientific. These considerations will prepare the reader for the tentative gropings and qualified statements contained in the chapters in question. What will be found in this section is thus, first and foremost, evidence that some *attempt* has been made to find the truth. There will be no sign of any infallible knowledge, capable of solving all problems whatsoever, for in so far as scientific certitude depends upon research, it is built on successive approximations.

The basic idea which the following papers aim at elucidating is the importance of the influence exerted at all points in the spiritual life by psychosomatic reactions at various levels. The book also gives a prominent place to the theory that these reactions were not nearly so conscious or so active when civilisa-tion was predominantly rural and the tempo of life was slower, even if not necessarily healthier.

As always happens with a new enterprise, this attempt to facilitate the harmonising of the moral life with the inflexible demands of the Catholic faith leaves gaps to be filled. We hope that its imperfections will not hide the issues at stake but will stimulate other research-workers to complete what we have left undone.

CHAPTER I

ASCETICISM AND MORTIFICATION IN THE NEW TESTAMENT

THE aim of this brief essay is to set forth the teaching and, when occasion offers, the practice of the New Testament with regard to asceticism. The sort of study we are trying to make—a purely factual thing—should if possible be undertaken without any preconceived ideas about the concept of asceticism, still less about the word itself, the overtones it may set vibrating in the mind or emotions, or the philosophical or historical factors involved in it; and preconceived notions about the value of asceticism would be even more out of place. Taking the term for the moment in its broadest and most generally accepted sense, we shall try simply to consult the text of scripture and let the facts speak for themselves.[1]

The texts which will enable us to get a preliminary idea of the New Testament attitude to asceticism fall into two main divisions.

In the first place, we find St Paul frequently and insistently putting his correspondents on their guard against certain ascetic practices. He warns the Romans not to attach any

---

1 Little has been written on this subject. To mention the most easily accessible works, there are a few pages in P. POURRAT, *La spiritualité chrétienne*, Paris, 1918, i. pp. 2–8, 38–40; M. VILLER, *La spiritualité des premiers siècles chrétiens*, Paris, 1930, p. 7; J. LEBRETON, *Lumen Christi, La doctrine spirituelle du Nouveau Testament*, Paris, 1947, pp. 171–196, 'Le renoncement'; J. HUBY, *Mystiques paulinienne et johannique*, Paris, n.d., pp. 47–51. The treatment of the question in these books does not seem to be directly relevant to the problem we are trying to state here. See also: L. BOUVET, *L'ascèse dans saint Paul*, Lyons, 1936.

This chapter was written before H. VON CAMPENHAUSEN's clear and illuminating article, *Die Aszese im Urchristentum*, 44 pp., Tübingen, Mohr, 1949, came to my knowledge. His conclusions are practically the same as mine, viz. that the New Testament does not recommend any specific ascetic practice and that it rejects any dualistic or gnostic contempt or condemnation of matter or the flesh, but requires Christians to go through a stripping process, especially where poverty is concerned, in order to become as free as possible to follow Christ and bear their cross after him.

importance to the observances concerning food which some
people 'of over-delicate conscience' (Rom. 14: 1–2) were
making much of, people no doubt who had remained faithful
to the tendencies of one or other of the Jewish or pagan sects.
'The kingdom of God is not a matter of eating or drinking
this or that' (Rom. 14: 7). Charity and peace are worth more
than anything else. The apostle returns to the charge with still
greater vigour when he writes to the Colossians, in whose
case these rules about food and drink seem to have been bound
up with gnostic practices (the 'worship of angels'—Col. 2:
18). '[These prescriptions] will win you, no doubt, the name
of philosophers, for being so full of scruple, so submissive,
so unsparing of your bodies; but they are all forgotten, when ·
nature asks to be gratified.' (Col. 2: 23.)[1] He had previously
reminded the Corinthians, too, who may perhaps have gone in
for both licentious living and an unhealthy practice of exaggerated asceticism, that marriage and marital relations are
perfectly legitimate (1 Cor. 7: 3–5, 27–28, 36–38). The pastoral
epistles in turn reveal an acquaintance with the 'pretensions
of . . . teachers [who] bid them abstain from marriage, and
from certain kinds of food, although God has made these
for . . . grateful enjoyment. . . . All is good that God has
made' (1 Tim. 4: 2–4). Christian asceticism does not depend
on the speculations embodied in any cosmogony, any more
than it implies contempt for the 'flesh' or for creation, since
'all is good that God has made' (cf. Gen. 1: 4, 10, 12, etc., 31),
and God has given it to man for man's enjoyment.[2] Radical
contempt for the flesh is always more or less consciously bound
up with dualistic beliefs, whereas nothing can defeat the
fundamental optimism that Christians, like the Jews before
them, derive from their faith in creation—and one might add,
from their faith in the incarnation and the resurrection.
'Verbum *caro* factum est . . . Credo *carnis* resurrectionem.'[3]

1 'But they are all forgotten', etc. P. Benoit translates. 'In fact, they are of no
  value for taming the insolence of the flesh.' The phrase might be rendered
  just as well, perhaps, as 'They turn out to be for the satisfaction of the flesh.'
2 Cf. *Didache*, lo. 3.
3 The old monastic custom of abstaining from 'flesh' and the Church's prescriptions perpetuating the memory of this among us are thus the residue of some sort
  of pythagorean theory. As soon as a flesh diet is considered more nourishing
  and heating to the body than other food, abstinence is looked on as a means of

Another factor which must be taken into account by anyone wishing to arrive at an estimate of asceticism in the light of the New Testament is the attitude of Jesus himself. The facts are well-known. How is it that his disciples are seen to eat and drink, when John's and the Pharisees' fast 'so often'? (Mark 2: 18 and the parallel passages). Together with prayer and alms-giving, fasting was a widespread practice among pious Jews (Tob. 12: 8). As a sign and symbol of repentance and return to God, *metanoia*, it was the almost necessary accompaniment of any particularly earnest prayer.[1] The Pharisees, who affected austerity, and the disciples of the stern ascetic of the wilderness both gave themselves to it with special earnestness. But this fasting by way of mourning and penance belongs to the period when the Jews were awaiting salvation. Jesus himself undertook a fast lasting forty days and forty nights. Not of course that he needed to do penance on his own account; he was fulfilling what had been prefigured in Moses and Elias—both of whom had used prayer and fasting as a prepara-tion for receiving a revelation from God (Exod. 34: 28; Deut. 9: 9; 3 Kings 19: 8)—and showing what it was to live in entire freedom from the needs of the body, spending all his days in silent prayer to his Father and opening his soul wide to the action of the Spirit (cf. Mark 1: 23 and the parallel passages).

He had chosen his disciples himself and he was still with them; to them he was the ever-present friend, by whose means the kingdom of God had been brought into their midst (Luke

---

'crucifying the flesh' (Gal. 5: 24) and quelling its revolts. It would no doubt be true to say that in these times the observance of abstinence-days has become chiefly a gesture of obedience to the Church and a sort of profession of faith.

1 When the child that Bathsheba had given him was ill, David prayed and fasted for seven days (2 Sam. 12: 15–17). The Jews fasted, wept and lamented when they heard of the edict for their extermination issued by Ahasuerus (Esther 4: 3). Esther fasted for three days and three nights before she went into the king's presence; so did her women and all the Jews present in Shushan (Esther 4: 16). Daniel prepared for prayer and supplication by fasting and wearing sack-cloth and ashes (Dan. 9: 3). Before leaving for Jerusalem, Esdras proclaimed a three days' fast: 'We would do penance and ask of the Lord God a safe journey for ourselves' (Esd. 8: 21). When Nehemiah learned that Jerusalem was in ruins, he fasted and prayed to the God of heaven (Neh. 1: 4). The Acts show that this practice still continued under the new dispensation. In circumstances of special gravity the Church supplemented prayer with fasting (Acts 13: 2–3, the choice of Barnabas and Saul; Acts 14: 23, the laying-on of hands to ordain presbyters). Cf. J. BEHM in *Theol. Wörteb. z. N.T.* vol. 4, pp. 925–935 (νηστεύω.)

17: 21); so why should they give themselves up to the practice of penance? 'Can you expect the men of the bridegroom's company to go fasting, while the bridegroom is still with them?' (Mark 2: 19 and the parallel passages). Inevitably the visible presence of Christ filled them with joy, the sort of joy that virgins have, the joy that married people have in each other, joy so intense and pure that of itself it excludes all mourning and penance. Jesus himself gave unreserved approval to the usual simple expressions of it: he went to the wedding at Cana, and he took part in the joyous feast with which Levi celebrated his conversion (Luke 5: 29)[1] and the one with which Zacchaeus showed his delight at having him in his house (Luke 19: 6). John announced that the kingdom of heaven was at hand and urged men to prepare for it by doing penance; he himself was neither to eat nor to drink (Matt. 11: 18). The presence of Jesus in the midst of his own people was as it were an anticipation of the kingdom and the joy of the kingdom; it was a sort of foretaste of the messianic feast. Hence, in his delight that publicans and sinners had obtained pardon, Jesus was willing to be treated as a glutton and a lover of wine like them (Matt. 11: 9).

As long as they had the Bridegroom with them his disciples could not be expected to fast. But the day would come when the Bridegroom would be taken away from them. When that happened they would fast (Mark 2: 19; Luke 5: 35); they would weep and lament then, while the world rejoiced (John 16: 20). And indeed, after his death we do find 'those who had been of his company' mourning and weeping (Mark 16: 10). He was soon to be restored to them and their distress would be turned into joy (John 16: 20), but after that he would leave them again. He was taken from them for three days, and this 'little while' (John 16: 19) was a sign and indication of the time when he would be taken from them once more. Those days of separation and mourning, too, would last only 'a little while'—for a thousand years count as a day (2 Peter 3: 8) —and he would eventually return in glory, just as they had seen him in the light of the first Easter morning (cf. Acts 1: 11).

1 The Pharisees' question about fasting evidently arises out of the events mentioned in this passage.

These are the two poles, so to say, of the Christian view of asceticism. All created things are good; we must not despise, condemn or mutilate them, and we can gratefully make full use of them. But the Bridegroom has been taken from us, and like the apostles after the ascension (Luke 24: 52), we are waiting, full of joy and hope, for his return. Yet our joy is not complete and definitive; we are still waiting for the coming of the Lord and his salvation. Hence if we take advantage of what the world offers, we must not take full advantage of it (1 Cor. 7: 31). We must patiently pass the time in fasting and weeping and doing penance, deriving our powers of endurance from hope in Christ (cf. 1 Thess. 1: 3).

* * *

'Was it not to be expected that the Christ should undergo these sufferings, and enter so into his glory?' (Luke 24: 26). Christ's cross is the central fact resolving the apparent autonomy between the two poles mentioned above, the initial and predominant fact in the Christian view of mortification and asceticism.

'*Proposito sibi gaudio, sustinuit crucem.*' Instead of choosing the joy that was offered him, Jesus chose the cross (Heb. 12: 2). Theologians whose special business it is to discover 'reasons' for the truths of faith, will say that a single act of love proceeding from the heart of Christ could have merited salvation, grace and glory for the whole of humanity; but *in fact* Christ chose to suffer in the flesh (1 Peter 4: 1) and redeem mankind through the pain of the cross. Scripture presents us with the *fact* of the cross, and this fact towers above all the mental structures we can erect ourselves and in its sheer starkness compels the attention of our proud little minds (cf. 1 Cor. 1: 17, 23). Here again theologians will find considerations, *rationes*, to justify the course of action Christ pursued. His overflowing love wanted our love in return. And since all that he did was meant for our instruction, he no doubt intended to teach men, too, that as they had turned away from God in spiritual rebellion and rebellion of the flesh had followed in the train of this, the only way they could return to him who is their beginning, their end and their beatitude, was to turn back

B

through repentance, *metanoia*, and walk along the hard road of humility of heart and mortification of the flesh; walk, that is, along the way of the cross. 'Christ . . . suffered for our sakes, and left you his own example', St Peter writes; 'you were to follow in his footsteps' (1 Peter 2: 21; cf. St Thomas, III, 46, 3). No Christian can possibly 'dwell in Christ' unless he walks along the road Christ trod himself (cf. 1 John 2: 6). Christians have to take Jesus for their model and be of the same mind as he—and he 'lowered his own dignity [and] accepted an obedience which brought him to death, death on a cross' (Phil. 2: 5–8).

Since Christ took our sinful flesh on himself, sin received its death-warrant in his flesh (Rom. 8: 3). Christians must henceforward live a new life 'through the powers of the Spirit'. They owe no debt now to the flesh, they have to mortify the ways of the flesh and follow the leading of the Spirit, as befits God's sons (cf. Rom. 8: 12–14).

'Christ therefore having suffered in the flesh, be you also armed with the same thought' (1 Peter 4: 1). But is it enough just to think about it? And are Christians free to think about it or not, as they please? There is no question here of a law imposed on men as it were from without and requiring their free acceptance. Or, to change the metaphor, there is no question of an external model which men must try and reproduce within the limits of their powers and their generosity. The necessity of dying is in the Christian himself, in his own flesh, in the life that became his at his baptism. The moment he was baptised, the scars of the crucified Jesus were printed on his body (cf. Gal. 6: 17): as he was baptised in Christ's name he has put on the person of Christ (Gal. 3: 27), the person of Christ crucified. The ultimate reason why this law of dying is written in the hearts of Christians is to be found in baptism, like the ultimate reason for the law of life which also should be theirs.[1]

Christ of his own accord went under the waters of death

---

1 It is surprising how often treatises professing to deal with spirituality or even with asceticism and mysticism devote hardly any space to baptism. When they consent to mention it at all, they give it at most a paragraph among the 'means' of furthering the spiritual life. Whereas in fact it is the real starting-point; the whole of asceticism and mysticism could be deduced from it.

(Luke 12: 50) and we can never know what torments he suffered in consequence (*ib*. and *cf*. Ps. 70: 2–3). But he came out again alive and victorious over death and the devil, as the Hebrews came victorious out of the waters of the Red Sea, which had swallowed up the entire Egyptian army. When Christians go under the waters of baptism they are plunged into Christ and immersed in his death. This immersion buries them in the death of Jesus. And when they come up again, with the holy water streaming from them—like Christ raised from the dead by the Father's power—they emerge in this Easter dawn into a new life, a risen life. They must henceforth live and move in a new kind of existence; it is as though they were stepping into a bright spring morning (cf. Rom. 6: 2–4).

The Christian lives for God in Jesus Christ, but before he can do so he must consider himself 'dead to sin'. As we said before, this death had already taken place in Christ, and the Christian becomes like Christ through baptism. 'Our former nature has been crucified with him' (Rom. 6: 6); but there is a mysterious law which God in his wisdom has seen fit to make, and in consequence of it our 'body of sin' (*ib*.) was not completely cleansed and made new when we were baptised; the 'flesh' in us is at war with the 'spirit'. This warfare is sometimes open, sometimes covert, but however it may be conducted it never stops. We too must suffer if we would attain to glory, and we shall not be fitted into the pattern of Christ's resurrection unless we have first been grafted on to him by being fitted into the pattern of his death (cf. Rom. 6: 5–12).[1]

Thus the man who belongs to Christ must 'deaden . . . those passions . . . which belong to earth, fornication and impurity, lust and evil desire, and that love of money which is an idolatry' (Col. 3: 5). He has 'crucified nature with all its passions' (Gal. 5: 24). He carries about continually in his body the dying state of Christ, so that Christ's living power too may be manifested in his body and manifested now (2 Cor. 4: 10). He is nailed to the cross with Christ (Gal. 2: 19); he has renounced the 'world' which is nothing to him now or he to it; he means no more to the world that the body of a

---

1 St Thomas in all humility probes this law to see if he can discover why it was fitting that God should make it (I. II, 85. 5. 2.; III. 69. 3).

condemned criminal does, hanging on the cross. 'The world stands crucified to him and he to the world' (Gal 6: 14).

He knows that the time is drawing to an end (1 Cor. 7: 29) and that the fashion of this world is soon to pass away (*ib.* 31). Hence, if he wants to have the best facilities for following the Lord and to give him his undivided attention, 'the best counsel in such times of stress' (*ib.* 26)[1] is to stay like the apostle himself, free, that is, from slavery to the flesh (*ib.* 8: 29–35). St Paul's preaching and example are here in line with the teaching of the gospel summarised above: now that the Bridegroom has been taken from them, Christians cannot just enjoy the world without giving the matter another thought.

*   *   *

The apostle, then, reminds the faithful that mortification is absolutely essential, and he gives an example of mortification in his own person. 'Follow my example, . . . as I follow the example of Christ' (1 Cor. 11: 1). Is it possible to go into greater detail and try and see what this mortification amounted to in the concrete? It would be unwise to aim at a higher degree of completeness and precision than the material warrants, but we can be fairly certain that the main thing involved is the warfare between the spirit and the flesh. This warfare never ceases; the fighting never slackens. The Epistle to the Romans and the Epistle to the Galatians are alive with the sound of it. It is perhaps the most searching of all 'mortifications'. If the 'pitiable creature', Paul, is to be freed from his 'death-doomed nature' and the effects of its corruption—the things that make a slave of him—and so allow love, joy, peace and purity, the harvest yielded by the Spirit, to reign in him in the glorious freedom of God's sons, he must 'mortify the ways of nature', 'crucify nature, with all its passions, all its impulses' (Rom.

---

1 *Propter instantem necessitatem* (1 Cor. 7: 26). It is tempting to see in these 'present' or 'imminent difficulties' an allusion to the *parousia*. Whether the second coming is close at hand or not has nothing to do with the question; the point is that it *will* come. We are therefore living in the last days of the world already, even if this period lasts for thousands of years, and we must all the time be on the watch for the Lord's coming. Many commentators, however, including modern ones like P. Allo, P. Huby and Canon Osty, take the phrase to mean 'the difficulties of this present life'.

7: 24; 8: 13; Gal 5: 24; Rom. 8: 21). As Methodius says, it is a contest worthy of Olympus.[1] The Christian has to wrestle like the athlete in the stadium; like him too he must voluntarily undergo privations of every kind. He does not waste his blows on the air; he buffets his own body and makes it his slave, for fear he should be disqualified (cf. 1 Cor. 9: 25–26).[2]

Then again, the apostle's labours and sufferings are a form of asceticism, and a very severe one too. He has been imprisoned and beaten, whipped and scourged; he has met with toil and weariness, hunger and thirst, he has repeatedly gone without food, borne cold and nakedness. . . . On top of it all there is the burden he carries every day, his anxious care for all the churches (2 Cor. 11: 23–29); and then the mysterious disease that inwardly tears him to pieces like a thorn pricking his flesh, or a shower of blows raining down on him and so keeping him humble (2 Cor. 12: 7). He needs no discipline or hair-shirt; all he could wish for in that line he finds in the insults, hardships, persecutions and distress he never ceases to suffer. But it is all 'for Christ' (*ib.* 10), and that changes everything; that alone can give real meaning to his sufferings: he accepts them out of love for Christ. That too is the meaning of the trials every Christian has to face. They are an education in themselves, *paideia*, a means by which God instructs his true children (cf. Heb. 12: 5–7) and moulds them to the likeness of his only Son.

Can we go further still and say that the apostle not merely accepted suffering for Christ's sake but even sought it out and embraced it of his own accord? The Epistle to the Philippians seems to imply that he did. Paul has consented to lose everything for the love of Christ and treat everything but him as refuse in order to win him and be 'found in him'. (Phil. 3: 8–9). His aim is to learn to know Christ and the virtue of his resurrection and what it means to *share his sufferings;* he wants to be *moulded in the pattern of Christ's death,* in the hope of achieving resurrection from the dead (*ib.* 9–11). What does this

1 *Banquet of the Ten Virgins,* 7. 3.
2 On this passage see F. PRAT, *Un aspect de l'ascèse dans saint Paul,* in the *Revue d'Ascétique et de Mystique* 2, 1921, pp. 3–22. It is difficult to see why this text should be taken, as it is by L. Bouvet (op. cit. pp. 158–161), to be an allusion to the practice of voluntary 'maceration' by St Paul.

mean? Does sharing the sufferings of Christ and being moulded into the pattern of his death mean anything more than communing with Christ in his death and resurrection through faith and love? Or will the 'despoiling of the natural body' (Col. 2: 11), a process begun at baptism and continued through all the conflicts mentioned above, be carried under the influence of love to the point of spontaneous imitation of the suffering crucified Christ? 'Carrying continually in our bodies the dying state of Jesus' (2 Cor. 4: 10), and 'In this mortal frame of mind I help to pay off the debt which the afflictions of Christ still leave to be paid' (Col. 1 : 24) are not just fine figures of speech. St Ignatius carried the principle to the length of passionately desiring death and the sufferings of martyrdom so as to 'imitate the passion of his God' (Rom. 6: 3).[1]

*   *   *

And so from these two consummate followers of the gospels we come back to the gospels themselves. On two separate occasions Jesus formulated for his disciples and, if St Mark is to be taken at his word, for the people as well, the all-embracing claims of the cross. 'He is not worthy of me, that does not take up his cross and follow me' (Matt. 10: 37–29 and the parallel passages). 'If any man has a mind to come my way, let him renounce self, and take up his cross [St Luke says 'let him take up his cross daily'], and follow me' (Matt. 16: 24–26 and the parallel passages).

This is the ultimate foundation of Christian asceticism, the ultimate basis of the law of mortification, the letter and spirit of which are handed down to us by St Paul. A disciple is not better than his master. Christ took up his cross and the disciple

1 Attempts have been made to prove that St Ignatius and St Paul held opposite views on this point, St Paul holding a mystical theory based on communion with Christ, St Ignatius one centred round imitation of Christ. This would seem to be mistaken. Communion in the Saviour's death by faith and love and by the sacraments of faith and love, baptism and the eucharist, surely tends of itself towards actual imitation and reproduction of the mysteries of Christ's sufferings. The germ of the idea so beloved of the medieval ascetics and mystics—the folly of the cross—is clearly contained in this principle. And St Paul himself declares that he is following or 'imitating' Christ's example (1 Cor. 11: 1). Wanting to imitate Christ's death does not imply a desire to shirk the immediate duty of charity. Again St Paul declares: 'I long to have done with it, and be with Christ' (Phil. 1 : 24). See the *Lettres de saint Ignace d'antioche*, ed. T. CAMELOT, *Sources chrétiennes* 10, Paris 1945, p. 29, and cf. infra.

must take his, too, and carry it every day. Christ's love will suffer no divided loyalties; when need arises he can demand the most far-reaching and painful of sacrifices. 'If any man comes to me, without hating his father and mother and wife and children and brethren and sisters, yes, and his own life too, he can be no disciple of mine.' That is how the *logion* stands in St Luke, who has doubtless preserved the ruggedness of the original semitic text in this instance, as in others (Luke 14: 26). St Matthew, who tones down the harshness of it, perhaps brings out the spiritual significance more clearly: 'He is not worthy of me, that loves father or mother *more*; he is not worthy of me, that loves son or daughter *more*.' (Matt. 10: 37).

The Christian's love for his master requires him to give his master preference over everything else. If he is to follow after Jesus, he must make a choice, and choosing means renouncing. To try and 'save one's life', i.e., no doubt, to insist on leading a life of one's own and 'preserving the independence of one's person, ideas and tastes' (Lagrange), is to lose it. To save one's life one must renounce everything—give up all attempt at making an impression on the world and forego the flowering of one's own personality—'for Christ's sake and the gospel's' (Matt. 16: 25 and the parallel passages; 10: 39; Luke 17: 33; cf. John 12: 25).

'For my sake and the gospel's.' If the Christian undertakes renunciation such as this—and Jesus has made it quite plain how far any disciple of his may have to carry it—he does not do so in the same spirit as the athlete, who aims at keeping fit because he wants to win the perishable crown awarded to the victor on the sports-field. He is not like the stoic or the epicurean, who practises renunciation in order to attain perfect serenity— *apatheia* or *autarcheia*—by rooting out all desire. He does not despise the 'flesh' or disdain the joys of life and the heart's affections. No; he gives up everything 'for Christ's sake and the gospel's'. There is nothing relative about the 'good news' that Jesus preached and illustrated in his own person; it is so absolute a thing that everything else may well be sacrificed to it.

The poverty set before us in the gospels fits into the same perspective. It is not just a question of selling all one's belongings and giving to the poor (Matt. 19: 21 and the parallel passages), but of doing this in order to be in a better position to follow Jesus. Brothers and sisters, father and mother, children, house and lands are not to be renounced merely for the sake of renouncing, but 'for my name's sake' (v. 29 and par.). If we are asked to give up everything, it is in order that we may be independent of everything, free to follow Christ and learn here and now what the good news of God's kingdom really implies.

So too with the chastity Jesus sets before those whose 'hearts are large enough to take it in'. The power to continue their own life in their children, the offspring of their body and fruit of their love, is perhaps the greatest of all the powers given to men; it is at any rate the one whose roots go deepest in their hearts and even in their flesh. Jesus suggests that his disciples should forego the use of this power and 'make themselves eunuchs'—but with 'love of the kingdom of heaven' as their motive (Matt. 19: 11–12). Those who are granted the strength to do this will be all the freer to follow Christ and live according to the gospel. Even now, in the weakness of the flesh, they will be living as the angels live (cf. Matt. 22: 30) and as it were knowing the kingdom of heaven by anticipation.

As P. Bouyer shows below, the sermon on the mount takes the practices of prayer, fasting and almsgiving then current in Jewish asceticism and transposes them into another key by declaring that they must henceforth be prompted by charity, must spring from a principle inside the soul and not simply be imposed from without (cf. Matt. 6: 2–8). In the same way poverty, continence and abstinence were not unknown to the wise men and ascetics of Palestine, Greece and India, but they are here given an entirely new vital principle, are literally transfigured by Christ's example and love.

Thus, as is well-known, poverty and continence, with all the 'mortifications' they imply, were the main forms taken by asceticism in the early days of the Church;[1] and as far as their spirit at any rate is concerned they always will be the lot of those who aim at going all the way with Christ.

*   *   *

1 M. VILLER, *La spiritualité des premiers siècles chrétiens*, pp. 25–30: 'Virginity is of necessity accompanied by mortification.' See also T. CAMELOT, *Virgines Christi*.

To conclude. We have tried to show—and the demonstration would be doubt have been clearer if we could have gone into greater detail—that the New Testament teaching about asceticism is thoroughly original. No doubt the practice of fasting was known to pious Jews, especially perhaps to those who fervently awaited the coming of the Messiah, as John the Baptist did. No doubt the Essenes practised abstinence in matters of food and drink and sexual intercourse, did without baths and eschewed all comfort. Doubtless too, the philosophers 'went into training' in accordance with the rules of one or other of the various spiritual techniques, to obtain perfect mastery over their bodies and their passions.[1] But all this was completely transformed by the cross of Christ.

To Christians, the Saviour's cross is a continual reminder that they are sinners and that they have been redeemed; but it also reminds them that this redemption is not yet theirs for good and all. Their salvation is only 'founded on hope' (Rom. 8: 24), and their 'flesh' remains enslaved to sin. They do not despise the 'flesh'; if they carry about in their bodies the 'dying state' of Christ, it is because they want to dig up the root which is everlastingly putting forth new shoots of sin. By 'mortifying' the flesh they obtain freedom, the freedom which Christ asks them to aim at until the time when the life of Jesus, the living power of Jesus, shall be manifested in their mortal bodies (cf. 2 Cor. 4: 10).

Christians are in mourning because their Lord has been taken from them; they fast and do penance while they wait for him to come back in glory. Of course, this mourning is not the despairing grief of men without hope. Together with their sorrow Christians possess the joy that goes with the assurance

1 The Greeks did 'exercises' in virtue just as they did physical 'exercises'. There are countless examples of this in Xenophon, Epictetus, etc. (See H. WINDISCH in *Theol. Wörterbuch z. N.T.*, vol. 1. pp. 492–494. A fuller lexical summary will be found in H. DRESSLER, *The usage of ἀσκέω and its Cognates in Greek Documents to 100 A.D.*, Washington, 1947). St Paul urges Timothy to 'train himself in holiness' rather than to bother about 'training of the body', which avails but little. He is no doubt thinking of 'physical culture', perhaps too of dubious ascetic practices inspired by dualistic beliefs (1 Tim. 4: 7–8). See C. SPICQ: *Les Epîtres Pastorales, in hoc loc.* and *excursus VII, Gymnastiques et morale* pp. 155–162; also also *La vie chrétienne est comme un sport*, by the same writer, in the *Revue des jeunes*, 1935, pp. 150–159. Spiritual techniques aimed at the production of psychological balance are one thing, Christian asceticism quite another.

hope gives (Rom. 12: 12), the joy of Easter, which began with baptism and is renewed every year, every Sunday, every day at the Lord's table. But even so, 'it is the Lord's death that they are heralding . . . until he comes' (1 Cor. 11: 16), and so they can never become attached to the 'fashion of this world that is soon to pass away' (1 Cor. 7: 31).

Being saved, then, by Christ's cross, they are brought by faith and love and the sacraments of faith and love, baptism and the eucharist, into *communion* with the Redeemer's sufferings. But their love goes further than that; of its very nature it tends towards *imitation*. The early sources are extremely reserved on this point, doubtless because at that time Christians could so easily find perfect imitation of the Crucified in martyrdom.[1] When the prospect of martyrdom ceased to be an ordinary feature of Christian life, its place as the great means of 'following Christ' to the very end was taken by monasticism. No doubt there was much that was excessive in the harsh asceticism of Egypt and Syria: platonism and even hinduism exerted a corrupting influence and there was always, perhaps, the temptation to 'beat the record'. But there was something more than that. The old monk who in ecstasy was present in spirit 'where holy Mary the Theotokos stood near the Saviour's cross' and 'would have wept like that for ever if he could'[2] was not a platonist; he was a Christian.

It is well-known that asceticism was sometimes carried to amazing—perhaps one should say excessive—lengths in the middle ages. Yet what was it but the folly of love, the folly of the cross?[3]

---

1 M. VILLER, *Martyre et perfection* in *Rev. d'asc. et de Myst.*, 6, 1925, pp. 3–25; *Le martyre et l'ascése, ib.* pp. 105–142. It is well-known that the ancient accounts of martyrdoms delight in bringing out in detail the parallel between the sufferings of the martyrs and the passion of Christ. Polycarp's martyrdom is a true 'martyrdom according to the gospel' (*Mart. Pol.* 19, 1). The martyrs of Lyons 'imitate and emulate Christ' (EUS., *Hist. Eccl.*, 5. 2. 2.)

2 *Apophthegmata Patrum*, Poemen., 144.

3 St Thomas shows that the abstinence of the philosopher, whose object is to keep himself in good health, and the abstinence of the Christian who 'buffets his own body and makes it his slave' (1 Cor. 9: 27) cannot be measured by the same standard. By the philosopher's standards the Christian might well seem to be overstepping the mark.

Chapter II

ASCETICISM IN THE PATRISTIC PERIOD

By L. BOUYER

THE outstanding feature in the history of Christian asceticism in the patristic period is the rise of monasticism. This novel thing cannot be understood unless it is seen in relation to the factors which prepared the way for it in the earliest days of Christianity. We must therefore mention at least the elements of Christian asceticism as they existed in the earliest period of all, for the sake of their links with patristic asceticism in general and monastic asceticism in particular.

It could be said that in the final period of judaism, just before the coming of Christianity, asceticism consisted of the three fundamental practices of almsgiving, prayer and fasting (cf. Tob. 12: 8); and it is worth noting that these three practices survived, in the sermon on the mount (Matt. 6), as the basis of Christian asceticism. Only our Lord made them look different by giving them a new scope and bearing. He brought them into the service of deliberate, conscious charity. Genuine love of God and of our neighbour for God's sake, a product of the discovery of God's love for our neighbour and for us, was henceforth to be the mainspring of almsgiving, prayer and fasting, and it was through them that our love would attain reality. It is most striking to see how these Jewish practices reappear in a work like the *Didache* with their motivation entirely transformed.

But although Jewish asceticism survived under another form in early Christian asceticism, there are two things which seem to give Christian asceticism an entirely new stamp. These are the appearance of martyrdom and virginity as focal points for the whole ascetic effort. It could be said that if the thing that made

Jewish asceticism specifically Christian was its polarisation by *agape*, the way this new orientation found expression in the life of the Church was through the emergence of these two new types of sanctity. At first sight they seem wholly unexpected, the martyr and the virgin seem to be merely ideal beings. Not only were they unknown in fact to judaism but they give the lie to some of its calmest convictions. It is undeniable that all the lasting elements that give Christian asceticism its originality go back to them.

Yet closer examination of the question soon brings the conviction that however revolutionary these innovations may have been, they were not without fore-runners in Judaism itself. Although judaism could never bring itself to abandon its initial conviction that the enjoyment of life and the goods of this world is a gift from God, the natural accompaniment of piety and wisdom, it nevertheless took a more mature view after the exile, when it showed at least some glimmerings of awareness that a very different outlook was possible. The heroism of the three young Israelites in the furnace (Dan. 3) and the death of the Macchabees for their fidelity to the one true God did more than foreshadow Christian martyrdom; they were real instances of it, although the thing itself had not yet made its appearance.

At first sight one would think that nothing of this kind prepared the way for the Christian ideal of virginity, at any rate. But one cannot be too sure. It is significant that when St Paul recommends continence (1 Cor. 7: 25 sqq.), he seems like Christ before him (Matt. 19: 10–12) to be approving an existing practice rather than introducing something new. It must be admitted that very little is known about the Jewish background against which Christianity made its appearance. Or rather, what is known about it concerns those parts of judaism (pharisaism particularly) which survived outside Christianity. It is not surprising that hardly anything stands out of this, like a toothing-stone, to bind the unfinished building of judaism to the new structure of Christianity. But through the mysterious apocalyptic sects—groups like the Essenes[1]—we get

---

1 The recent discoveries in Palestine may reasonably be expected to do something towards lifting the veil under which the Essenes are at present hidden. See the article by P. DE VAUX in *La Vie Intellectuelle*, June 1949, pp. 583–595.

an inkling of the presence of quite different elements in judaism. The gnostics, too, who were contemporary with the earliest generations of Christians, clearly reveal in their literary productions their debt to various trends of Jewish opinion which show that judaism was at once more mystical and more ascetic than it is commonly represented as being. It is beyond all doubt that the first disciples, starting with John the Baptist, came from circles where all these ideals were in ferment. Christ's connection with the Baptist makes it certain that he too was at any rate in close touch with these circles. It was moreover, only in a milieu of that sort that Mary's vocation to virginity, Mary's practice of continence in her married life with Joseph, could escape being regarded as a scandalous absurdity.

This throws light on the origin of the connection between continence and preparation for the end of the world, which comes out so clearly in what Christ and St Paul say about virginity. Those Jews who were not satisfied with judaism as it then was were ready to give a sympathetic hearing to the new message preached by Christianity, whereas those who were content with the established religion would have nothing to do with it. The distinctive thing about the members of the first group was that they were preparing for the end of the world, an event which they considered was more or less imminent and would coincide with the Day of Jahweh, the great day of judgment, the day, above all, when justice would be restored to a world that had come adrift from its centre. The innermost core of this group was composed of people who, like those congratulated by Jesus in the gospel, had become as eunuchs 'for love of the kingdom of heaven' (Matt. 19: 12). And the way Christianity first struck men was as an answer to the longings of people such as these.

These considerations are important because they alone can show what virginity really means to Christianity. There was never any question of condemning the life of the body, still less of condemning marriage. Both Jesus and St Paul preached the resurrection of the body, and their teaching about marriage was based on so sublime a concept that no one had ever had the slightest idea of it before. But marriage is bound to involve ties with this world; it gives a man obligations first to his wife and then to his children if he has any. For anyone wanting to abandon everything to do with 'this world' and prepare for the 'world to come', these obligations are an insuperable obstacle, all the more so because of their sacred character. While there is no belittling of marriage, then, in Christianity at all (in view of its enhanced dignity under Christianity and the consequently greater weight of its obligations, one might say because there is no belittling of marriage in Christianity), it is still quite understandable that virginity and continence should be *recommended* to Christians. Marriage is perhaps the holiest thing there is in this life, but the gospel message is addressed to those who realise that if our hope belongs to this world only, we are unhappy beyond all other men (1 Cor. 15: 19).

Some generous souls, then, had found out this other way of life through their longing for the Kingdom and embarked on it without waiting until the Kingdom had actually come in the person of Christ. But with the actual presence of Jesus the Kingdom of God ceased to be a thing of the near future and became an immediate reality. There was also the example of Jesus himself to serve as a stimulus. Hence it was natural that what had been an exceptional way of life should become a normal one, because it was the most logical one.

This explains the connection between virginity and martyrdom. Just as Christ's virginity prepared him for the all-embracing sacrifice of the cross, so the renunciation of this present life which is involved in virginity, would prepare Christians to walk in Christ's footsteps and bear witness to him by engaging in the same mortal combat against the powers that rule this world. Since these powers kept the world in a constant state of hostility to the world to come, i.e. to the Kingdom of God, all who were living for the Kingdom could expect to do battle, as Christ did. But as the Epistle to Timothy says, 'The soldier on service, if he would please the captain who enlisted him, will refuse to be entangled in the business of daily life' (2 Tim. 2: 4).

All this provides the perspective necessary for seeing what the transformation effected by the sermon on the mount in the old Jewish practices of almsgiving, prayer and fasting amounted to.

As far as the Christian ascetic was concerned, the natural tendency would be to refrain from using present goods. This training in holding aloof from the good things of life would prepare him for leaving them altogether when the peremptory summons came to the 'witness' of martyrdom. The goods he did use he would employ in accordance with the parable about base wealth (Luke 16): he would use them only for the practice of charity towards his neighbour and thus as a means of fitting himself for entry into the Kingdom. Almsgiving brings *agape*, the sole law of the Kingdom to come, into action by anticipation; abstinence creates independence and freedom. With these as a basis the Christian would be free to pursue the occupation proper to him, viz. to pray for the coming of the Kingdom, to say the Our Father, the prayer Jesus taught his disciples, and to pray the Maranatha to Jesus himself. His life would be all longing for the Kingdom, which he would find in Jesus; it would be devoid of all ties with this world or else would so transform them that they became nothing but occasions for the sacrifice charity inspires.

In these few words we have as it were a synthesis of the factors constituting the motive power of monasticism and all the apparently novel practices found in it.

To understand patristic asceticism as it was systematised in the fourth and fifth centuries, it is essential to realise that fundamentally it was nothing new. It simply applied the tendencies that had their roots deepest in primitive Christianity to changed circumstances.

It presupposed as ever-present and inescapable the conflict between this world and the world to come, the world as we know it and the world which is to be the Kingdom of God. Not that it condemned the created universe; far from it. The universe was considered to be good in itself, but it had fallen into the hands of the powers of darkness, which were subjecting it to a fundamentally ungodly government or 'economy'.

Consequently the Christian ascetic would be one who prepared for the necessary, inevitable conflict, not by condemning the good things of this world but by detaching himself from them, to prevent them from serving as bait to catch him with or fetters to hold him captive. In so doing he would, as St Paul says (1 Cor. 7: 31), be taking advantage of what this world offers but not taking full advantage of it. In other words, he would as far as was humanly possible use the good things of this world only when he could do a real act of charity with them; he would refrain from using them when the purpose in view was his own exclusive benefit or when he feared he might divert them to that end.

Once again, these principles were transmitted from the primitive Church to the Church of the Fathers without the slightest change. What had changed in the meantime was the historical conditions into which the principles had to be fitted, the circumstances to which they had to be applied.

In the period stretching practically from the beginning of Christianity to the age of Constantine, the question seemed extremely simple. The only choice a Christian had lay between the strict application of his principles and apostasy pure and simple. The fundamental antagonism between the 'economy' of this world and the Kingdom of God, which was the one Christians belonged to, took palpable form in the relations between Church and State, owing to the deliberate policy of the State. An avowed Christian was *ipso facto* a candidate for martyrdom. Clearly the idea of a life in which allegiance to the Kingdom was compatible with allegiance to this world could not but appear entirely chimerical. Caesar himself undertook to remind those who were faithful to Christ that they could not acknowledge Jesus as the sole *Kyrios*, the only Lord, without incurring the enmity of the Lord who ruled on earth.

It was all quite different, of course, when the Emperor declared himself the first of all the worshippers of the heavenly Lord. No conceivable change could have been more disconcerting to Christian thought and practice than that; in fact it could be said that in all its subsequent history Christianity has never again had to face any upheaval like it. We may add that the problems created by this change were so delicate and complex that they have not been fully solved even now and they probably never will be. And as many of the controversies among Catholic Christians in our own day show, we are still hesitating over some of the alternatives consequent on this revolutionary event.

It was only natural that a reaction should set in and that men should think, or tend to think, that the conflict was now over. As the world had become or was on the way to becoming Christian, it was difficult to see how there could be any antagonism between it and the Kingdom of God. If Caesar had declared for Christ, he ought surely to be considered not as Christ's rival but as his instrument or even as his image. Far from being an obstacle to God's Kingdom, Caesar's empire might be expected henceforth to prepare the way for the Kingdom; it might even be itself the beginning of the Kingdom. This line of thought seems to have been carried to its logical conclusion almost from the start, as it was by Eusebius of Caesarea in his *De Laudibus Constantini*. But his easy acceptance of arianism as well reveals the fundamental misunderstanding on which this conciliatory attitude in theology was based. The world was thought to have been converted to Christianity, but in fact it was Christianity that was too easily giving way to the world. The world was still the same, the change was only superficial. Though Christians thought they were still worshipping Christ, they were really venerating the hellenistic *Logos* and calling that Christ.

It was no accident that monasticism was born and came to maturity just at this time. It was no accident, either, that its followers also formed, on the whole, the most dependable battalion in the fight against arianism. They represented the reaction of the Christian instinct against the fallacious reconciliation with the world which the Emperor's conversion had seemed for a time to justify. At a time when the political organisation of the world seemed to have lost its hostility to Christianity, the rise of monasticism was evidence of a feeling that had its roots deep in the Christian conscience. This was the feeling that the antagonism between 'this world' and the 'world to come' was a wider thing than the particular problem of the relations between Church and State. It mattered little that for the moment this problem had been solved or seemed to have been. The conflict between the two 'economies' would

c

take other forms; it would always be there, would never be broken down. Monasticism began as a spontaneous protest of the Christian spirit against the insidious temptation to come to terms with a world no longer seen with the same clarity as being out of harmony with the Kingdom of God and essentially incomparable with it. At a time when the world had ceased to exact a militant attitude towards itself, because the State had been converted, monasticism and the ideal it bore witness to showed Christians that they must maintain that attitude all the same, or deliberately resume it if they had dropped it.

This brings us to the one genuine novelty in patristic asceticism. In the patristic age Christians had become keenly aware of their position with respect to the world, because they had given considerable thought to the question, and this awareness formed the starting-point of their asceticism. Hitherto their attitude to the world had been automatically determined for them by circumstances; from now on they began to reproduce by various deliberate techniques the practical equivalent of conditions which had formerly prevailed in the ordinary course of things. It goes without saying that this development did not take place all at once. There was no sudden transition from the period of continual persecution to the period of peace under Constantine. In the same way, before peace with the state became an accomplished fact, Christians had already begun to see the dangers it might lead to. It brought certain problems to a head, but those problems had begun to make themselves felt beforehand and attempts had already been made to grapple with them. The new form of asceticism which crystallised round monasticism had many forerunners both in the speculative order and in the practical. It is worthy of note that most of them came from the same centre of Christian life and thought, the church of Alexandria.

Origen's *Exhortation to Martyrdom* had represented martyrdom not as a chance occurrence due to circumstances, a thing that would disappear with the conditions that had produced it, but as the normal culmination of the Christian life. It followed that Christians ought systematically to shape their lives by detaching themselves from the world, even if the world itself should in the end cease to force them to. Origen's treatise thus contains the germ of a special system of asceticism, the one, in fact, that was to be developed in monasticism.

Again, Clement's presentation of the ideal of ἀπάθεια as the goal facing the 'gnostic' was big with consequences. Both the word and the idea were adopted by Evagrius and his successors in their speculative writings of monasticism, and they came to form the core of ascetical theory.

At first sight it might seem that we were here plunging into the thick of the fatal confusion between Christian and pagan spirituality, in spite of having said that monasticism came as an antidote to that confusion. Anyone who thought this would be taking a grossly material view of the relations between Christianity and paganism. The use of a term or even a concept taken from the contemporary vocabulary of the spiritual life cannot be the deciding factor in the question of the preservation or loss of the original element in Christian belief. The important thing is to see how the word was understood, how the concept it expressed was used. Careful examination of ἀπάθεια in Clement, and particularly in Evagrius and his successors, is enough to show that far from representing the surrender of Christianity to hellenism, it is a sign of the conquest of hellenism by Christianity. When they use the word ἀπάθεια, the Christian moralists and ascetics of the period of the Constantinian revolution mean by it something quite different from what the stoics before them had seen in it. For the Christian writers there never was any question of trying to reach a state of 'insensibility' in the sense we should now attach to the term. The proof is that in works as early as Clement's ἀπάθεια is presented as subordinate to ἀγάπη; it is to be brought to perfection solely in order to ensure that ἀγάπη too shall reach its full development. What is more, in the sense in which Clement takes it, ἀπάθεια cannot be attained at all unless there is a supernatural basis of ἀγάπη in at least a nascent state. Thus the gnosis, the process that leads to ἀπάθεια, starts from the divine seed of charity and again, in Clement's view, finds its term in charity, the full flower of charity this time.[1]

In the monastic theory of asceticism, ἀπάθεια was the ideal

1 Cf. *Stromata*. 2. 9. 45 and 6. 9. 78 for gnosis and agape in general. *Stromata* 6. 9. 71–79 is the clearest and most decisive passage on agape and apatheia.

state in which a man ceased to be the plaything of his natural
instincts and became capable of arranging his whole life and
the conduct of his soul in accordance with the new instinct
implanted in him by ἀγάπη. In other words, he ceased to be a
'child of this world' (Luke 16:8) and was in a way to becoming
a 'son of the kingdom' (Matt. 8: 12).[1]

Having looked at the historical context of the monastic form
of asceticism as it was in the earliest days and seen what the
lines of thought were that presided over its development and
systematisation, we may now ask what in the last resort were
its distinguishing features.

After what we have said, the first will be quite obvious—
ascetic effort of the kind made by many Christian humanists
at the present day with a view to the immediate sanctification
of this world and its goods was quite unknown in the patristic
period. It would be ambiguous and an over-simplification to
say that the asceticism of the fathers was primarily a flight from
the world. But it is essentially true to say that it was a process
of liberation from the world.

This does not mean that it gave up the attempt to sanctify
the world and consecrate it to God. But in the opinion of the
early monks and the fathers who gave it expression, this
sanctification and consecration would be the work of the resurrection. They thought that men ought to prepare the way for
it, or rather, perhaps, prepare themselves for it. The world had
already been redeemed, and the way to prepare yourself for
its ultimate sanctification—the only way to do so—was to
keep yourself apart from the world here and now. *If you wanted
to save the world, you had to begin by saving yourself from the world.*
In these few words lies the justification of the anachoretic life,
the deliberate separation from the world which is the starting-
point of monasticism. If we have made our meaning clear,
this will appear a mere consequence of the fundamental conviction of the Christian faith that the cross of Jesus is the road to
the resurrection.

Thus the statement that the ideal later adopted by the type
of humanism dignified by the name of Christian—the ideal of

---

1 For Evagrius cf. P. HAUSHERR's two articles on the *Traité de l'oraison d'Evagre
le Pontique* (Pseudo-Nilus) in the *Revue d'Ascetique et de Mystique*, 1936.

positive and immediate sanctification of the world—was unknown in the asceticism of the patristic age, must not be understood to mean simply that no one had thought of it at that time. No, the position then adopted was taken up quite consciously and deliberately; it definitely, though implicitly, anticipated the modern ideal mentioned and excluded it. The patristic ideal embodied in monasticism took the form of systematic separation from the world not because the fathers failed to realise the possibility of reconciliation with the world but because they rejected the offer, attractive though it was and never made so persuasively before or since.

A second distinguishing feature may at once be added to the first, viz. the physical or material character of asceticism in the patristic period. Modern theorists have often been captivated by the idea of a 'purely spiritual' form of asceticism or one tending that way. This theory, like the patristic one, requires a good deal of renunciation: that is the point where it differs from the idea of asceticism through acceptance alone (if there still can be said to be room for asceticism in such a conception). But the renunciation is interior: in short, you keep what you renounce and you renounce it while you keep it. If this is possible and can ever take on some sort of reality, we shall have to say that the entire patristic conception of asceticism becomes sheer nonsense. Monasticism, the embodiment of the essential element in patristic asceticism, would never have come into being unless the spiritually-minded men of the time had been firmly convinced that you cannot really renounce a thing without actually, physically, giving it up. The institution of the anachoretic life must be regarded as a deliberate step, taken after mature consideration by Christians intent on the spiritual life, at a time when the world was insinuating that they could very well be Christians and yet keep (or acquire) what until then it had forced them to do without—if they insisted on remaining faithful to Christ. In other words, the formal rejection of this reconciliation with the world is one of the most striking marks of patristic spirituality. You may of course think, if you choose, that the authors of that spirituality were mistaken. But if you do the opposite of what they did, you cannot claim that you are thereby following and perfecting their method. Either you believe, as they did, that there can be no 'spiritual' asceticism without a foundation of 'material' asceticism, or you do not. If you do, the way they opened up is the one you must follow, unless you want to dream your life away; if you do not, the patristic way must seem to you an aberration.

The third distinguishing feature is of the greatest importance for clarifying this point. The actual, non-hypothetical renunciation demanded by patristic asceticism never aimed at suffering for suffering's sake; the end in view was always liberation and liberation only. Savage mortifications such as those later introduced by the Irish monks and men like St Peter Damian were entirely unknown at this time. *A fortiori*, there was not the slightest leaning towards the attitude characteristic of men like Henry Suso at the other end of the middle ages and of certain trends of thought more or less closely linked with St Bernard and St Francis and culminating in the modern devotion to the Sacred Heart—the mystical intoxication produced by the idea of suffering with Jesus.

Doubtless the monks of the fourth and fifth centuries often set themselves exhausting and exceedingly painful physical penances; they fasted for long periods, deprived themselves of sleep, and so forth. But throughout this struggle against physical difficulties which to us seem almost insurmountable, the object always was to master what normally masters the spirit; it was never suffering as such. Quite the contrary, as the notion of ἀπάθεια is there to show—there was no question of injuring the body and stifling the feelings, still less of intensifying this sense-life through pain; the aim was to bring it into subjection. Hence the ascetic practices known to the desert fathers, even the most rigorous of them, did not positively afflict the body but simply refrained from satisfying its normal needs. They deprived the body of food, comfort and sleep. But there was nothing corresponding to or foreshadowing the discipline and the whole armoury of penitential instruments which during the middle ages came to symbolise a form of asceticism meant to crucify the body.

One other feature remains to be considered. What exactly in psychological terms did the liberation or ἀπάθεια we have been trying to define amount to for those who put the patristic theory of asceticism into practice? We might say that it was a kind of cleansing or decanting process; it purified and at the same time intensified the consciousness. The vegetative element was deprived of nourishment because too copious a diet, especially of fleshmeat, makes the mind heavy. Comfort was refused because it eliminates the necessity for adaptation to changing circumstances and conditions and enables a kind of somnolent bliss to be prolonged throughout the day. Above all, the time reserved for sleep was cut down as much as possible, because the whole aim was to keep the mind awake, or rather, positively to wake it up. The business of asceticism was to free men from the trammels of life in this world, and life in this world was seen by the monks as something clogged and dulled by matter. Far from being a help to the mind, something the mind could see out of, matter had in his opinion become a leaden carapace, stifling the mind's aspirations and making movement impossible to it.

That is yet another reason why the desire for suffering (*aut mori aut pati*) was entirely foreign to the monk. Suffering invades and masters the consciousness, whereas the monk aimed at emptying his consciousness and lightening the weight it had to bear. *A fortiori*, the element suggestive of intoxication in the romantic notion of suffering with Jesus or for Jesus would have aroused misgivings in the fathers, irresistible though it was to prove in the middle ages. The objective the fathers had in view was not *Schwärmerei* like that, but ἡσυχία, i.e. not the peace enjoyed by a satisfied body but the serenity and light possessed by a soul set free from its slavery.

But there is still a final question, and it is the most important of all. What was to fill this lucid emptiness, to obtain which the monk had lived withdrawn from the world and avoided spending himself for worldly ends? What could fill it but prayer? Reading of the Word of God with its announcement of the coming of God's Kingdom in him whom Origen calls by the splendid name of αὐτοβασιλεία, the 'Kingdom Personified', would nourish this prayer, would as it were entice the soul into praying. And this prayer itself would be guided and borne along by the prayer inspired by God's Word, the prayer of the psalms. We can do no more than mention this subject; to develop it fully would take us too far. But if it is passed over or denied the central position that rightly belongs to it, the harmony between the unity at the heart of patristic asceticism and its extremely rich complexity is destroyed; the whole orchestration of the symphony suddenly becomes meaningless. The ultimate reason for the phenomenon we have stressed so much—the continuity between the earliest form of Christian asceticism and the monastic form of it in the Church of the fathers—is that they both represent a whole-hearted effort at listening with all the powers of the soul to absolutely everything contained in the word of God, so as to be caught up into it and penetrated by it through and through.

Even now we have not all the essential features of patristic asceticism before us. There is still one more. At first sight it may seem inconsistent with the strict 'other-worldliness' that comes out in all the others we have mentioned up to the present, but in fact it provided them with a complement which was indispensable if monastic asceticism in those early centuries was not to lose its 'eschatological' character and degenerate into mere dreaming. This feature was work, the necessity for the ascetic to labour with his body. The stress laid on this point in the *Apophthegmata Patrum* gives the key to the exceptional commonsense which is no less distinctive a feature in the fathers than their radicalism in the mystical sphere. Although the kind of spirituality they recommended to others and proposed to follow themselves may be said to have rested in a way on flight from the world, all they were in fact fleeing from was the hardening and stagnation the world brings about; they never shunned the responsibilities or even the legitimate anxieties which are the lot of man in general. However deliberately they set out to live with another world as their goal, they well knew that until they died they had of necessity to live in this world and, materially at least, by this world. They utterly refused to live in the world as parasites. Here again, particularly, it is clear that they were not taken in by the comfortable but questionable spiritualisation of asceticism which some centuries later was to be represented as an advance.

'If a man will not work, he ought not to eat either.' Few

maxims sprang to the lips of the early monks more often or more naturally than that one. A monk seeking to live on alms and offering his prayers and mortifications in return would have been the object of their most pitiless sarcasm. A man living exclusively for God and his Kingdom ought to avoid making a burden of himself to others where his personal wants were concerned; and, moreover, when he had reduced those wants to a minimum, he would be in a much better position than most people to help his brethren, and that was what he ought to do. The monk had to apply himself to work, the *labor improbus* that brings sweat to the brow, not only to ensure his own subsistence but to aquire the means of practising charity with a liberality unknown to those who refuse nothing and have a wife and children to support into the bargain.

This point is of the utmost importance. Once again, to over-look it would spell total failure to understand the asceticism of the fathers. Its eschatological character shows that monasticism did not proceed from subconscious resentment at the world's treatment of Christians or camouflage an attempt to shirk the task that all men have to face, but rather was a virile effort to go beyond ordinary requirements. If the life the early monks aimed at was indubitably angelic, it was not because they had failed to live like mere men but because they realised that a merely human existence, even in all the fulness it is capable of, can never be enough to satisfy the 'children of God'.

NOTE: I have refrained from supporting the statements I have made in this brief sketch by quotations from the fathers. They would have lengthened the essay out of all proportion. I may be allowed to refer the reader to my book, *La Vie de saint Antoine et les origines de la spiritualité monastique*, in which evidence is given at length for each of the points treated in the second part of this article.

Chapter III

ASCETICISM IN THE MIDDLE AGES

By F. PETIT, O.PRAEM.

THERE seem to have been two sharply defined creeds in medieval asceticism—on the one hand a manifest and deliberate continuation of the old tradition, on the other an ever-growing desire from the eleventh century onwards for strict conformity with Jesus crucified. The two tendencies were superimposed one upon the other and never came into conflict. We shall examine each separately and in a third section look at some of the tentative efforts that were made to bring asceticism from the cloister, where it was most at home, into the world of the laity.

1. *Continuation of the Old Tradition*

The dramatist who made one of his characters talk about 'us people of the middle ages' was well laughed at for his pains. The fact is that the people of the middle ages thought they were still living in the ancient world. Actually, the tradition had come sharply with the barbarian invasions. Comfort had quite disappeared. But that was of slight importance as long as the language remained the same—which it did (the literary language at any rate) until the sixteenth century, when the popular forms of speech officially won the right to exist (when Francis I, for instance, ordered the official documents to be written in French). Language is the main thing in any civilisation. Where religion was concerned, all hearts were still set on the primitive Church. Longing looks were cast at the early Christian community at Jerusalem, and all community life, whether among monks or later among canons, was an attempt to allay this longing. Above all, where asceticism was concerned, the law in force practically everywhere was the one laid down by St Benedict, whose remarkable powers of discernment had enabled him to condense in his Rule all the lasting contributions made to asceticism in that early period. Further, in nearly all religious houses, the staple reading of the monks, canons and mendicant friars was holy scripture, and to this the reading of Cassian's *Conferences* was added nearly every day. No doubt there was a taste for novelty too in reading-matter; otherwise so many new works would not have been written. But most of what was produced when the middle ages were at their height was composed almost exclusively in the patristic tradition. It is therefore not surprising that the asceticism of the early Church should have continued to prevail. St Norbert's disciples had such an enthusiastic admiration for their master that they wanted no rule but him; yet the saint said to them, 'Unless you have a rule, and the canons, and the regulations the holy father made, you will have no direct road to heaven.'

In Gaul, the influence of the fathers may have been out-weighed at the beginning of the middle ages by Irish influence, particularly by the Rule of St Columban, which puts asceticism well to the fore: *Maxima pars regulae monachorum mortificatio est.* This mortification was to apply chiefly to the will, but as it bore on the source of all the monk's actions it affected the whole of his life. 'He must not do as he likes', the Bobbio manuscript says; 'he must eat what he is told to, do whatever work he is given, submit to people he dislikes. He must go to bed tired out, fall asleep standing, be forced to rise before he has had his due measure of sleep, and if he is wronged, keep silence.'

St Columban's pentitential code is still more severe. If the poor man is so worn out that he becomes careless over some detail, he is to be punished for it. If he forgets to say *Amen* or *Benedicite* he will receive six strokes, and six if he forgets to make the sign of the cross over his spoon; if he loses a crumb of bread, he will have to say a *Pater Noster* in church. If he knocks against an altar the punishment is fifty strokes; if he makes excuses he will be kept in confinement in a cell until he repents. If he forgets to close the church door he will have to say twelve psalms; if he goes into a house with his head covered he will receive fifty strokes. And there are more serious offences than these. If, for example, he loses the sacrifice, i.e. the consecrated

host, and cannot find it, he will have to do public penance for
a year. In short, nothing is passed over. As the penitential
code itself says in conclusion, at all costs the monk must leave
the earth and its base deeds behind him and cleave to God
alone, *relicta humo cum flagitiis, uni adhaerere Deo.*

Little by little, Irish influence gave way before St Benedict's.
With him we come back to the earlier tradition. The patriarch
of the western monks had lived the life of the desert fathers, and
the monks of the east themselves venerate him as one of their
great models. But he saw that if he wanted to adapt the older
form of monastic life to the capacities of his disciples, he would
have to eliminate from it all that was too severe and burden-
some for them. This he hoped had been done in the programme
he eventually presented them with. If the life still seemed hard
and narrow at first, they were not to let that make them run
away from it. Their hearts would become capable of more,
and they would eventually find themselves running in the way
of God's commandments and delighting in them beyond words.

Asceticism occupies a prominent place in the Benedictine
Rule. Mortification of the body, love of fasting and avoidance
of custom appear among the 'instruments of good works'.
But asceticism is not the beginning and end of the spiritual life.
In the 'school where he is trained in the love of God', the monk
will also learn to rate nothing higher than the love of Jesus
Christ and to desire eternal life with all the spiritual intensity
he is capable of.

If we ask what Benedictine asceticism consists of, we shall
say that it is first of all a matter of keeping clear of sin by observing God's commandments and so avoiding what we now
call the seven deadly sins: the monk must not be proud, a
drunkard or a glutton, lazy, much given to sleeping, envious
or a grumbler. St Benedict is well aware that if you want to be
perfect you must start by keeping the commandments. For
use after this he puts forward a scheme for self-reformation,
a programme as shrewd psychologically as it is effective of
humility—shunning one's own will, being obedient even
when the thing commended is unpleasant, stamping out bad
thoughts, being content with little, believing oneself to be of
less account than other people, following the accepted rules and

customs, keeping silence, not often laughing and never laughing loudly, always showing gravity, having a modest bearing in church, during the office, in the oratory, in the monastery, in the garden, when travelling and in the country, like the publican in the Gospel. It is all based on holy scripture, which Benedict quotes at every turn. You can easily tell whether it is being carried out, because it is bound up with external practices; yet it makes great demands and is capable of taking those who practice it right to the heights.

It may cause some surprise that the common observances providing the framework for this asceticism should look so mild. As a matter of fact, if St Benedict's monks had fewer psalms to sing than the monks of the east, they still had a considerable number, and anyone applying himself properly to the task would find it tiring. But prayer, reading and manual work were so judiciously blended that monotony and excessive fatigue were avoided and the body received its measure of physical exercise. The amount of food allowed was as much as would normally be taken in the world: a pound of bread, a hemina of wine, two main courses and even dessert, if the garden could provide any. Life went on in peaceful silence, which the monk was to prize because it was a condition of attaining union with God. Lent stood out in contrast to the rest of the year by reason of its austerity: the monk was then to curtail his food, drink, recreation and manifestations of merriment, so as to prepare for the holy feast of Easter with the joy that comes of spiritual desire. And so, as one reads St Benedict's Rule, one begins to wonder why so often in the course of history people have torn themselves in two to add things to it.

It is all the more surprising in that the proper balance is not easily kept. As early as the time of St Benedict of Aniane, the offices were celebrated in such a way as to lengthen the time required for them, because the monks did not care much for manual work. At Cluny the number of psalms became endless, not that any change was made in what the Rule lays down about the body of the office, but preparatory psalms were added. Thus in Lent Psalms 119-150 were said before matins, psalms were added after the concluding prayers at each of the hours, there were psalms for the brethren who had recently died, the *Quicumque* was said at prime every day, there were two processions a day to the church of our Lady, and so on.

A requiem Mass was sung daily in addition to the Mass of the day. It is true that on great feasts there were not quite so many psalms, but one cannot shut one's eyes to the fact that the office was lengthened in order to shorten the time available for the manual work.

The order of Cîteaux was founded in reaction against Cluny, with the quite definite idea of returning to the letter of the Rule and practising all the observances as originally laid down. But the balance that had been lost was not to be recovered by that means. No doubt monks were now to be seen morning and afternoon on their way to work in the fields. Led by their prior himself they walked two by two together, with spades on their shoulders and habits of unbleached cloth, like farm-hands too poor to afford the expense of having their wool dyed. But they could not rest content with the office as it had been appointed by St Benedict; they must needs say the little office of our Lady and the office of the dead every day as well. St Benedict had ordered that anything approaching buffoonery should be avoided, but they eliminated recreation altogether. St Benedict had allowed the two courses of the meal to be followed by dessert, but they withdrew the concession.[1]

The main thing they were after was poverty: *cum Christo paupere pauperes.* They wanted to live by the work done in the abbey, and for that reason they took lay-brothers, *fratres barbati,* who were experts in agricultural work. There were to be no more crosses of gold or silver, no gold chalices or silk chasubles, no dalmatics, tunicles or copes. But this poverty did not take the joy out of the Cistercian life; they quoted the Canticles as often as they did the psalms. The days were light enough at Cîteaux and Clairvaux and the other monasteries, for angels came to see them and they saw the Virgin smiling.

From the ascetic point of view, some of the reformed canons regular, the congregation of Premontré and Arrouaise, for example, may be compared with Cîteaux. They did not follow the Rule of St Benedict, but they kept to the old ascetic tradition

1 P.L. 166, col. 1507.

with as much respect and affection as if they had been Cister-
cians.

Some of the old practices—solitude, the discipline, the hair-
shirt and pilgrimages—were even to receive a much more
extensive application at this time.

St Benedict had composed a Rule for cenobites. However,
he rated cenobites less highly than anchorites or hermits,
people who had outlived the fervour of their noviciate and after
a long apprenticeship in community had learned from the
example of others how to fight against the Devil. Hence the
monks were in the habit of retiring into solitude during Lent,
in imitation of the solitaries of the Jordan. Some wanted to
restore the anachoretic life, in a form that would provide safe-
guards against its possible disadvantages.

This was the position of St Romuald and the Camaldolese.
As St Peter Damian, the most famous of them, says, though
St Benedict put his monks in monasteries he was all the time
showing them the way to the desert: *dum in monasterio hominem
ponit ad eremum dirigit; hic quidem collocat sed illuc exhortatus
invitat.*[1]

It was also the position of St Bruno and the Carthusians, who
lived in the same enclosure but in separate cells—a novel
practice at that time—and met together only for the night office
and the conventual Mass.

Both the Camaldolese and the Carthusians lived in community, but there were innumerable cases where a recluse
was immured in a cell built against the wall of a church.

Grimlac's Rule gives picturesque details of the life led by these
recluses. In his view the active life, which is for beginners, is
the one in which a man learns to live under the authority
of a superior, in community. The contemplative life, while
still, of course, requiring love for God and love for men, makes
those who live it despise all visible things and set all their
desires on the things of heaven. It is lived on earth but will be
made perfect only in heaven, and the rules of the anachoretic
life were drawn up by the early fathers with the sole object
of making the contemplative life easier to follow. Grimlac
thought that as a general rule a man wishing to live the

[1] P.L. 65, col. 252.

contemplative life should serve a probationary period in the cloister and not leave the monastery until he had obtained permission from the bishop or from his abbot.

The recluse was to be provided with a small cell carefully protected against the outside world. If he was a priest, the bishop would consecrate an oratory for him adjacent to the church, and there he would follow the chant, make his offering and receive communion. The window between this oratory and the church would enable him to talk to his visitors, give them advice if they came to consult him or hear their confessions if he was a priest. Whenever possible, space would be left for a little garden, in which he could plant a few vegetables. He was to take the air from time to time, *tangi ab aere*; that would do him good: *multum ei proderit tactus aeris*. If he had any disciples they would have a separate cell of their own and he would give them his instructions through a window. As in the monastery the time would be divided between psalmody, *lectio divina* and manual work. The recluse was advised to be as circumspect as possible when directing women or hearing their confessions.

Recluses were recommended to live in twos and threes rather than entirely on their own. Priests were not to be accepted for the life unless they had first made a two years' noviciate in a monastery. Young men could be accepted if there was evidence that they had been leading a really religious life. The recluses seem to have carried on apostolic work fairly steadily through the spiritual direction they gave: they were sought after by the more fervent, as their sanctity was well-known and gave them great prestige. They easily obtained permission to communicate or celebrate the holy sacrifice every day. Reading must have been a frequent occupation of the solitaries, but it can hardly have extended beyond the Bible. They had to work hard enough to earn their living, but Sundays and nights were not working times and there was nothing but prayer and reading to fill them.

If it happened that the faithful brought them offerings, they could make use of them, just as the poor would make use of their alms. But their life would always be frugal. Frequent fasts were prescribed for them. They were never to eat before noon. Most of the time their meal was either after noon or after vespers. The quantity and quality of their food was regulated in accordance with the Rule of St Benedict.

For clothing, they were to have two tunics and, if they were monks, two cowls as well; otherwise they would have two furred capes instead. If they were priests, they would have a chasuble at their disposal, together with two albs, two amices, two stoles and maniples, two corporals and two lavabo-towels, all this to be kept spotlessly clean the whole time.

Their bedding was to be poor, and they were to sleep fully dressed, even to their belts. They were to shave and cut their hair and, if they were priests, take a bath from time to time. Foreseeing the objection that St Anthony never bathed, Grimlac replies that it was because he never had to say Mass. This way of life was not reserved for men only, and in the twelfth century St Aelred, abbot of the Cistercian house of Rievaulx, wrote a Rule for Recluses for his sister's use. People embark on the solitary life, he says, because they want to avoid the danger of sinning and the numerous obstacles to spiritual progress to be found in the world, and above all because it gives them greater freedom for paying court to Christ. But bodily seclusion is not enough; the imagination and the senses must be kept under control too. Garrulous old women should not be encouraged to call, and the recluse should be careful not to talk too much to herself and not hoard on the pretext of wanting to give alms.

It is not her business to give hospitality or teach little girls their letters, and she is not to hold long and frequent conversations with her confessor.

She is to recite the monastic breviary and the office of the Blessed Virgin. If she finds the office too long, she is to leave off and take up some reading instead. Thus, like the monk-solitary, she will spend her time in saying psalms, reading and working with her hands. She is to fast often. Her diet, too, is to be of the utmost frugality. The main meal will consist of one course only, which will be a dish of vegetables or something of the sort with a little oil or butter. In the evening there will be a little milk, cheese or fish and some fruit or salad.

The clothes the recluse wears are to be warm but they should be made of coarse stuff. As a protection for her chastity she is

D

to think of Christ her Betrothed, pray to the Blessed Virgin, St Agnes and her guardian angel, and mortify herself. In short, she should strive to be as pure as a fine linen corporal.

The rest of the Rule is a method of prayer and meditation, an aid to meditation on the life of Christ and the four last things, especially the glory and bliss of paradise.

It would seem that whereas the early Church had moved on from the anachoretical life to the cenobitic, the Church of the middle ages began with full acceptance of the cenobitic life and gradually discovered the value of the solitary life. And although there had always been hermits properly so-called, a sustained effort is discernible in the middle ages at providing a stable framework for the solitary life, so as to remove its possible drawbacks.

From the beginning of the middle ages there is a noticeable tendency towards the use of another penitential practice, the one we now call the discipline. In the Benedictine Rule the word 'discipline' denotes the entire process by which an offence is corrected: the preliminary warning and the subsequent reprimand, penalty and scourging. Scourging was prescribed for many offences, whether shouting and brawling, lying, treating what the monastery owned in common as though it were one's own private property, fornication, theft or even conversation with a woman in private. The child oblates, particularly, were liable to be whipped if they made a mistake in choir. But what we call the discipline at the present day is quite another thing. We now use the term to denote a whipping given or received not in punishment for a specific offence but as an act of atonement for one's own sins in general, or an act of reparation for the sins of the world. The discipline in this sense seems first to have been prescribed for the Camaldolese by St Romuald. He ordered his hermits to fast three days a week on bread and water, recite the whole of the psalter and the canticles every day, keep unbroken silence and take the discipline, *disciplinas flagellorum in cella facerent*.

When the practice was attacked, St Peter Damian came forward in its defence and thus helped to spread it further.

Another kind of penance which also spread widely during the middle ages was the wearing of the hair-shirt. The hair-shirt was not used in the Jewish way as a sign of mourning, but as a means of mortifying the body. Breastplates and belts of iron and crosses furnished with sharp points came into use at the same time. Thus in the Carthusian statutes Guy provides that every monk shall have two hair-shirts.

The most popular way of doing penance in the eleventh century or thereabouts was to go on pilgrimage. It remained so until the end of the middle ages and after. Jerusalem, Rome and St James of Compostella exerted a strange pull on men's hearts and made them ready to leave their families, homes and possessions and set out for the shrine of their choice, sometimes going barefooted, always begging their bread, facing all weathers, arousing suspicion and liable to have their most necessary requests refused. When they reached the goal of their pilgrimage they sometimes stayed there for years, like St Gerlac, who spent seven years at the hospital of St John of Jersualem as a swineherd. This kind of devotion was, however, forbidden to monks, for, as St Bernard writes, they were on pilgrimage to the heavenly Jerusalem. The councils of York in 1191 and London in 1200 gave similar decisions.

2. Conformity with Jesus Crucified

The ascetic tradition we have just analysed remained in existence after the end of the eleventh century and throughout the rest of the middle ages. It is well known that Cassian's *Conferences* were a favourite book with St Thomas Aquinas. It is perhaps not so well known that in very many houses they were regularly read by the monks, or the canons, as the case might be, before compline.

Yet the late eleventh century and the twelfth saw the appearance of a new spirit. Just as the twelfth century was an age of innovation in the fields of thought, piety, art and literature, so was it in asceticism. In a very real sense it marked the beginning of a new era in the history of Christian civilisation.

As far as the ascetic practices themselves were concerned there was scarcely any change, but the background against which they were considered was seen in another light. Asceticism became a matter of reproducing the likeness of Christ, copying his poverty and humiliation, suffering as he did on the cross. It was a touching idea and one that was to leave its mark in no uncertain way on the Christianity of the modern period.

Of course, an attentive study of early Christianity would belie the impression that this devotional approach to asceticism was unknown in the primitive Church, for it is based on the mystery of the incarnation. But from the time of St Anselm, John of Fécamp and the first crusades it comes out with such force that it quite alters the general outlook of things in the religious sphere.

The great change that then occurred was in connection with poverty. Poverty had always formed part of Christian asceticism; wealth with its deceptive promises, *fallacia divitiarum*, had always been the enemy. However, in the early days of monasticism, poverty simply meant living by manual labour; it did not exclude ownership altogether, because the solitaries used to give alms on a generous scale. Under the cenobitic system poverty strictly speaking came to mean having everything in common, to the consequent exclusion of all private ownership. St Augustine took the ideal from the Acts of the Apostles and defended it with great zeal; and from his time onwards all the monastic Rules dwell on it at length. Yet it may be that the term *paupertas* was never used to denote this virtue. The only instance I have found of it in Greek is in the typikon sent by the Empress Augusta to the nuns of St Mary's at Constantinople. There the phrase, 'Strive after the greatest possible poverty' occurs. But if the word itself was not used, that did not prevent many great abbots—SS. Euthymius, Sabas, Isaac, Richimirus, Corbinian, Vitalis—from refusing offers of income for their monasteries, because they wanted to live by their work alone.

But in the twelfth century all this underwent a change. Partly through the constant hard work put in by the religious and in consequence of the peace then prevailing in the west, precarious though it was, a certain degree of wealth was once more in evidence. Such a thing had not been seen since the barbarian invasions had destroyed the splendours of the Roman Empire. It was revealed now not so much through comfort as through luxury, and this unaccustomed luxury cut the true

Christian instinct to the quick. It turned to the cross and reacted strongly. 'God forbid that I should wear a crown of gold', Godfrey of Bouillon exclaimed, 'where my Saviour wore a crown of thorns.' And poverty was now represented as a virtue enabling men to live as Christ had lived.

Itinerant preachers were to be seen on the roads of France and Northern Europe, travelling in pairs and doing what Christ had told them to do in the gospel—giving as they had received the gift, without payment (Matt. 10: 8).

St Robert of Arbrissel, St Stephen of Muret, St Vitalis of Savignu and St Norbert were of their number. They kept their eyes on the gospels and wanted to carry out to the letter the directions Christ had given the apostles. And they preached perfection to everyone they came across. Men, women and children left their all to follow them and monasteries had to be built to house them. The orders of Fontevrault, Grandmont, Savigny (later affiliated to Cîteaux) and Premontré were the result. The cult of poverty flourished in them all. 'If when the Son of God was on earth, he had known of a better way back to heaven than poverty', St Stephen of Muret writes, 'he would have taken it.'

It was the same with St Norbert. He was always talking about *paupertas spontanea* and *paupertas voluntaria*, and his disciples who were proud to call themselves *pauperes Christi*, were so anxious to look poor that they were seen putting patches on their new habits.

The famous phrase about following naked the naked Christ, *nudus nudum Christum sequi*, is much older, because it comes from St Jerome; yet it was not until the twelfth century that it was first put into practice in every part of Christendom. And all this striving after poverty was to be crowned by the betrothal of St Francis of Assisi to Lady Poverty and by the prayer he said so often. 'Lord', he used to pray, 'have pity on me and on Lady Poverty. She is the queen of the virtues but she has to sit on a dunghill now. She complains that her friends will not look at her and have become her enemies. . . . Remember, Lord, that you came from where the angels live to take her as your bride, and have very many perfect children by her. She was the one who made you welcome in the cattle-shed and at the crib; she it was who went about with you all your life long and saw to it that you had nowhere to lay your head. When you began the battle for our redemption, Poverty followed you like a faithful squire; she stayed beside you while you fought and did not leave you when the others fled. Your mother followed you to the end and bore her share of all your sorrows; but when the time came that even she could come no closer, because the cross was so high, Lady Poverty held you tighter than ever. She would not have your cross elaborately wrought or the nails sharp and smooth and sufficient in number: she made them rough and coarse, the better to further the aim you had in undergoing this torment. And when you were dying of thirst, she took good care that you should be refused the slightest drop of water. So it was in the embrace of this bride that you breathed your last. Who would not love Lady Poverty more than any other creature?'

Anyone unable to see that this belongs to the heights or realise how stupendous an effort it represents at becoming like Christ through asceticism is to be pitied.

It was inevitable that the peak should be followed by a decline. Very few Franciscans really had the Franciscan spirit; there were not many like St Clare and St Antony of Padua, who managed to keep to the primitive ideal. For the most part, human weakness went downhill in one of two ways. Some drifted into seeking comfort (though this 'comfort' did not amount to much); others fell into an Ebiomistic frame of mind which led them to condemn all wealth as evil and all wealth in the Church as a monstrosity. As was to be expected, this latter party was condemned.

Devotion to Christ's suffering humanity also found expression in flagellation. The thought of Christ scourged at the pillar was often present to the saints; they dwelt on it with loving attention. If disciplines were often wet with blood, it was not because the bodies of the ascetics and virgins who wielded them were in particular need of chastisement. It did not mean, as a rule, that a passion for cruelty was seeking appeasement that way instead of on another's body. It simply came from the urge to be as Christ was when his flesh was torn by the rod and the lash.

The story of Henry Suso's mortifications provokes a shudder
as one reads of the horsehair shirt with its straps fitted with
five hundred sharp points, the bracelets that crushed his hands
at night, the gloves with their projecting pins, the cross set
with thirty iron nails that he wore on his bare flesh, between the
shoulders, and the disciplines wet with blood. Sometimes he
saw himself what a pitiable object he was, and then he wept;
but he went on all the same, setting before his imagination
the picture of the Lord he loved, bound to the pillar and cruelly
beaten with rods.[1] And he was not the only one who acted so.

Thus from the twelfth century onwards, the effort to reproduce what Jesus had suffered from his poverty and his scourging
came to occupy a prominent place in asceticism.

We may mention in passing one ascetic practice not connected
with this idea—or so, at any rate, it would seem at first sight—
yet gaining ground more and more as the thirteenth century
wore on, especially with the Dominicans. This was the pursuit
of knowledge. It was undertaken not as a deliberate piece of
ascetic training but as a means of supplying the Church's needs
in the way of preaching and teaching. Yet in practice it came
in many houses to be substituted for the manual work which had
played so large a part in the older asceticism. There is scarcely
any need to point out that study made quite as many demands
on the religious and was just as painful as manual work.
St Thomas stresses the fact when he dwells on the mortification
implied in the study of theology. Pride, which seeks knowledge
only to bolster itself up, vain curiosity and laziness, desire for
secular reading or reading outside the scope of the precise
subject being studied at the moment, the inclination to seek
supernatural knowledge to the detriment of rational and the
tendency to centre all learning on the self, must all be resisted
and mortified. Unfortunately, this mortification was often
wanting towards the end of the middle ages, and many students
found that their work brought them spiritual dryness and
cut off their prayer at its source.

All these varieties of asceticism were on the whole contemplative in tendency. Until the thirteenth century, it was
considered that spiritual life consisted of two parts, the active

1 H. Suso, *Oeuvres poetiques*, trans. Thiroui, Paris, 1899, i. p. 66.

life and the contemplative life. The classification is several
times mentioned by St Thomas. But it was not taken then, as
it is now, to apply to two distinct ways of life, the one arranged
with a view to contemplation and the other existing for the
sake of the apostolate and the works of mercy. The active and
the contemplative were successive phases of one and the same
life. The active life was the one lived by beginners and those
who had made a certain amount of progress, the life, that is,
of those who were working to acquire the Christian virtues by
means of set exercises and mortifications. It amounted to
what is now called asceticism. The contemplative life was the
one lived by those who had already reached perfection. Its
symbol was the psalm *Beati immaculati in via* in the canons'
office, while the other was symbolised by the gradual psalms
which the monks recited at the little hours.[1] But the two
parts fitted closely together to form one whole. As Adam Scotus,
the Premonstratensian (later Carthusian), put it, in the active
life you search for the lost silver piece (Luke 15: 8), while in
the contemplative life you look at the likeness stamped on it.
This is a point of view which must never be lost sight of when
reading the spiritual writers of the middle ages.

The spiritual writers are in fact our next subject of discussion.
It is easy to find works embodying the ascetic tradition derived
from the early Church, the tradition we discussed in the first
part of this article. The whole thing is as it were summed up
in the Rule of St Benedict. But the second tradition, the one
beginning at the end of the eleventh century, will be found
scattered in a host of saints' Lives, collections of monastic
statutes and theological treatises. There is no end to these
works, and the fact that Migne's *Patrologia* finishes with the
thirteenth century does not make them any easier to come by,
in spite of their relevance to our purpose. Hence the most we
can do will be to take a bird's-eye view of the country and
pick out the most conspicuous features from afar.

St Bernard will detain us a moment. He is likely to prove

---

1 In actual fact, the controversies between the monks and the canons turned on
more fundamental things than these, but neither party could say what they were.
The monks would not realise that ministerial work, which requires the priest
to be at his neighbour's disposal all the time, constitutes a very great mortification. That was at the bottom of the dispute.

disappointing to anyone approaching him for the first time
with no more than a knowledge obtained from hearsay.
What the critics always draw attention to in connection with
him is the element characteristic of the new devotional spirit,
especially its demonstrative affection for Christ and the
Blessed Virgin, which attains its full intensity in him. Yet
passages bearing the stamp of this exceptional delicacy of
emotion are by no means common in his works. Taken as a
whole, his writings reflect the Benedictine tradition more
than anything else, the tradition of the monks. The mere
fact that the *De Ordinatione Vitae* of the 'man of God', John,
Abbot of Fruttuaria, who is perhaps the best representative of
the old tradition, and the *Scala Claustralium*, which is probably by
Guy the Carthusian, could be attributed to him without
any inherent improbability, is enough to show that this was so.

His theory of asceticism is the result of a very careful study
of the relationship between grace and free will. Grace is useless
without the co-operation of free will. Grace and free will work
in concert and not separately; they act together and not turn
and turn about. There is no question of their each contributing
part of the force required to produce a given effect; both together produce the whole effect.[1]

Bernard deals with the necessity of grace in his treatise
De Gratia Et Libero Arbitrio. He does not very often return to
the question elsewhere; most of the time the point he stresses
is that essential requirement for spiritual progress, the conviction that however perfect you may be, you must never stop
trying to become still more perfect. *Nemo perfectus qui perfectior
esse non appetit.* If you stop trying to go forward, you go back-
wards. *Nolle proficere deficere est.* And the means he most recommends for making progress is the cultivation of humility.
In that respect he comes into line with the oldest tradition of
all in asceticism: his treatise *De Gradibus Humilitatis et Superbiae*
is nothing but a commentary on one of the chapters in
St Benedict's Rule, enlivened with psychological examples.

Bernard did not deny that perfection could be sought in the

---

1 *De libertate et gratia* is a problem frequently discussed by the spiritual writers of
the middle ages. It is evident that their interest in the question turns not so
much on the theological issues at stake as on the spiritual ones.

world, but he regarded the religious life as the normal means of attaining it. In this he shared the views of all the other writers of the twelfth century. The religious life he thought of as constituted by poverty, obedience and mortification. He laid particular stress on this last point: the more austere a particular kind of religious life was, the better it must be. In the controversy between the monks and the canons regular he naturally sided with the monks. Notwithstanding his friendliness towards St Norbert and the Premonstratensians, he could never see that the cure of souls and the anxieties arising from it implied just as much renunciation and mortification as the practices followed in the monastic life.

His idea of the religious life was so traditional that even at that time it seemed a little out-of-date. It is thoroughly monastic and does not clearly distinguish the three religious virtues.

At the same time the modern idea of life in common under the vows of poverty, chastity and obedience was gradually coming out in the new orders.[1] The Canons of the Holy Sepulchre promised to live chastely and obediently without private property. St Norbert said in his Sermon that his religious ought to be quick to obey, poor by their own choice and noted for their chastity. If these three things were absent, the essence of the order would be missing. A little later St Francis of Assisi wrote, 'The rule, the life of these brethren [the Friars Minor] is to live obediently and chastely without anything of their own.' In the light of this new idea, the religious life came to be regarded as capable of supplying help to the Church in all her needs. This was the concept defended by men like St Bonaventure and St Thomas Aquinas.

These two great theologians were the chief representatives of ascetic theory in the middle ages, though the treatises of such men as David of Augsberg and St Vincent Ferrer were widely copied and exerted considerable influence on ascetic practice.

It is not, perhaps, in his spiritual treatises that St Thomas

---

1 The idea took shape only gradually. Though its development was fairly rapid in the twelfth century, it was not so rapid as we are inclined to suppose. When St Bernard was asked what the essence of the religious life was, he said, 'Poverty, obedience and mortification.' The idea is very close to ours, but it is not quite the same.

Aquinas makes his most noteworthy contribution to the subject, although the *Contra Impugnantes Dei Cultum Et Religionem* is a magnificent apologia for the religious life and lays down the fruitful principle that one religious order is superior to another not primarily because it is more austere but because it has a superior end. But the whole of the second part of the *Summa Theologica* contains a complete and balanced theory of asceticism. It goes thoroughly into the question of the disorder existing in our tainted nature and the importance of the passions as a force for good or evil. It carefully analyses the workings of the will. It provides a clear and searching account of the Christian virtues, their respective values, their relationship to one another and the means by which they may be practised.

Although St Bonaventure wrote more on asceticism than on mysticism, his works nevertheless provide the reader with a mass of important ascetical teaching. The pseudo-Denis's division of the spiritual life into the three stages of *purgatio*, *illuminatio* and *perfectio* obtained lasting acceptance in the west thanks to him, with the difference that marked emphasis was now laid on the ascetic side. His two Lives of St Francis and his minor writings on the religious life also deserve attention.

The end of the middle ages saw the rise of the school of Windesheim in Holland, founded by Gerard Groot and counting Gerlac Peters and Thomas à Kempis as its two main writers. Gerard Groot's spiritual journal seems to have provided Thomas à Kempis with the ideas and the plan for the *Imitation of Christ*, which he cast in that elegant rhythmic form that makes so deep an impression on the memory.

The *Imitation* may be said to provide a synthesis and epitome of medieval spirituality (though with a trace of sadness, perhaps, in the formulation), just as the Rule of St Benedict does for the spirituality of early monasticism.

3. *Tentative Efforts to Lead the Ascetic Life Outside the Cloister*
If of all places the cloister is the one most favourable to the pursuit of the spiritual life, the call to perfection is nevertheless made to all Christians and not just to religious.

It must be admitted that no movement will be found in the

middle ages at all like the one started by St Francis de Sales for bringing people in the world to the pursuit of the perfect life. All the same, there was nothing in the west comparable to the moral attitude of Russia in the east, where the laity so often resigned themselves to mediocrity or sin in their moral life because the spiritual support of monasticism was beyond their reach. The third orders, for instance, did much to raise the moral level of the hosts of Brethren and Sisters of Penance who joined them.

Later, John Gerson raised the question of the kind of religious training suitable for small children, *de parvulis ad Christum trahendis*, and suggested means (or *industriae*, as he called them) for preparing the soul for contemplation by a kind of advanced asceticism. He showed how the soul ought to be made simpler, purer and more stable, so as to become capable of forming a much higher and purer idea of God. And this ideal was not restricted to the cloister. Gerson had no hesitation in setting it before his sisters for their guidance in the celibate life they were living in the world. The secular saints—people like St Louis and St Joan of Arc, for instance—carried their asceticism to the point of heroism. Their anxiety to fulfil the duties of their state of life properly made them live what was in essence the religious life, though they never imitated its observances, or if they did, it was with very wide modifications. Solid habits of faith and austerity had been handed on to them by their families, and these served to prepare them for their ascetic way of living. Anyone giving more than a merely superficial attention to their lives will soon become aware of all this. But the history of medieval asceticism outside the religious life and among the laity deserves to be studied in greater detail. The absence of such a study forces us to limit our observations to an outline so general as to be of very little use.[1]

1 All the same, there was a degree of asceticism in the middle ages which would seem astounding today. The life of St Joan of Arc will serve as an example of it. We know that she fasted every Friday—the practice was common enough. She was forced to sleep next to the men-at-arms when she was campaigning, and we find her doing so without unlacing her armour. It must have been very painful, though it was no doubt done from motives of prudence as well. And in prison, where she might reasonably have considered herself dispensed from some of her penitential practices, she would not avail herself of any dispensation at all. She was asked whether she had done penance through Lent, and although she

Such, then, as far as we can see, is the history of the main features of medieval asceticism. With very few exceptions, asceticism was evidently considered at this time not as an end but as a means. There was no question of annihilating the self, still less of satisfying a sort of sadistic urge by crushing one's own body; the aim throughout was to keep the soul free for the prayer and contemplation that would unite it with God. The place occupied by asceticism in medieval spirituality is really very modest. If all the strictly ascetical passages in the spiritual writers were collected together, they would make a very small book in comparison with the passages on contemplation, methods and models of prayer, meditation on the literal and allegorical senses of scripture and mystical theory. It is a far cry from this to the spiritual literature of today. It was largely because asceticism was both practised with vigour and kept in its proper place in the middle ages that the period saw such a flowering of childlike joy, tinged with compassion for Christ's sufferings and his mother's. For the same reason, this joy never failed, in spite of all there was to try it so cruelly towards the end.

All the same, the later middle ages, just before the end, present a somewhat different appearance. They were characterised by an impoverishment in the spiritual life of the clergy and religious, a decline in fervour eventually leading to a marked reaction in favour of asceticism.

This slackening in the spiritual *tonus* came in part from the substitution of scholastic studies in the religious houses for the old *lectio divina*, which was as much an exercise in praying and loving as a means of learning properly so-called. As the new ways of learning were directed at the mind alone, some sort of compensation ought to have been provided, some means of giving the soul that personal converse with God which was now denied it and for want of which liturgical prayer became mere formalism, however solemnly it might be celebrated.

In the second place, the system by which benefices were given to graduates in law and medicine as well as to those with

was told that she was not bound to answer, she said that she had kept the fast the whole time. At one point in Lent she had sent for a doctor, because it was feared that she would die a natural death and so escape burning. Yet that had not stopped her from fasting every day.

degrees in theology led many clerks to forsake theology for
canon law, a subject which had not nearly the same power
of turning the soul Godward.

Again, many abbeys and convents were burned or plundered
during the Hundred Years' War. It thus became necessary
for the religious to seek what refuge they could, with their
families or elsewhere, a circumstance far from propitious to
religious fervour. Even where the monasteries survived, there
was such want of the necessities of life that it inevitably made
the religious preoccupied with material worries and so did
harm to the spirit of poverty. Further, the exile of the popes
at Avignon, and then the great schism and the Council of
Bale, seemed to have turned the world quite upside down,
while the Turkish successes in eastern Europe made men
tremble for the very existence of Christianity.

Hence the reaction of the saints in the direction of asceticism.
Vincent Ferrer led processions of flagellants. Colette brought the
Poor Clares back to the austerity of the primitive Rule.
Catherine of Siena did without food almost entirely.

Hence too the distrust felt by the school of Windesheim for
the decadent scholasticism of the time. Hence the efforts to
invent spiritual exercises distinct from the liturgy—things
like the rosary, for example—so as to make possible the
genuine prayer which the singing of psalms ill-understood
and never digested through meditation could no longer
provide.

The men of the renaissance took a long time to find their
feet in the fields of art and thought. It was the same in the
field of asceticism. The medieval practices had aged with the
society they had helped to mould. Men now wanted less social
means of perfection, things more personal to themselves.
These were to be worked out by the doctors and saints of the
sixteenth and seventeenth centuries.

CHAPTER IV

CHRISTIAN ASCETICISM IN FRANCE FROM
THE XVIth CENTURY TO THE XVIIIth
CENTURY

By L. COGNET

THERE can be no doubt that at the very end of the middle ages a certain lack of balance is discernible in every field of spiritual activity—in art and mortality, in philosophy and in religion. In every case there was a gap between the formal elements and the ideas underlying them, a gap which was bridged only with the greatest difficulty. The cleavage is particularly evident in the case of the questions we are concerned with at the moment.

The estrangement between spirituality and theology which had begun when the middle ages were at their height came to a head in the *devotio moderna*. Theology now became a science, an affair for specialists, a set of speculations barren of consequences for the Christian life. Conversely, the problem of union with God was stated without reference to an intellectual context; in fact spiritual writers often went so far as to consider knowledge an obstacle to that union. Nothing could be more typical of this point of view than the Imitation of Jesus Christ. The anti-intellectualism and contempt for knowledge evident in that work certainly express a state of mind that was becoming more and more common at the time.

Further, in the fifteenth century people everywhere tried to externalise and objectivise their vague inner awareness that all was not well, by making pain as such an integral part of their system. The cult of pain came in, both in art and in religion. The tendency to make pain one of the chief subjects for representation and to confer an absolute value on it, independent of any correlation with the religious sphere, was already

51

clearly manifest. The idea that suffering is a noble thing in itself and bestows something almost sacred on the sufferer also began to appear. Late medieval poetry is particularly sympto-matic of this attitude.

Hence, from this time onwards the painful side of asceticism becomes particularly marked. People had not been unaware of this side of the question in previous ages, but they had thought of suffering chiefly as being a necessary concomitant of certain actions; it had certainly not seemed to be itself alone the basis and principal means of asceticism. The tendency had shown itself long ago in St Peter Damian and the flagellants, but it did not appear in all its fulness until the fifteenth century. There were two factors which helped to keep it within due bounds and preserve its specifically Christian character. The first was devotion to Christ's humanity. This was real enough to ensure that the cult of pain, in spite of its seductive nature, should always be referred to the Saviour's passion. The second was the ardently mystical character of fifteenth-century piety, which meant that the asceticism it inspired flowed spontaneously all the time and escaped the dryness that comes from too rigid an application of rules. All the same, lives like St Lydwine of Schiedam's and Bl. Henry Suso's make one feel a trifle uneasy in spite of one's admiration for them. Their mortifications were really terrifying and their orgies of suffering were sought after a little too much for their own sake.

*   *   *

Into this troubled atmosphere burst the great thunderbolt of the renaissance. The literary side of the renaissance is undoubtedly the one that makes the greatest impression today, but in fact it was never of more than secondary importance, relatively speaking, at any rate. The really significant thing was that the scale of values had been turned clean upside-down and every field of mental activity transformed in consequence, so that man was once more the focal point of all speculation on intellectual and moral matters. The medieval theorists may have hesitated over the question and changed their minds about it, but they always regarded man as a creature with an end higher than himself, a supernatural, transcendent end.

But the humanists refused to see in man anything more than man, and would not assign to him any end but his own nature.

As the very idea of Christian asceticism is essentially bound up with the supernatural view of man, the rejection of this view, whether in theory or in practice, was bound to lead to the abandonment of asceticism. Humanism provided a substitute of sorts, however, in the shape of the cult of human perfection, for the effort a man would have to make if he wanted to develop his natural powers to the full, cultivate all his faculties one in harmony with another and make use of all his potentialities, was considerable. Although the ideal was a purely human one, it could be very exacting. But it was none the less incompatible with Christian asceticism, in so far as Christian asceticism entails the restriction of natural activity and almost the mutilation of nature.

For the man, then, who was a humanist and nothing more, asceticism ceased to have any meaning or justification at all. But those who still remained devoted to Christianity and claimed that their humanistic pursuits were compatible with it—as many did—saw the problem in a different light.

They failed to grasp the dynamic element in Christian asceticism, which makes it essentially a kind of folly, folly inspired by the cross. Many of them tried hard to prove that the demands it made, if complied with, produced the conditions necessary for a balanced human life, produced even the ideal conditions for full human development. In short, on this hypothesis, Christian virtue at its highest amounted to little more than ordinary natural virtue; it surpassed it only by reason of its higher aims and objects. Such, in broad outline, was the position taken up by Pierre Charron, Guillaume de Vair and the 'devout humanists' as a whole. It amounted to a thorough humanisation of Christian asceticism.

But other professional ascetics went further still in the directions of reconciling humanism with Christian asceticism. In their anxiety to conform to the prevailing fashion, they did not hesitate to undermine the traditional principles. Their basic argument was that man was the noblest creature that had come from God's hands and human activity the most perfect praise that could be given to the Creator. It would

E

therefore be wrong to allow any kind of asceticism which might
diminish or even simply restrict the free exercise of that
activity. Christians would thus be well advised to give themselves
without reserve or misgiving to worldly activity in all its
forms. The mortifications of the saints were permitted or even
willed by God to show what man was capable of, but care should
be taken not to regard them as models to be copied. There
can be no doubt that this was the attitude taken up by many
French Jesuits in the sixteenth century and at the beginning
of the seventeenth. P. Binet is probably the best example of the
school. Others, like P. Garasse, skirted the difficulty by using
the theory of the two ends. According to them, part of a man's
activity is meant for God and part for the man himself. Consequently, we are square with God when we have given him his
part. Hence P. Garasse has no hesitation in comparing the
relationship between God and man to that between one
businessman and another. Asceticism properly so-called thus
came to be superseded by devotional practices, which were
regarded by their adepts as pledges of salvation. P. Lemoyne,
the much-mocked priest of the *Provinciales*, is the prize specimen
of the brood.

*   *   *

In actual fact, all these fanciful theories constituted a serious
distortion of the Christian view of asceticism; they show how
superficial attempts to bring Christian asceticism into harmony
with humanism inevitably led to failure. The real solution
would have been to think out the whole ascetic problem
afresh in a humanist spirit. We shall see that the two really
new syntheses which saw the light in the sixteenth century—
those produced by St Ignatius and St Francis de Sales—did
work along those lines.

Of course, it cannot be said that St Ignatius was a humanist
in the strict sense of the term. But if he does not deserve the
title on intellectual grounds, he has a right to it from another
point of view, for no one understood the spirit of his age and
its concrete needs better than he. It is obvious that the Exercises
are anything but a theory of asceticism, and it should not be
forgotten that first and foremost they constitute a method of

converting the soul and bringing it spiritual renewal. It is precisely because they are a method that they are relevant to our present purpose. For through their wide circulation they have in no small degree helped to make asceticism into a technical process. The Exercises are like a recipe for making something. They have this characteristic to a marked extent, and although the text supposes that there will be someone to 'give' them and regulate their use, the feature remains a particularly striking one. The idea comes out very clearly that a given set of acts and considerations, if judiciously chosen in view of a desired end, must almost necessarily lead to a certain state of mind and of will. This point of view was entirely new, all the more so as the choice and manipulation of the acts and considerations seems to depend much more on accurate knowledge of human nature than on the dictates of Christian dogma. The traditional ascetic practices are used in the Exercises as means, but these means are taken in themselves, without any essential reference to the religious content which is their ultimate justification. Those of the Additions at the end of the first week which concern penance are typical in this respect. The letters of St Ignatius and his biography show that the saint himself could apply his principles with a great deal of flexibility and shrewd insight. But in the hands of his spiritual sons the procedure eventually took on a certain rigidity and in the end was canonised for its own sake. Many contemporary works on asceticism still bear traces of this attitude. The Ignatian system does not attempt to reduce the various kinds of ascetic effort required of men to codify them. That was what gave it an affinity with the humanist outlook and enabled it to be grafted on to that outlook.

Unlike St Ignatius, St Francis de Sales really was a humanist and he relied to a large extent on his literary and philosophical attainments. But to insist on crediting him with a theory of asceticism at all costs would probably be to misrepresent him, for the most noticeable feature of his teaching is its synthetic character, an evident consequence of his great concern with apologetics. His contacts with the protestant reformers must have speedily convinced him that a purely intellectual form of apologetics was useless. He very soon came to feel that the most pressing need was to show the world the spectacle of

Catholics living a fully Christian life and so provide an effective
counterpart to the example given by the protestants. His chief
aim throughout the *Introduction to the Devout Life* is to show how
the ordinary actions of life as it is lived by ordinary people in
the world can be christianised. This presupposes a decrease
in emphasis on the external side of asceticism and a corresponding concentration of attention primarily on the internal side.
It then very soon comes to be considered that the essential
thing to bother about is the state the mind and will are in.
Thus the saint's asceticial teaching bears a strongly psychological stamp. Consequently the idea of spiritual direction plays
a considerable part in it: a really dependable guide is an
absolute necessity for a safe passage through the subtle mazes
woven by the mind and will, and much more is required of him
than is expected of an ordinary confessor. In this respect,
St Francis de Sales is unquestionably the source of the views
we hold today on spiritual direction. It should be noted, too,
that he also remained faithful to the traditional ascetic practices. He has acquired a reputation for a rather insipid sort of
mildness, but this is belied by the fact that he used the old
practices to an extent that would seem very severe today.
Yet he never regarded those practices as anything but a more
or less indispensable means of bringing about a certain psychological state, which was the only thing that really counted.
He applied all this with a degree of flexibility and a shrewdness
of insight that justify his tremendous reputation as a director.
Nevertheless it is quite clear that his asceticism was psychological
in character; it bore on internal conditions. That is the point
where it fits in with humanist culture, which was just as
psychological. The saint also joins forces with humanism through
his pronounced optimism, which makes him carefully hunt out
and enumerate everything in our nature that has escaped
corruption by original sin. He goes far in this direction and the
effect of asceticism, as he sees it, is much more to develop
already existing potentialities than to put a fundamentally
corrupt nature on to a sound basis again. Hence the essentially
balanced, human and almost rational note in his asceticism.

*   *   *

It is a curious thing how little influence the asceticism produced by the renaissance had on the cloister. The phenomenon is strange enough. Until the sixteenth century the development of ascetical theory, the thorough study and, to a certain extent, the practice of it, had been carried on almost exclusively in religious houses, and the faithful in general had only been allowed to share in something not directly made for them. The immediate objective of St Ignatius, however, and still more of St Francis de Sales, in their ascetical writings, was to reach people outside the religious houses; and if their systems acquired any importance at all for the professional ascetics shut up in the cloister, it was only indirectly. The period of secular asceticism as distinct from asceticism in the religious life, was beginning. It is the period we are still living in.

The phenomenon in question was chiefly due to the advanced state of decay affecting the religious orders in the sixteenth century. The fact is well known and there is no need to dwell on it here. It eventually amounted to almost total failure on the part of the religious houses to fulfil their spiritual mission. Another cause, however, is undoubtedly to be found in the humanist spirit, which directed attention to man considered in himself and naturally did not take kindly to the slightly artificial framework of conventual life.

Thus the religious revival evident in France at the end of the sixteenth century was first and foremost the work of secular priests and lay people: the very important part played, for instance, by Mme Acarie and her circle will at once come to mind. It is true that the religious houses soon came into the movement, which indeed in a few years produced a reform of the orders; but all the same, they did not initiate the movement, and from this time onwards the almost exclusive control they had exercised over the theology of the spiritual life was lost to them for ever.

The effervescence of ideas caused by the revival was certainly not without consequences in the field of asceticism. Yet the initial effort of the reformers had not borne on that: their first concern had been to synthesise contemporary ideas about the spiritual life with the traditional ones and then to spread their synthesis. Thus their intervention in the ascetic field needs to be considered in relation to their spirituality.

The dominant figure throughout the period is of course the great Berulle. Yet in fact his importance in the history of asceticism is of the slightest. He simply accepted the results of previous thinking on the subject. He also accepted the traditional methods, though he was influenced to some extent by St Francis de Sales. His works contain nothing original from this point of view. What is much more interesting is the way he grafts the traditional asceticism on to his own Christological spirituality. He definitely parts company with St Francis de Sales on that point. As we have seen, St Francis had aimed at working out a psychological form of asceticism. But this side of the matter was of slight importance to Berulle, who was not much of a psychologist and was not much interested in the individual. The thing that mattered to him was that the soul should be made to take up a certain attitude. This attitude was essentially dogmatic: the soul was to reproduce in itself the various dispositions found in the soul of the Incarnate Word. Asceticism with him all boiled down to his theory of abnegation and had no other object but to promote the attitude of mind just mentioned. From this point of view, then, he makes asceticism entirely an affair of the reason. No doubt there is a strongly affective element underlying it, but it none the less remains a means of inducing a certain state of mind and spirit, a means in which mental conviction plays a large part. The same tendency is found in P. de Condren, his successor, though in his case it is deeply coloured by special insistence on the annihilation of everything but God in the soul.

*   *   *

Much more novel ideas came in with another of Berulle's disciples, Jean Duvergier de Hauranne, abbot of Saint-Cyran. Saint-Cyran's spiritual training had given him a thorough knowledge of Berulle's Christological system, and on the whole he took up the same position as his master with regard to the place of asceticism in the Christian life. But he had a perceptibly different angle of approach: the problem of human salvation was a much more urgent question to him. His characteristically Augustinian pessimism was practically the same as Berulle's. Only he carried it much more nearly to its logical extreme and considered that conversion, a moral revolution, was a radical necessity. That was the starting-point of his ideas on asceticism. What he concentrated on in the Christian life was the spiritual condition a man was in and not his acts, at any rate not directly, because in his eyes these were only signs of the spiritual condition which had produced them. Thus no idea could be more foreign to his mind than the notion of a life spent in a continual round of falling into sin, obtaining forgiveness and then committing the same sin over again. As he saw it, the problem of conversion was to bring the sinner out of the state of sin into another state, a relatively stable one in theory, the state of grace. This is where Saint-Cyran's psychological propensities came in. In many ways they invite comparison with St Francis de Sales, and they gave Saint-Cyran the idea that conversion was impossible unless the mind was given a good jolt. The method he advocated for changing the sinner into a penitent was to make him conscious of his moral indigence by means of a certain number of external signs, especially the withholding of the sacraments. (Saint-Cyran himself intended that the sacraments should be withheld for a short while only—a few weeks or at most a few months; but his later disciples did not always apply the principle with the same moderation.) Then, when the desired psychological effect seemed to have been obtained, when the conversion seemed complete, the penitent was reconciled by absolution and admitted once more to communion. Such was Saint-Cyran's technique of 'renewal'. But even after this spiritual renewal, the newly-reconciled penitent still had to remain a penitent in the wider sense of the term. He had to go on doing penance so as to avoid suffering a counter-attack from concupiscence, for concupiscence is at the very root of human nature and our spontaneous bent lies that way. By continuing his penances, the penitent would of course atone for his sins but he would also be sure—with God's help—of persevering to the end of his life.

This accounts for the severity of tone in Saint-Cyran's asceticism, born as it was of intense concern with the problem of salvation and characterised by a marked distrust of nature.

It was undoubtedly psychological in form at the beginning, but Saint-Cyran and Arnauld after him later struck the historical note with no uncertain force and made out that the process of 'renewal' was a return to the practice of the early Church, though in so doing they were only following a general Counter-Reformation tendency.

It is a fact, too, that Saint-Cyran showed a marked preference for archaic forms and made an obvious attempt to return to primitive techniques when he came to put his theories into practice. The Solitaries he sent to Port Royal regarded themselves to some extent as heirs of the desert fathers. Hence the thoroughly traditional character of their penitential practices. Solitude came first—withdrawal from the world, separation from the social group because it was enslaved to pride and covetousness and regarded as evil and an enemy of God. Prayer was first and foremost liturgical and vocal, mental prayer being considered good but of secondary importance. Abstinence and fasting were practised and the time allowed for sleep was cut down. Manual work was done as a penance but more as an exercise in humility, a challenge to the proud prejudices of the contemporary world. The only concession to more recent practice lay in the use of instruments of penance: the hair-shirt and the discipline were used, but with the greatest moderation. In short, the life Saint-Cyran devised for his Solitaries was very like the kind of life lived by the Carthusians he so much admired.

Such methods were perfectly suited to the monastic life, and when Saint-Cyran came to direct the nuns of Port Royal, he had no great change to make in his point of view. The conventual life seemed to him to be the very type of the life of penance. Hence he did not like the nuns to add anything to what was prescribed by the Rule: anything at all personal, any penance undertaken as a work of supererogation, was apt to be suspect in his eyes. It is strange to see how his ideas were kept alive at Port Royal. Mère Angelique Arnauld had more to do with it than anyone. Her strongly-marked personality, sharp temper, stubborn self-will and remarkably extensive influence enabled her to keep Port Royal in an atmosphere of poverty, austerity and absolute fidelity to the Rule; and even her death did not arrest the movement she had set going.

She influenced Port Royal in person for a few years only, but even after that the house still remained the ideal place where Saint-Cyran's ideals could be seen carried out in practice. It continued to be the intermediary between those ideals and the religious world in general, which it thus brought under their influence. Life was still rough at the time, much blood was shed over questions of honour, morality was none too strict. Hence the sight of people practising all this austerity, humility and poverty from choice took hold of men's imaginations and made a great impression on public opinion. The Solitaries and the nuns became a sign which was contradicted. But the polemical side does not concern us much here. The thing that matters for our present purpose is that Port Royal left its mark on the age it belonged to, both through its friends and through its enemies. The famous austerity of the Grand Siècle comes from Port Royal, is simply the stamp Port Royal impressed upon it.

But how is this austerity to be defined? As a matter of fact, on its ascetic side it seems at first sight to imply nothing very original: it amounted to this, that the practices followed at Port Royal and the severity and exacting demands of the place spread beyond the nuns of the Solitaries and were increasingly taken up by ordinary Christians. Yet on closer examination it will be seen that it all had one note in common —a sort of general distrust of nature, a quasi-instinctive need for restraint and contempt for compromise on moral questions. These were the specific features in the asceticism of the classical period, quite apart from any question of doctrine. They were no doubt more marked in the Jansenist party, which had been to a large extent responsible for them in the first place, but the people directed by St Vincent de Paul and M. Olier were not a whit behind the Jansenists in this respect. While the *Provinciales* were flaying the causists for their over-indulgent attitude in moral matters, the rigorists had already won the battle on the spiritual front, and the Jesuits themselves had presented the world with moralists as strict as any Pascal speaks of before ever Bourdaloue appeared. Here again the theological controversy involved is not of much concern to us in our present enquiry: distrust of nature and the desire for a pattern of restrained living were common to all schools.

* * *

However, in proportion as seventeenth-century asceticism acquired a recognisable shape of its own, it came to be marked by a further feature which, like the others, extended to all schools irrespective of their opinions about doctrine. It gradually fell under the sway of that tendency to psychologise about the spiritual life which we saw in its early stages in St Francis de Sales and Saint-Cyran.

It is a truism to say that the seventeenth century was an age deeply interested in psychology and reason. By the end of Henry IV's reign, the desire to plumb the depths of what was called the human heart was beginning to be consciously felt. Men wanted to unpick the threads of its motives and analyse the obscurest forces behind its actions. And if this imperious desire was to be satisfied, it was also necessary that people should be able to give an accurate account of all their reactions, even the slightest. It was an accepted principle that these always had an intelligible cause and that a properly-conducted dialectical process ought to reveal what it was. This psychologising was essentially concerned with the reason; it may even be called rationalist. As it found the subconscious embarrassing, it strove to reduce the field in which it operated, and if it sometimes touched on the subconscious in its descriptions, it did so in spite of itself.

Asceticism could not, of course, escape this tendency. Before this time St Francis de Sales, Berulle, Condren, Saint-Cyran, Olier and many others had each in their own way stressed the importance of the inner states of mind and will in the Christian life; they had made introspection a necessary means to the attainment of the end of asceticism. A slight increase in emphasis was all that was needed in the later period to make it the fundamental and almost the only method. The essential difference between the two periods, however, is that none of the theorists we have mentioned ever thought of making introspection an end in itself where asceticism was concerned. As they saw it, it was always subservient to a religious end and, in the last analysis, to a dogmatic one.

Whereas the habit of psychologising on an exclusively rational basis introduced a prejudice which came to underly all speculation arising from it. This was the idea that all a man does, all that occupies his mind, all his reactions are spontaneously and of their nature directed towards the furthering of his personal interests; the idea that in psychology everything is governed by what La Rochefoucauld called self-love. The moralists of the period did their best to furnish detailed proofs of this thesis. The ascetic writers used the material thus provided more or less as it stood, but they were not limited to the descriptive point of view: they tried to devise a technique for healing psychological disorders as well.

Thus the pessimism of the earlier writers had eventually led to distrust of nature—a position ordinary and traditional enough—but in the present case this distrust of nature had crystallised in an essentially psychological form and issued in the struggle against self-centredness and self-love. The writers of the second generation, then, set out to do two things: to unmask self-seeking, however subtle its disguise, and to point out methods for curing it. Needless to say, they all had a background of dogma and religion behind their psychological pursuits, and the road they mapped out was meant to be followed out of real love for God. Yet this suggested method of self-stripping may not have rested on a specifically Christian basis. It was essentially a repudiation of the cult of nature, but in some ways it was only the other side of the same medal; it remained on the same level as the thing it repudiated and never succeeded in freeing itself from it. Hence it is not surprising that the methods and technique of the 'self-culture' which was one of the products of humanism should sometimes be found in it, though as it were turned inside out. But, I repeat, traces of this sort of thing were scarcely perceptible, the tendencies involved scarcely present even in outline. On the whole, these writers were saved by the Christological cast of their thought and the anxiety for union with the incarnate Word which was so marked a feature of French piety at that time.

The first name that comes to mind in connection with the practice of psychologising is Nicole's, whose *Essais de Morale* delighted so many people in the seventeenth and eighteenth centuries, though now they lie in undeserved oblivion. It would be an exaggeration to say that Nicole wrote nothing of importance besides his ascetic treatises: he had a very good mind and was unquestionably one of the abler theologians of his time. All the same, it was mainly by his ascetic treatises that he made his name, and it must be admitted that it would be difficult to carry the form of psychological analysis he uses in them to greater lengths. Their subtlety, in fact, is doubtless the chief ground of criticism that can be urged against them. Nicole was the means of introducing the method at Port Royal, where it was destined to find highly talented exponents. The most interesting is no doubt Mère Angelique de Saint Jean, a niece of the original Mère Angelique. She did not like Nicole, but all the same, her writings are not a whit behind his, either in subtlety of analysis or in literary merit. Her curious *Examen de conscience a l'usage des religieuses de Port-Royal* is probably the best of the works written in the style whose possibilities had been shown by her aunt, Mère Agnes, in her *Image d'une religieuse parfaite et imparfaite.* The whole of the second generation of writers at Port Royal, moreover, was deeply marked by the psychologising tendency—Pascal, the mild M. Hamon and Le Maître de Saci all alike. And the tendency remained constant throughout the Jansenism of the eighteenth century. No doubt Quesnel stresses the rational side in his *Reflexions morales*, but the psychological side comes out in his letters. The tendency showed itself with considerable charm a little later in J. J. Du Guet but lost its flexibility and freshness under the great Jansenist directors of the eighteenth century, the school of which Paul Collard, Jerome Besoigne and René Cerveau are the best examples.

But it spread very much further than the school of Port Royal. As it sprang from thoughts that were uppermost in most men's minds at the time, it affected practically all parties. The school of St Sulpice produced a writer who shows it in a quite typical way—M. Tronson, whose disconcertingly shrewd and detailed *Examens particuliers* have trained so many generations of priests in the delicate art of introspection. The most illustrious exponent of the method outside Port Royal was, of course,

Bossuet. It is curious to see how much evidence there is of it in the letters he wrote to the people he directed. Even the Jesuits did not escape the tendency. The first of them to begin on these lines was one whose thought was marked by particular originality and beauty: P. Lallemant. He was under way in Berulle's time, and he was succeeded by a group of extremely able disciples. A little later, in the person of Bourdaloue, the Jesuits produced one of the most searching analysts of the workings of the soul in the spiritual life, and they continued the tradition until the eighteenth century with P. Grou, P. Croiset and P. de Caussade, who, for all their mysticism, were just as psychologically inclined as the others.

It is evident, then, that the tendency to treat of the spiritual life in psychological terms showed extraordinary vitality, since it managed to survive throughout the eighteenth century, though it gradually declined as its intellectual and dogmatic basis weakened. The fact of its survival shows eighteenth-century religion—a little-known subject and one usually judged with scant sympathy—in an unexpected light. In spite of the moral decay evident in some quarters, the persistence of the tendency is a sign that there were still many people living as austerely as anyone in the seventeenth century had done. The letters on points of spiritual direction often to be found in the files of dusty muniment-rooms show that there was no lack of people in the eighteenth century who still kept their purity and their regard for higher things. And some religious communities would be proud of the rules of life that come from the same sources, meant though they were for ordinary lay-folk. But it was all a trifle chill and uninspired, all the same. There was severity in eighteenth-century asceticism and its piety was sound enough, but there was no enthusiasm to serve as a ferment and give new life. Signs were not wanting of something dangerously like a hardening of the spiritual arteries.

* * *

It was only to be expected that this systematic and sometimes exaggerated emphasis on the rational side should very soon lead to a reaction in the opposite direction, a movement towards the non-rational. It might have been supposed that this counter-attack would come from the mystics and particularly from those belonging to the school of spirituality known as quietism. But paradoxically enough, the quietist view of asceticism was closely connected with the tendency described above, the tendency to stress psychological factors, especially the reason. (It should be borne in mind that my present remarks apply only to the French side of the question.) From Bernieres to Malaval and P. Lacombe and then on to Mme Guyon, not a single quietist writer rejected asceticism; most of them, in fact, claimed that it was a necessity, for they regarded it as an indispensable means towards the self-stripping which had to be accomplished before any mystical union could take place. They were entirely in agreement with the outlook of their age as far as that point was concerned; they differed from it in looking on asceticism as a preliminary phase which would eventually be outgrown. When the soul reached the perfection of the unitive life, it would not need to bother about asceticism any more, in fact it would not be able to. They ruthlessly subordinated asceticism to mysticism, but within the field of asceticism itself they made no innovation at all.

The real reaction came from another quarter. It appeared in circles influenced by the Visitation order, when the new devotion to the Sacred Heart introduced by St Margaret Mary Alacoque began to gain ground to a noticeable extent. With the new devotion came a new form of asceticism, one centred round the idea of reparation.

Hitherto, in all the different schools mentioned, asceticism had always been regarded as a means of furthering the perfection of the person who practised it; in one way or another it would in the end help to bring the soul to a certain type of perfection. Of course it was also regarded as penance, as a means by which a man might atone for his sins. But the purifying of the soul counted for at least as much in the process of atonement as the placating of God's justice; and in any case, there was no question of anybody's sins but the penitent's. Again, the idea of reparation was older than the seventeenth century. It is well known what importance was attached in the middle ages to self-inflicted suffering as a means of sharing in Christ's Passion; and at the beginning of the seventeenth century, after the religious wars, the offering of adoration to God in atonement for human sins and failings was the central point in the cultus of the Eucharist. The idea of reparation was familiar, too, to Bernieres de Louvigny and his school, though in an exclusively mystical context. But quite a new theory came in with the devotion to the Sacred Heart as it was understood at Paray-le-Monial—the idea that self-imposed mortifications and sufferings should be offered purely and simply to placate God's outraged justice, and, moreover, that they should be offered for sinners in general, without any special reference to one's own personal guilt. The idea became the starting-point of a whole theory about the value of the victim-state and the importance of a perpetual self-oblation as a holocaust to God. In some instances, when asceticism was regarded as a means of atonement, it was directly associated with Christ's sufferings and looked on as a way of sharing in them. This was the case, for example, with the holy hour, one of the practices which became popular in circles influenced by the Visitation. But very often it was simply considered that suffering of this kind was of itself a way of appeasing God's anger, quite apart from any other consideration. This is obviously clean contrary to the methods worked out by the school that relied for its asceticism on the conscious use of the reason. There was no personal result in view here, no immediate progress at all. The reaction was a purely affective one.

But it had all that was needed for widespread popularity, because it touched a region of the human soul which no form of asceticism based on reason alone could ever reach. The idea of asceticism as reparation and the theory of the victim-state were often the subject of attack and the occasion of passionate controversy, but they went on gaining ground all the same and they gave rise to a whole devotional literature. The tendency is still alive, in fact, in our own day; it is a feature of Christian psychology that has to be reckoned with. It would be interesting to follow its progress throughout the eighteenth century, when it found its way into the devotional life of many of the faithful, led to new religious foundations and even affected religious orders like the Carmelites, although at first sight it seems quite foreign to their spirit. Curious passages are to be found in the writings of eighteenth-century directors, telling Carmelite nuns that their main purpose in life is to offer themselves as victims to God's justice—which is quite surprising. When the revolution broke out, still more people came to be possessed by the desire to make amends for human sin, and extraordinary penances were performed in consequence. This explains the fact that at the present day it is often hard to separate the idea of asceticism pure and simple from the idea of asceticism as reparation.

*   *   *

These were not the only forms taken by the reaction in favour of the non-rational. There were others, odder and disconcerting, and this even in Jansenist circles, devoted though they were to the traditional ascetic methods. And so we come to the strange story of the Convulsionaries.

Francis Paris, a Jansenist deacon of the recalcitrant party, a man who had lived a very austere, holy life in great poverty and charity, died on May 1, 1727, and was buried in the little cemetery of St Medard. Crowds came in increasing numbers to pray at his tomb; cures took place and were thought to be miraculous. During the summer of 1731, some of the sick people who went to the tomb were seized with nervous convulsions. The phenomena became more and more frequent, and as they were catching, like all such conditions, they infected some of the onlookers. The cemetery sometimes looked like a mad-house. In January, 1732, it was closed by the police on the King's orders. But the Convulsionaries, as they were henceforth called, met in private houses instead and managed to go on holding their assemblies right into the nineteenth century, in spite of being hunted and sometimes run to earth by the police.

In spite of its pathological character, the movement is relevant to our present purpose on more grounds than one. The Convulsionaries used to meet and say psalms and prayers in front of a crucifix or a relic of Francis Paris, and one or more of the congregation would go into a trance and begin to prophesy. The gatherings are strangely like Quaker-meetings and Welsh revivals. The pronouncements of the makeshift prophets often turned on the conversion of the Jews or the return of Elias, eschatological questions which were much to the fore at that time in Jansenist circles; but often too they were just exhortations to Christian perfection. There were, however, more disturbing phenomena mixed up with these. Cases soon occurred in which the ecstatics went into trances and then asked people to strike them, make them feel pain or even stick nails or swords into their bodies. Some went so far as to persuade people to crucify them. Doing violence in this way was called 'giving relief'. It was not long before real orgies of sadism took place, with strange phenomena in the way of invulnerability and instantaneous healing. The people who 'gave relief' regarded these strange events as miracles meant to confirm the recalcitrants in the attitude they had taken up. But the sufferers themselves generally looked on their self-chosen sufferings as means of atoning for the sins of bad Christians. However much these phenomena may have owed to fraud, they nevertheless helped to make the practice of asceticism for purposes of expiation a common one in Jansenist circles. The attitude they were responsible for was in every way the counterpart of the one described above and it was just as non-rational.

Towards the end of the eighteenth century people began to revive the oldest forms of asceticism again. This movement too started in circles influenced by the Convulsionaries. Hermits were once more to be seen, in fairly large numbers, living in the most isolated conditions. There were still some, in fact, in the nineteenth century. And there were pilgrims who spent their whole lives in going from one shrine to another, begging their bread as they went. The movement affected many besides Jansenists and even gave the Church a canonised saint in the person of St Benedict Labre.

*　　*　　*

Any consideration of the history of ascetic theory in the nineteenth century would be outside our present scope and would not, alas, yield much of value. We should have a long way to go before we met with any book on the spiritual life which could be said to have real merit. The books recommended to the devout at the time of the Empire and the Restoration were simply bad imitations of eighteenth-century works, and

F

then the romantic movement came and flooded everything with sentimentality.

This heartrending void shows only too well how very dangerous the tendencies were whose historical development we have just analysed. The religious revival of the early years of the seventeenth century had been made possible by the appearance of an essentially dogmatic type of spirituality, a synthesis, that is, between devotion and dogma, a factor which is obviously of paramount importance in the Christian life. Decay set in when excessive emphasis on the rational side began to separate devotion and asceticism again from theological enquiry and when theology itself became dry and fossilised. The result was the stagnation of the nineteenth century. Could anything show more clearly where the solution is to be found?

CHAPTER V

MORTIFICATION IN THE BODY OF THE CARMELITE ORDER FROM ST TERESA OF AVILA TO ST THÉRÈSE OF LISIEUX

By FRANÇOIS DE SAINTE-MARIE, O.C.D.

I. St Teresa and St John of the Cross; (*a*) austerity part of the Rule; (*b*) dispensations from the Rule; (*c*) additional penances. II. Restraining influence of St Teresa and St John of the Cross on the Carmelite reform; (*a*) exaggerations; (*b*) intervention of the two saints in favour of moderation; (*c*) the Italian Congregation; (*d*) introduction of the Carmelites into France; (*e*) the Carmelites in modern times; St Thérèse of Lisieux.

THESE few pages will belie the promise of the title, as it is impossible to treat such a subject in so small a compass. All I will attempt to do is to point out some of the landmarks in the three centuries of Carmelite life under review.

* * *

I.

The real inspiration of the Carmelite reform came from St Teresa. The first steps towards it were taken by the saint and a few nuns in her confidence on the evening of July 16, 1560, in her little cell in the Convent of the Incarnation. We must not suppose that she looked on the step she was taking as a mere return to the austerity prevailing in the earliest days of the order. No, as she saw it the end of the Carmelite order was not penance. What attracted her was the idea that one of her companions had just put forward in the conversation. 'Let's all go somewhere else', the nun had said, 'all of us here now; let's look for a place where we can live a more solitary kind of life, like hermits. . . .'[1] The ideal the future reformer had before her was the one which is the very essence of the Carmelite life: continual prayer. 'Mental prayer and contemplation are the first things.' But even at this time she realised the necessity of renunciation as a basis for contemplation, a truth she was to state in telling terms later in her life. 'But observe, daughters that if you are to gain this, he would have you keep back nothing; whether it be much or little, he will have it all for himself.'[2] And as she also said in another work, self-indulgence and prayer do not go together.[3]

This motive for austerity was reinforced by another. The pursuit of individual holiness is not the only thing that Carmelites aim at; they are expected to be eaten up by apostolic zeal as well. But their work for souls will be barren unless it is rooted in mortification, for the seed can bear no fruit unless it dies. This last consideration led the saint to undertake more in the way of austerity than she had meant to at first. 'When this convent was originally founded', she said in the *Way of Perfection*, '. . . it was not my intention that there should be so much austerity in external matters.' It was only when she learned of the havoc wrought by the protestant heresy that she 'determined to do the little that was in her—namely, to follow the evangelical counsels as perfectly as she could, and to see that those few nuns who were there should do the same'.[4]

Like all the saints, Teresa of Avila was the first to practise what she preached. We are told that she used to try out instruments of penance on her own body before she would let her nuns use them. She went in for vigils, took little sleep and most of the time worked at her correspondence far on into the night. Some of the devices she invented for subduing her senses were of the kind that we are now more inclined to admire than to imitate, such as eating her gruel (and even less inviting things) out of a human skull. (She lived, remember, in the sixteenth century and in Castile.) At one time she gave up this excessive penance on account of her great physical

---

1 *Histoire de sainte Thérèse d'après les Bollandistes* . . . Lethielleux, vol. 1, ch. 12. Mme. Auclair's lively biography of St Teresa had not been published when this article was written.
2 *Interior Castle*, 5, 1; ed. Peers ii, 248.
3 *Way of Perfection*, 4; Peers ii, 16.   4 *Ibid.*, 1; Peers ii, 3.

infirmities. But the 'holy man who heard her confessions' said that perhaps it was because she had stopped doing penance that God had sent her so much illness, and he prescribed several penances for her. She owns that they were scarcely to her taste, but without saying a word she prepared to obey.[1]

But this side of her life need not detain us any longer. We are not concerned with her own personal life so much as with the instructions she gave her daughters about the mortifying of their bodies.

Broadly speaking, her position was this. The austerities prescribed by the Rule had to be faithfully carried out. Plenty of courage would be needed and a nun might have to go beyond her strength, though she ought never to go so far as to ruin her health. Any persistent desire for extra penance was to be regarded with grave suspicion, and in any case such penances were to be carried out only under strict obedience.

In addition to these considerations relating to individuals, St Teresa seems to have been much concerned to prevent the introduction of extra mortifications into communities as such.

(a) In her various writings the saint comes out strongly in favour of the austerity required by the Rule and she wages war against what might be called the bourgeois spirit.

In the *Conceptions of the Love of God*, she denounces the false peace which the flesh, with its fondness for self-indulgence, may bring us. 'How is it', she asks, 'that people can spend their days so happily in feasting and sleeping and in pursuit of recreation and of all the ease they can get? I am astounded when I think of it. . . . The body grows robust, but the soul becomes so enfeebled that if we could see it we should think it was at the point of death.'[2]

Hence she was extremely shocked when she heard that out of mistaken kindness the confessor of the nuns of St Joseph's at Avila was trying to get the whole convent to eat meat.[3] She was even indignant at the excessive caution people were showing about health at the time, the sort of thing that made them say, 'People's health is feebler nowadays and . . . times are not what

1 *Life*, 24; Peers i, 153.
2 *Conceptions of the Love of God*, 2; Peers ii, 370.
3 *Letters* 352 (369); Peers ii, 817.

they were'.[1] She was annoyed, because she had seen from her own convent that austerity could be practised 'quite easily by people who were not in the least robust, but really delicate, if they had sufficient spirituality'.[2]

The zest with which she unmasks the temptations put in the soul's way by the flesh, ever bent on keeping its precious peace, reminds one of St Bernard. (Who says that the saints have no sense of humour?) 'On [one] occasion it may harm you not to wear linen, but because you wear it for several days you need not make a regular practice of doing so. On another day it would disagree with you to eat fish, but, if you get used to taking it, your digestion accustoms itself and it does you no harm. It is so easy to think yourself so delicate that you cannot do without eating meat, and that your weakness requires you never to do a day's fasting. I have experience of all this and of much more; one does not realise how important it is to do these things even though in themselves they may not be really necessary. My point is that we must not allow ourselves to be persuaded into relaxations but test ourselves from time to time.'[3] Nature is so deceitful.

Therefore, 'do not think of complaining about the weaknesses and minor ailments from which women suffer. . . . They come and go; and unless you get rid of the habit of talking about them and complaining of everything (except to God) you will never come to the end of them.'[4] It would not even be a bad idea, she thought, for the nuns to revive their spirits with the aid of the practical reflection that if they had been married they would have had to bear worse sufferings without saying a word, for fear of annoying their husbands.[5]

Carried away by her subject (though afterwards, speaking from another standpoint, she contradicted herself), she fearlessly made the bold assertion, 'I also know that we can desire no better kind of sight or health than to lose both in so good a cause.'[6]

(b) But prudence had no intention of relinquishing its rights, and the saint did not hesitate to assert that discretion was of the

---

1 *Life*, 27; Peers i, 176.   2 *Ibid.*, 36; Peers i, 261.
3 *Conceptions of the Love of God*, 2; Peers ii, 370.
4 *Way of Perfection*, ii; Peers ii, 47.   5 *Ibid.*
6 *Life*, 13; Peers i, 76.

greatest importance.[1] Thus she counted on superiors to take care of the nuns' health. 'You are very foolish', she wrote, 'to go on worrying about perfection and thinking you are taking too much care of yourself, when you see how important it is that you should keep well.'[2] Besides, if the nuns who were made to look after themselves more were really fervent, they would be so crestfallen at being reduced to such a position that the mere fact of being in it would be a mortification to them. Nuns were not to undertake long fasts, then, if they were weak and ill. Woe betide the 'melancholic', particularly. St Teresa found them hard to bear and even thought of putting them in prison. Her kind heart prevented her. But her wish was that while they should be kept well in hand, they should also be excused from prolonged fasting.[3] False mystics were to be treated in the same way. In one of her letters the saint says how pleased she is that two nuns supposed to be far advanced in prayer have been ordered by their confessor to eat meat. If they had been with her, she says, they would not have had so many visions.

Yet, wide though these dispensations from austerities prescribed by the Rule might be, they were never to exceed certain limits. Thus nuns were not allowed to keep food in their rooms if they were ill.[4]

(c) St Teresa was too experienced not to put her nuns on their guard against the classical illusion by which the Devil leads the generous to practise a whole host of extra penances, often in secret, with the result that they exhaust their strength and cannot even continue to observe the Rule itself. 'He inspires a sister with yearnings to do penance', she wrote, 'so that she seems to have no peace save when she is torturing herself. This, in itself, is good; but, if the prioress has ordered that no penance is to be done without leave, and yet the sister thinks that she can venture to persist in so beneficial a practice, and secretly orders her life in such a way that in the end she ruins her health and is unable to do what her Rule demands, you see what this apparently good thing has led to.'[5]

But even if obedience had been safeguarded and the superior

1 *Foundations* 18; Peers iii, 89.   2 *Letters* 60 (71); Peers i, 149.
3 *Foundations* 7; Peers iii, 40.   4 *Letters* 352 (369); Peers ii, 817.
5 *Interior Castle*, Bk. i, ch. 2: Peers ii, 211.

had approved a penitential practice additional to those laid down in the Rule, the greatest caution had to be exercised in carrying it out. The instructions St Teresa gives about the use of instruments of penance are amazing in their way. You need a good deal of insight not to raise the cry of sybaritism when you find her saying: 'The hair-shirt will be a powerful stimulus to the love of God; only there is one thing I insist on, and that is that you must not wear it at any price after you have made your toilet or when you are going to bed. Wear it once a week. You may arrange it so as to get a little discomfort from it. [A delightful way of talking about an instrument of penance.] And even then I am rather afraid of recommending it to you. If the hair-shirt joins all the way down in front, take care to put a piece of linen on your stomach. Unless you take this precaution it will hurt you a great deal. Don't pull it too tight round the shoulders.' And again she advises a correspondent not to hit too hard when taking the discipline.

Where going without sleep was concerned—the other great penance in contemplative convents—she again advised prudence. She considered that all work, however important, and even prayer itself should be dropped so as to allow of the necessary amount of sleep. In one of her letters she writes that sleeping well is no small favour but a very great one, and she tells her correspondent not to try and curtail the time for sleep. We find her advising and even ordering at least six hours of sleep in one case and acknowledging the imprudence she has been guilty of in working at her correspondence until two o'clock in the morning. . . . The utmost she will allow (she provides for everything!) is that if a nun wakes up in the night in transports of love, she may sit up in bed for a moment but not get out of bed, because she must not lose her sleep.

The supernatural wisdom of this saint who, so her companions said, was 'just like everybody else', is a thing to marvel at. It goes from one extreme to the other. We have just seen her battling against false peace and asserting that no better use can be made of health than to lose it for God's sake; and now, in connection with extra penances, we find her declaring that care should be taken in all such cases not to destroy health. There is no contradiction between these two positions. The virtue of discretion, so dear to contemplative religious, is simply a harmonious balance between the spirit of penance and the spirit of ordinary common prudence.

In short, what St Teresa asked first and foremost of her nuns in the way of penance was that they should practise the austerities laid down in the Rule as loyally as possible. 'I am not asking anything new of you, my daughters—only that we should hold to our profession, which, as it is our vocation, we are bound to do.'[1]

She condemned innovators before there were any. 'God forbid', Mother Mary of St Joseph heard her say, 'that I should ever see my sisters substitute novel inventions for the real rules of holiness.' With God's help she had drawn up an austere rule of life and she was bent on having it kept as it was, without any additions or subtractions. Model of obedience though she was, she yet felt greatly distressed when the various apostolic visitors took it upon themselves to revise the constitutions and sometimes to add new burdens. 'If you think well', she wrote to Father Gratian, 'will you delete Father Fray Pedro Fernandez's rule that the nuns are not to eat eggs or take bread at collation: he *would* make the rule and I could never prevail upon him to omit it. It is sufficient if the obligations of the Church are fulfilled.'[2]

If she stood up, albeit respectfully, to the powers that be, it was only to be expected that she would be annoyed with inexperienced prioresses who took it into their heads to add to the Rule by prescribing new penances on their own initiative. There was the case of Malagon, where the prioress would sometimes tell a nun to go up to another when she was not expecting it and slap her face, and the nuns used to pinch one another to test their virtue.[3] This was absurd and not at all to the foundress's taste. Her retort was that nuns were not slaves. It was much better not to 'give the nuns more to do than their obligation required, . . . for any prioress might impose whatever special duties she liked, and be so exacting about them as to overwork the nuns and ruin their health'.[4] The saint remembered that she

1 *Way of Perfection* 4; Peers ii, 15.   2 *Letters* 351 (368); Peers ii, 815.
3 *Letters* 131 (146); Peers i, 340.
4 *Method for the Visitation of Convents*; Peers iii, 248.

had herself lived in a convent where the superior was greatly drawn to penance (unfortunately) and used to make all the nuns follow her in that respect. Thus on certain days the whole community took the discipline for as long as it took to say the seven penitential psalms and several prayers after them. And the rest was in keeping.[1]

We will not dwell on St John of the Cross's own personal penances. The saint was very hard on himself. He used to spend the greater part of his nights before the Blessed Sacrament, was merciless with the discipline, wore an iron chain about his loins, and so on.

But he showed himself just as sensible as St Teresa where penance was concerned. In the *Ascent of Mount Carmel*, he protests violently against what he calls animal penance. People are attracted to it like animals, too, he says, by the relish they find in it. As all excess is bad, penance like this promotes vice rather than virtue. The Evil One leads the imperfect to act along these lines so as to confirm them in the pursuit of their own wills.

II.

If we may be allowed to compare the two great saints behind the Carmelite reform, we shall say that St Teresa seems to have carried discretion in penance to greater lengths than St John of the Cross, at any rate where other people were concerned. She seems even to have restrained St John of the Cross himself.

While on her way to make a foundation at Toledo in the spring of 1569, she stopped at Duruelo and went to see the little hermitage where St John of the Cross and Father Antony de Heredia had launched the reform in the midst of incredible austerities. She was a brave woman, but all the same she was horrified by the way they were living and she implored them to be more moderate. It had cost her so much in prayer and desire, she said, to get the Lord to provide the right men for starting this new way of living, and now she was afraid she might see the Devil shortening their days before her hopes were fully realised.[2]

1 *Foundations*, 18; Peers iii, 89.
2 Fr BRUNO, O.D.C., *St John of the Cross*, London, 1932, p. 89.

Her intervention does not seem to have diminished the ardour of the early reformers to any notable extent. On the 13th July, 1569, they founded their second house at Pastrano, and the mortifications there were on such a scale that she said she would leave others to describe them, as the task was beyond her own powers.[1]

The challenge was taken up by Father Francis of St Mary, who writes at length about Pastrano in his history of the reformed Carmelites.[2] As the good father is just the least bit inclined to exaggerate (though with the best of intentions), his descriptions of life at Pastrano are apt to be hair-raising. The reader may judge for himself. Abstinence was practised with the utmost rigour. A meal usually consisted of a basin of herbs, not as a rule of cultivated varieties (i.e. not vegetables) but generally of greenstuff gathered in the country (nettles and such-like). The great treat for feast-days was to put oil on the vegetables, but as there was so little of it, the gesture could be said to be a mere formality. If chick-peas or lentils happened to be served, there were so few that it must have been possible to count them in the bottom of the bowl. Cod cooked without seasoning was kept for great feasts. As if this were not austere enough, some of the fathers fasted on bread and water all through Lent as well. Others, considering the food too dainty, came to the refectory equipped with wormwood and ashes to sprinkle on it.[3] Meals were taken in the refectory amid skulls and plates of ashes, which served as reminders of the last things and sufficed to remove all temptation to flatter the body.

There was the same severity in all the other exercises. The discipline was taken three times a week, with such force that the sound of the blows falling could be heard at a distance and the fathers had blood-stains on their faces and hands.

Ordinary hair-shirts would have been like silk to these ascetics who wore thistles laced together on their flesh and used chains with sharp incurving points on them. There was a sufficient

1 *Ibid.*, p. 105.
2 *Reforma de Los Descalcos de Nuestra Senora del Carmen de la Primitiva Observancia*, 6 vols., Madrid, 1644-1710. The French translation, *Histoire générale des Carmes et des Carmelites de la Reforme de Sainte-Thérèse*, by Fr Marie-Rene de Jésus-Crucifié, Lerins, 1896-1897, is more accessible.
3 Bk. 2, ch. 33, *passim*.

stock of these instruments in the novitiate to meet all tastes. The novices had to ask permission to use them, but the others were freer to follow their own inclinations. These austerities were supplemented by other practices exhausting to the body, such as continual prayer day and night, carried out by all the religious in turn. 'Some stayed so long on their knees that you would have thought them brazen statues rather than men of flesh and blood. You could scarcely hear them breathe.'[1]

Allowances must no doubt be made for over-writing in this presentation of the facts. But no one who bears in mind the iron will and ardent temperament of the Castilians, the fervour of the reformed friars and the example of the desert fathers which exerted so strong a pull on them, will have much difficulty in reconstructing the atmosphere.

Pastrano is an excellent object-lesson. The excessive severity of the place stood self-condemned even before St Teresa and St John of the Cross intervened, by reason of the abuses it had led to. Many of the religious had paid for their imprudence with their lives, and one, a certain Brother Benedict, had become so absorbed in prayer that he had forgotten his mother-tongue and was forced to 'invent words of his own to reply to questions with' (and it would be surprising if he made himself understood even so!).

Worse still, this intemperate mortification produced serious aberrations in the spiritual sphere. The young novice-master at Pastrano, Angelo of St Gabriel, thought that in spite of all their austerities they still had not done enough. 'To his mind, perfection lay in penance and austerity, and his favourites were not the most talented, spiritual or virtuous but those most eager to practise mortification.'[2] This man eventually reached the point of introducing customs clean contrary to the spirit of his order, such as making the novices go round the neighbourhood teaching Christian doctrine and perform spectacular penances in public.

(b) At this juncture St John of the Cross was sent from Daruelo to Pastrano to correct these excesses and restore order. He relieved the novice-master of his office, whereupon Angelo showed that although he was very mortified in bodily matters,

1 Bk. 2, ch. 31.   2 Bk. 2, ch. 50.

he was not very indifferent where his honour was concerned. He was mortally offended with the saint and he set out to bring as much discredit on him as he could. He appealed to St Teresa, who was universally regarded as their Mother and foundress. One of his arguments was that he would fall a prey to melancholy if his wishes were not granted. But there can be no doubt that he was 'melancholic' already.

St Teresa evidently remained faithful to her usual line of conduct, intervened in favour of discretion and upheld St John of the Cross. But out of humility she asked for expert theological opinion, and for once she wanted to know the grounds for it. Father Banez wrote her an excellent letter in reply, a balanced, illuminating document emphasising that recollection and humility were more important than spectacular penances. 'The desire to imitate the Fathers of the Company', he said, with reference to the sending of young Carmelites to teach outside the house, 'amounts to a desire to found another order quite different from Carmel. . . . As this friar wants mortifications, a good one for him to practise would be for him to believe himself mistaken. . . . Your Reverence should soothe him', he added tactfully, 'and advise him to obey and keep quiet, like our Lord, who was silent for more than thirty years and devoted only two years to preaching.'[1]

Even after this decisive intervention, St Teresa was still concerned about the friars' health. In an letter to Father Mariano (December 12, 1576) she wrote that she had strongly urged the provincial, Father Gratian, to feed his friars well. And it is to be supposed that in saying that to the ardent hermit, she was quietly giving him a lesson.

But the spirit of Pastrano was not dead. It was to be revived, in part at least, by Father Nicholas Doria, who succeeded Father Gratian as head of the reformed Carmelites. Father Nicholas was a great champion of strict observance but he seems to have been an extremist and to have taken things too literally. He went to Pastrano, and where Father John of the Cross had spoken of discretion he 'roared' (the expression is not too strong to use of one who was known as the Lion of Carmel), 'We must have strict observance, fathers. With the laxity that must be

1 *Ibid.*

obvious to Your Reverences we are heading straight for disaster. Yesterday we rivalled Theibaid and Scete; today the mere names terrify us. . . . If we want our reform to prosper we must keep the Rule. If we want to save our souls, we must keep the Rule. If we want to edify our neighbour we must keep the Rule. . . . Even when I am dead, my bones will jump together in my grave and shout out, "Keep the Rule, keep the Rule".'[1]

In the desert of La Penuela, a new house founded by the Order in 1577, the most savage mortifications flourished once more.[2] There is no need to repeat Fr Francis of St Mary's highly-coloured descriptions of them. The point to note is this —what the good father complacently stresses is that the solitaries of La Penuela outdid Nitria and the Theibaid and even the monk-penitents of the famous house described by St John Climacus and called by him 'the prison'.[3] This shows what the ascetics' weakness was, viz. a rather vain spirit of rivalry after the style of the desert fathers. As if mortification of the body ought to be like a test of endurance—which in fact is the very thing to deprive it of all merit in God's sight.

One of the still extant sources of information about the early days of the reformed Carmelites is the *First Instruction For Novices*, by John of Jesus and Mary (Aravalles).[4] The book appeared in 1577 and was approved by Father Nicholas Doria and his council, including St John of the Cross. It has some excellent things in it, especially about prayer, and the influence of St John of the Cross, who had been Father John of Jesus and Mary's novice-master, is thought to be discernible in it too. But the chapter on mortification is permeated by the spirit of Pastrano. Thus, after matins, novices who have obtained permission may take the discipline an extra time before going back to bed. Permission is granted for wearing hair-shirts, fasting on bread and water and keeping vigil in numerous circumstances. Novices in good health are considered capable of praying before the Blessed Sacrament for nine hours at a stretch.

(c) The spirit of austerity was due in part to the Spanish

1 Fr BRUNO, *St John of the Cross*, cf. p. 297.
2 *Reforma de Los Descalcos*, Bk, 3, ch. 10, 14–16.
3 Bk. 3, ch. 14.
4 It was recently republished by the Editions du Seuil in the series, *La Vigne du Carmel*.

temperament. That may have been one of the reasons why the Spanish friars were so reluctant to spread the order beyond the frontiers of the Most Catholic Kingdom. They thought that no other country could live the Carmelite life as perfectly as Spain. However, in 1600 the Italian Congregation was founded with the help of members of the Spanish one. It too was very austere. Another John of Jesus and Mary (of Calahorra, an ex-novice of Pastrano) produced for it another *Instruction For Novices*, much more scholastic in tone but continuing the spirit of Pastrano in such passages as this: 'The more perfect a religious order is, the more does it treat the body with studied severity and prescribe rules for the flesh and enforce them with the utmost exactitude. . . . Such is the principle behind hair-shirts, fasting on bread and water, moderation in the use of wine and food, prolonged vigils, severity over the discipline, iron chains, etc.'[1]

(*d*) Eventually, in 1608, the first Carmel in France was founded at Avignon by some friars of the Italian Congregation, in an atmosphere of mortification and hardship. The novice-master, Peter of St Andrew, who felt the urge to confide the heroic deeds he had witnessed to posterity, says in his *Histoire générale de la Congregation de saint Elie* that the noviciate was a 'faithful copy of the noviciates of Pastrano and La Scala'.[2] The account given of it by Father Louis of St Teresa in his *Annales des Carmes Dechausses de France* will enable us to judge for ourselves. Here again we may find more to admire than to imitate, but it would be unseemly to scoff at it.

Some of the novices slept on boards, and to make them still more uncomfortable used to put sticks across them at various points. Others slept on the ground or propped up against a wall. Some of the more imaginative obtained permission to spend whole nights in the community burial-vault, so as to conquer their fear of darkness. A special room housed the instruments of torture kept for the noviciate, and recourse was had to pious fraud in order to reconcile the thirst for mortifying the body with the claims of obedience.[3] The teaching given to the novices was on the same lines as in Spain, the intermediary

1 Ch. 9, 2nd part, p. 168.
2 *Annales des Carmes Dechausses de France*, 1608-1665, Bk. 1, ch. 2; ed. Laval, 1891, p. 21.
3 *Ibid.*, p. 25.

between the two being the Italian Father John of Jesus and Mary's *Instruction For Novices*. The novice-master even went to the length of having some of the usages of the Spanish novices put in writing. They became famous under the title of Customs of Pastrano.[1]

We must be careful, however, not to view the French Carmelites from this angle alone. The novice-master at Paris, Alexander of St Francis (he was the nephew of Pope Leo XI and brother of Cardinal Ubaldini, the nuncio in France), seems to have been a spiritual master of the first rank. As a superior he governed with uncommon prudence. No doubt he was a stickler for observance, but at the same time he was full of charity to everyone. He had the tact, for instance, always to leave the door of his cell half-open, so as to make it easier for his novices to come and see him. When he sent them away, he had a playful habit of putting his scapular on their heads, placing his hands on top and saying, 'You must be holy and patient and commend yourself to God.'[2]

Moreover, in Brother Lawrence of the Resurrection (d. 1690), the province of Paris in the seventeenth century possessed an extremely engaging master of the spiritual life and a model of discretion, a man not altogether unlike St Thérèse of Lisieux. This friar began by practising mortifications of all kinds with the greatest generosity, but he eventually came to regard the question from an admirably balanced spiritual standpoint, as his maxims show. 'That he was not bold enough to ask God for mortifications, nor did he desire them. But he knew well enough that when God sent them he would also send him the graces to sustain them. . . . That all penitential practices and other mortifications were useful only in so far as they promoted union with God through love. He had given much thought to this, and was persuaded that the shortest way to come to God was by a continual exercise of love, doing all things for his sake. . . . That all possible mortifications would not serve to blot out a single sin, unless they were grounded in the love of God.'[3]

He even went so far as to maintain that 'many people get stuck in penitential practices and special devotions and neglect

1 *Ibid.*, p. 81.   2 *Ibid.*, p. 134.
3 *Practice of the Presence of God.* London, 1948, p. 9.

love, which is the real aim. This . . . is the reason why we see so little solid virtue.'[1]

He was eminently mystical in the stress he laid on the one thing necessary. Consequently, he has never dated. His discretion shows him to be of the same spiritual lineage as saints like Teresa and John of the Cross. We admire his brethren, certainly, but we see them as part of a vanished epoch. He alone stays ever young in their midst, young with the eternal youth of Love.

(c) In every great period in the history of the religious life, the need for a model has been felt. Like experienced scribes, who can produce the oldest of things from their treasures and the newest too (Matt. 13: 52), these gifted people adapt the ageless formulae to the times they live in, rediscover them for themselves and thereby give them a new interpretation.

What St Teresa of Avila and St John of the Cross were for their age, St Thérèse of Lisieux has proved to be for the Carmelites in the twentieth century. At a time when the majority of people would be hindered rather than helped in their spiritual life by such penitential practices as we have described above, Thérèse of Lisieux provides an example of the sort of renunciation everyone can manage. P. Petitot points this out in his book on the saint.

To estimate the credit due to her on this score we must remember that she began her religious life in an atmosphere of indecision. The old orders had reached a real turning point. The old tradition of bodily austerity was still very much alive, but when people put it into practice they were in danger of being crushed or broken by it, as constitutions were becoming weaker and weaker in consequence of a whole series of wars and other upheavals.

When the Carmelite order was restored in France in 1840 by some friars from Spain, the old penitential practices were restored with it. The 'Vade Mecum' des novices (translated by P. Ephrem de la Mère de Dieu, Malines, 1875), though containing excellent teaching on the life of faith and love and on obedience, etc., is not free from exaggeration when it comes to deal with penance.

1 Cf. *Ibid.*, p. 13.

G

Some of the mortifications recommended in the little treatise seem antiquated now because they are so systematic. Thus we are told never to look at people for long when we talk to them, to shut our eyes so as not to see things that might otherwise come to our notice, not to look up at the sky except for reasons of devotion, and to shun news of wars and treaties between temporal princes and conversations about them,[1] because they are things that poison the religious life. But in these days wars are not games played by princes; they turn the whole world upside down. And the method preached in the little book for mortifying the sense of smell seems lacking in simplicity. If you cannot do otherwise without drawing attention to yourself, it says, you may put sweet-smelling things to your nose but you should take care not to breathe in, so as to avoid catching the scent. (St Thérèse of Lisieux was not so artificial.) In the same way, we cannot see the necessity of imagining something we have a distaste for when we are eating food we like. We are generally prevented, too, by constitutional weakness for using a piece of wood as a pillow and making frequent prostrations. Our minds would be distracted rather than helped to recollection if we did.[2]

The *Point d'exaction des Carmelites*,[3] a collection of old customs which had almost the force of law in Carmelite convents in the last century, contains spiritual pearls like the sayings of the Bl. Mother Magdalen of St Joseph, and side by side with them other passages savouring of the spirit of the *Vade Mecum*. There is perhaps too much concern with 'regulating one's bearing in accordance with modesty and religious mortification, keeping one's eyes modestly lowered and speaking . . . edifyingly . . . in a low voice'. The act of eating could not at the present time be considered so base a thing as this work implies. It has been holy ever since our Lord sanctified it, and the humblest meal on earth, especially if taken in common, is a figure of the eucharistic banquet and the family table in heaven. St Thérèse of Lisieux formed the habit of offering to God the food she liked just as naturally as she offered him the food she disliked.

We come back to her, because she was the one who discovered

1 *Vade Mecum*, p. 4.
2 *Ibid.*, p. 23.
3 *Regularites ou Point d'exaction*, Agen, 1883.

how renunciation can and should be practised in the twentieth century.

Discovery is not too strong an expression, and the way the saint groped in the matter shows that it did not exactly come of itself. When she went into the convent at Lisieux, she found the same cruel penances and macerations there as in the other houses of the order. If the foundress, Mère Généviève, had shown discretion, Mère Marie de Gonzague, her successor, seems to have had a weakness for penitential practices. She was robust and had no experience of illness; she was an ardent creature into the bargain. Consequently she was quite at her ease in this sphere. 'Little Thérèse' seems scarcely to have thought of using instruments of penance before, but in such surroundings she too at first felt a desire to mortify her body. Stirred by reading the lives of the saints of the past, she tried to imitate them as far as obedience allowed. Hence she did her utmost, for example, to make her food insipid, in accordance with the traditional ideas of the way in which the taste should be mortified. After her profession, she got Mère Agnes to let her use an instrument of penance for three hours on the days when there was no discipline. And she put all her heart into this practice, as she always did with everything. Another nun once said to her, 'When I have an instrument of penance on, I take good care not to move too much'; but Thérèse replied, 'I don't; I act as though I had nothing there at all.'[1]

This little iron cross was the vehicle of an experience that was decisive for Thérèse on the ascetic question. In 1895 or thereabouts, after wearing the cross for a few hours, she fell ill. While she was resting, she saw light on the subject and realised that the macerations the saints had practised were not meant for her or the other little creatures who were to follow the same path, the path of childhood. However, she went on faithfully wearing the instrument until after her haemorrhage in 1896, when she was forbidden to use it any more. But the experience had been decisive from the first.

From this time onwards the example of the saints ceased to unsettle her. One day when returning a Life of the Blessed

1 *Sainte Thérèse de l'Enfant-Jésus et la mortification sous forme d'instruments de pénitence*, Carmelite Convent, Lisieux—typewritten document.

Henry Suso to Mère Agnes, she said she had realised that she was not meant to take the same path herself. God had not asked her to spend a long time mortifying her body like a private soldier in his army; he had given her a knight's armour straight-away, so that she could fight the battles of self-renunciation on the spiritual front.[1]

Like all true Christians in every age, St Thérèse of Lisieux lived on those timeless words of Christ's, 'If any man has a mind to come my way, let him renounce self' (Matt. 16: 24); but she understood and applied them in what is practically the only way possible in the twentieth century. Asceticism for her meant an intensely painful pursuit of exactitude inspired by love and extending to the smallest things, the minutest detail of the Rule and observance. The scope for renunciation was infinite. And if this infinity was often made up of tiny things, it was none the less infinite for that. As the saint's canonisation process says, 'God shows his power as much by creating the infinitely small as by creating the infinitely large, and it would seem that Soeur Thérèse showed her strength by making an enormous number of small or even microscopic acts.'

Thus if she happened to be writing a letter she would stop the moment she heard the bell and leave the word she was writing half-finished. She never complained of the cold and was careful not to show that she was cold by shivering or rubbing her hands. She never crossed her legs or her feet. When she had unpleasant medicine to take she sipped it slowly, drop by drop. She re-frained from reading a complimentary letter about one of her poems. She purposely went past certain cells so as to have an opportunity of putting herself out by doing some troublesome little service. When her 'little Mother' was prioress, she gave up her turn for spiritual direction to the others. And so on.[2]

We must be careful not to take these little acts one by one, in isolation, and attempt to codify them. They were the fruit of an unflagging inventiveness, they sprang from a love always alert and fresh. Nothing could be less systematic and at the same time more absolute, the aim being all the time not to let 'any opportunity' slip, 'any look' escape, 'any sacrifice' go by the

1 *Novissima Verba*, London, 1929, p. 103.
2 *Sainte Thérèse de l'Enfant-Jésus. Une Renaissance spirituelle*, by P. PETITOT, pp. 49–50.

board. But absolute though it was, it bore the unmistakable stamp of discretion. Unlike some saints in the past, Thérèse never had to bother about checking excess where mortification of the body was concerned, so as to give nature a little respite. She was discretion itself in that she performed the sort of penances that could not disturb her mental balance or undermine her health but nevertheless killed self-love just as effectively.

Moreover, all these different kinds of renunciation amounted to very little in her eyes in comparison with charity. She was fond of quoting the passage from Isaias in which God says, 'Fast of mine is: —— ease the insupportable burden, set free the over-driven; away with every yoke that galls' (Is. 58: 6).

The lesson went home and the influence of St Thérèse of Lisieux has been widely felt in our time, in this as in all other spheres. Many have come to realise, as she did, that if 'complete self-immolation is the only thing that can be called love', it must nevertheless bear the hallmarks of discretion and balance. Those who carry this kind of sacrifice into their lives, doing with the utmost fidelity what their duty requires of them moment by moment and giving themselves to others all the time, learn to make the thousand and one trifles of everyday life into occasions for practising a love that is by no means trifling. It is perhaps the best way for people today to make certain of going through the 'small gate' (Matt. 7: 14). In times of greater violence it was possible to force an entry; now we simply slip in underneath.

Chapter VI

ASCETIC PRACTICES IN USE IN THE CHURCH

By AUGUSTIN LEONARD, o.p.

I. Preliminary Observations: 1. Object of this outline; its relative character. 2. Multiplicity of methods. 3. Methods not all systematised to the same extent. II. Definition of Christian asceticism. III. Ascetic practices: 1. The special importance of the three vows. 2. Exercises of a general nature. 3. The particular points on which asceticism bears: (*a*) the body and the senses; (*b*) the non-rational tendencies; (*c*) the memory and imagination; (*d*) the affections; (*e*) the mind; (*f*) the will. IV. Some suggestions.

I MUST start by making it quite clear that this account of ascetic practices amounts to something like treason towards Christian asceticism. Treating asceticism as a string of different practices means emptying it at the outset of what is both its motive-power and its end—love of God and men carried to a point beyond the reach of unaided human powers. It thus means depriving it of its beauty and value and of its justification as well.

The present statement has been drawn up with one end only in view: it has the thankless task of pointing out the problems and debatable points arising from the subject and so of providing a basis for subsequent discussion. Making a list of ascetic processes is like taking a cross-section of a living being, whereas the only way to understand asceticism is to watch it in action in the lives of the saints and spiritual men and see it through the unity, forcefulness and charm of their personalities.

In the first place, these recipes for moral perfection are unintelligible unless they are considered in their doctrinal context and in connection with the dogmatic motives prompting their use. If I am to keep to my allotted subject, I shall be forced to

90

give a very inadequate and sometimes slightly ridiculous idea of Christian asceticism; it will be false through being too limited. Readers unfamiliar with the subjects we are dealing with may see just what Christian asceticism is if they will refer to the historical outlines in the preceding chapters and the theological discussion in the next one.

For in this case, as in all others—and this is the second reason why any listing of methods is bound to have something relative about it—the influence of historical development has been considerable.

Finally, although it may seem surprising at first sight, it is difficult to give a general outline of Catholic asceticism without losing all touch with reality because of the degree of generalisation involved. No such thing as Catholic asceticism has ever existed, except in the loosest sense or in so far as it contains elements distinct from the asceticism of other religions. What you do find is a single stream—the spirit of the Gospels—flowing through various channels, sometimes very different from one another, or a single tree with many branches.

Hence any general description we may give of the ascetic effort will need correction: we shall have to bear in mind that the methods by which it is carried out are in fact extremely varied. The same acts done in a different spirit will produce a psychological structure of quite a different complexion. *A priori*, this pluralism is bound to make any description of asceticism a very abstract thing. If we want unity, we must look for it not so much among the concrete manifestations of the moral life as among the dogmatic concepts inspiring them.

That methods of asceticism are extremely varied is evident from the existence of so many different 'schools of spirituality' —Benedictine, Victorine, Dominican, Franciscan, Flemish (*devotio moderna*), Carthusian; the Ignatian and Carmelite schools and the school of St Francis de Sales; the seventeenth-century French school, the school of St Alphonsus Liguori, etc.

A classification similar to the one recognised by writers on education could thus be made in the religious sphere as well; here too we could classify methods as didactic, intuitive or active. And in the same connection, we might perhaps ask whether the findings of modern educational research would not produce happy results if they were applied to this question of ascetic method.

Another reason why there are so many methods is to be found in the fact that asceticism in religion is the bond of unity between a great number of other factors. If it is true that the religious attitude is the 'most complete of all psychic syntheses', as is often agreed, that does not make it any the less surprising that deposits should be found in it incapable of explanation on religious grounds alone. Thus various features can be discerned in the religious type of asceticism as it has developed in the concrete in the course of history. Some of them depend on intellectual outlook and attainments, others on the moral education of the people using them; others again are specifically religious in origin (asceticism through the worship of God or through mysticism).

'Apart from the direct influence of the traditions associated with the great religious bodies, the shaping of religious awareness depends on many other factors, some of which pertain to intellectual development, some to moral and the most effectual to the cultivation of the artistic and emotional senses.'[1]

Asceticism in religion generally presupposes a certain intellectual and moral training or at any rate develops in conjunction with such a training.

The various methods may be systematised to a greater or lesser extent. Objectively, the degree of systematisation depends on the idea behind the method itself; subjectively, it is a result of personal vocation, which, with the boundless energy commanded by its freedom of choice and even whimsicality, may turn everything upside-down when once it steps in. One has only to think of St Francis of Assisi, St Philip Neri or St John Bosco.

Hence lack of method can itself be set up as a method. It would be very difficult to find a method, in the modern sense of the term, in St Thomas Aquinas or St Bernard.

Quasi-instinctive methods will also be found. The image P. de Guibert uses to describe them is a good one. 'Little by little', he says, 'and without thinking, an old navvy will have acquired a certain way of holding his shovel so as to make his

1 R. HUBERT, *Traité de pédagogie générale*, Paris, 1946, p. 455.

work easier. He never says to himself, "Why do I do it like that and not some other way?" but he has a vague feeling that it is best the way he does it.'[1]

The same writer—a classic—also speaks of empirical methods systematised by subsequent reflection, of scientific methods, and so on.

We thus come to the inevitable conclusion that any synthetic description of ascetic methods is likely to be untrue to the facts. I will try, all the same, to expound the current teaching as it is given today by the manuals and the *auctores probati*.

The object of our enquiry has to be defined, and that is the first difficulty, for asceticism is an extremely complex thing. The definitions at present in use hang rather in the void and are not anchored to principles—a phenomenon which seems to reflect the age-old hesitation as to whether the word should be used in the strict sense or in a broader one. The idea of methodical exercise denoted by the word $ἄσκησις$ was applied by Homer and Herodotus to artistic and technical work; Plato and Philo extended it to the physical, moral, intellectual and religious spheres; Christian tradition in turn took it up and used it in two different senses of its own. Clement of Alexandria used the term 'gnostic asceticism' to denote the whole life of the perfect Christian, while in Origen the word 'asceticism' has a narrower meaning and denotes the habitual practice of continence.[2] It is worth noting, as M. Olphe-Gaillard has shown, that the word occurs only once in the New Testament (Acts 24: 16).

Theologians today are thus divided between the idea of asceticism as a quality affecting the whole of personal religion and the moral life and indistinguishable from them, and the idea of asceticism as a special system of training in mortification.

In the first sense, it is not defined as a special virtue. It is 'not so much a virtue as an assemblage of virtues; it consists of the surmounting of obstacles with a view to restoring the balance of the faculties and their due subordination one to another'.[3] In a still wider sense, St Teresa of Avila used to say that ascetic-

---

1 *Leçons de théologie spirituelle*, Toulouse, 1946, i. p. 344.
2 M. OLPHE-GAILLARD, *Ascèse*, II, Development historique, in *Dict. de spiritualité*, Paris, 1937, vol. I.
3 A. TANQUEREY, *Précis de théologie ascétique et mystique*, Paris, 1924, p. 437.

ism was everything that enabled people to give themselves to God without reserve.

Generally speaking, it may be said that the prevalent idea of asceticism at the present day is that it is something separate and apart from other religious activities. It is a 'fight against evil inclinations, to bring them into subjection to the will and to subject the will to God'.[1] Another well-known writer says that 'except in individual cases, the task of asceticism is not exactly to annihilate the passions and feelings, destroy sensation or reduce the imagination and memory to inactivity; the object is rather to regulate and temper all these things, so as to make them serve the ultimate aim, which is the establishment of God's kingdom in and around us. Asceticism should be thought of as a kind of discipline for harmonising and as it were orchestrating all our capacities under the direction of the Holy Spirit. This harmony will result in inward peace.'[2]

P. de Grandmaison takes up a position midway between these two points of view. He regards asceticism as the 'sum-total of the means whereby a human being may be trained and exercised so as to become pleasing to its God and made one with him'.[3] He distinguishes two aims in asceticism. 'Spiritual exercises may be divided into two classes, according to their function. Some have the restraining, reforming function of setting the "old man" to rights by mortifying him; others have the positive function of building up the inner man, the "new man".'[4]

Thus on the one hand you have cultivation of the virtues and on the other a form of asceticism consisting of mortification properly so-called. Both follow the same method, which is that of using 'exercises costing a great deal to nature, things deliberately undertaken as being painful, as severe forms of discipline, but all of them used with the ultimate aim of promoting spiritual development and conducing to a higher and better life'.[5]

In order to avoid any possible misunderstanding, I must emphasise once again that in this article asceticism is considered from a strictly limited viewpoint. There are elements in

1 A. TANQUEREY, Précis de théologie ascétique et mystique, Paris, 1924, pp. 486–487.
2 H. PETITOT, La doctrine ascétique et mystique intégrale, Paris, 1930, vol. 1, p. 64.
3 L. DE GRANDMAISON, La religion personelle, Paris, 1940, p. 90.
4 Ib., pp. 92–93.   5 Ib., p. 94.

asceticism which are so alive and rich in vitality that when they are uppermost they send the question of methods into the background and diminish it almost to vanishing-point; but those elements are here left in the shade.

Many spiritual writers scarcely ever mention asceticism or spiritual exercises. What they stress is 'self-government by supernatural means', the continual effort at creation and adaptation required of the individual in the moral sphere when confronted with varied and unpredictable circumstances.[1] One writer emphasises the link binding moral and ascetic effort to the life that flows from the sacraments. 'In reality these two lines do not run parallel with each other, still less in opposite directions; they run in each other and are mutually interlaced. There is no sanctity in the Church which is not sacramental, and there is no sacramental act which is not at the same time a striving after sanctity.'[2] Another is content to remind us of the 'specifically Christian pattern of morality' springing from the great truths of Christian dogma and summarised by St Paul in the Epistle to the Romans (c. 12).[3] And the community outlook is not forgotten, for the aim is to train not just a good man but a 'Christian at one with other Christians in the one body of Christ'.[4]

Hence, in reading through the following list of ascetic methods, it is important not to lose sight of the fact that Christian asceticism itself has more the character of a whole than any of the methods subordinate to it, and not to forget that unlike gnostic, Stoic or Buddhist asceticism, it is inspired by specifically Christian motives.

There is no form of Christian asceticism that does not aim at something more than a merely human harmony of personality, and none, correspondingly, where grace does not come in and cradle the effort of the will. The saint's endeavour is made in quite a different world from the man's whose aim is only

1 A. GARDEIL, *La vraie vie chrétienne*, Paris, 1937; A. LEMONNYER, *Notre vie divine*, Paris, 1936.
2 K. ADAM, *The Spirit of Catholicism*, London, 1934, p. 213.
3 Dom A. VONIER, *The New and Eternal Covenant*, London, 1930.
4 E. MERSCH, *Morale et corps mystique*, 2nd edition, Paris and Brussels, 1941, p. 117. The article by Friedrich Wulf and Hubert Thurn on *Auffassungen und Fragen der christlichen Aszese und Zeit, Geist und Leben* in the *Zeitschrift fur Aszese und Mystik*, Feb. 1949, Heft 1, pp. 1–15, may profitably be consulted for what it has to say about present-day trends in Christian asceticism.

natural perfection, and consequently it looks quite different too. Detachment is never sought for its own sake or for any end but charity. In Christianity, asceticism is never more than a means; it is only a proof or a consequence of love.

Because asceticism can be applied to every side of the human personality, the practices used in it can be classified in various groups. Thus theologians distinguish a negative form of asceticism—detachment from certain things good in themselves or abstention from the satisfaction of certain desires—and a positive form—the effort involved in living virtuously. They also speak of forms of asceticism that restrain the natural impulses or give them pain, and again of physical, moral or intellectual asceticism, according to the region affected by it.

One of the most interesting classifications is the one that takes the headings for its subdivisions from the three evangelical counsels. The three vows of chastity, obedience and poverty are, it is true, the leading products of Christian asceticism. Even those Christians who do not actually make the vows must strive to acquire their spirit. The following analysis has recently been suggested.[1] Just as asceticism is practised at three levels, the physical, the moral and the spiritual, so poverty successively engenders rejection, independence and receptivity, chastity passes through the successive stages of reserve, abnegation and attention, and obedience begets strength for sacrifice, self-mastery and life according to the truth.[2]

To trace all ascetic practices to the evangelical counsels is of course an arbitrary proceeding. Yet it is true that in a sense poverty, chastity and obedience cover the whole field of Christian asceticism, for the three vows prescribe the simultaneous renunciation of all the main human tendencies, a fact which evidently corresponds to a psychological truth of great profundity and one well worth bringing out.

It goes without saying that vows are here considered not from the legal but from the human point of view, i.e. with regard to what they imply that the person making them is committing himself to. If this commitment is to be sincere and lasting, it

---

1 BERNHARD MARTIN, *Die neunfache Form der Aszese, Von der Einubung christlicher Vollkommenheit, Geist und Leben*, l.c. pp. 37–71.
2 BERNHARD MARTIN, art. cit., p. 69.

requires much more of a man than what is strictly necessary in law for the keeping of the vows. That is what the books mean when they say that you cannot keep a vow unless you have the spirit implied by it and the virtue corresponding to it. The initial refusal to live a merely natural life can only be the negative sign that you are deliberately committing yourself to something of greater worth than that.[1]

Before a man can enter on the inner or spiritual life, he must first free himself from vicious habits, either by performing some act that will cut right to their roots (as when William James says that you must throw yourself straight into the water, wholeheartedly and irrevocably), or, if the habits in question are not intrinsically bad, by gradually weaning himself from them. This is the case, for example, with the use of narcotics, drugs, alcohol, tobacco and the gambling habit. In some countries (Ireland, for example, Flanders and Switzerland), there are societies whose members make a public or semi-public promise not to take alcoholic drinks. When this is found, it is generally in countries where drunkenness is common.

[1] On the question of the vows, particularly the vow of chastity, see E. DE GREEF, *Notre destinée et nos instincts*, Paris, 1945, pp. 167–169. As a statement of the problem, though without adopting all its assertions, I take the liberty of reproducing the following passage from an article by John Layard. 'This raises the problem of celibate priests who come for psychological treatment because, for reasons unknown to them, they are inhibited in the conduct of their religious duties. It might by some be wrongly supposed that, when it comes to the sexual aspect of their problems, ordinary analytical methods might be inapplicable on account of their ideal of celibacy and its enforcement by an authoritarian system. Experience shows, however, that psychological concepts regarding the release of libidinous matter not only apply to them quite as much as to the ordinary layman, but are applicable if possible even more, since true celibacy, far from being an affair of sex-repression is itself, if rightly understood, the most complete expression of the transformed sex instinct. It is in fact the case that sex-repression in any form hinders the celibate even more than it hinders the married man. For what the celibate is seeking is deeper than sex, that is to say, a direct union with "the other" which is God. But, since he is human and endowed with sex instinct, without which he would be as nothing, and since individuation of any kind demands the fullest development of all desire, if sex desire is repressed the way to God is to that extent blocked also, and cannot be found until the unconscious inhibition is removed. This is so vital to the priesthood that it is astonishing how frequently it is overlooked. But the analysis of priests shows that it is the case, and that the sex instinct, far from being feared, has actually to be heightened to such a pitch that it bursts through the barrier of flesh and reaches the depths —or heights—which give access to the divine, bringing about a union formed not of flesh but of the spirit. And thus the incest taboo reaches its final goal, which is the anima within, divested of all projection in the form of fleshly desire upon the anima without.' *The Incest Taboo and the Virgin Archetype, Eranos Jahrbuch*, XII, 1945, Zurich, pp. 253–307, cf. pp. 285–286.

When a man has been converted to a better life, as far as his desires go, at any rate, he may use what P. de Guibert calls the 'means and exercises by which men tend towards perfection'.

(a) First come exercises to 'arouse, maintain and direct the striving for perfection'.[1]

The study of every kind of writing that has a bearing on the spiritual life is essential. The immediate purpose of this study is virtuous action and not knowledge for its own sake. It first takes the form of spiritual reading—reading of holy scripture, the writings of the great spiritual masters and the lives of the saints. This reading is supplemented by oral instruction in the shape of lectures and exhortations.

Next in the same connection come annual retreats and periodical days of recollection, short periods spent in solitude and devoted to thought and prayer, either alone or in common with others, under the direction of a master. The aim is to allow people to reconsider the ideal they are pursuing, take stock of the present state of their consciences and, with due regard to the circumstances of their lives, make with the proper generosity the resolutions required by their vocations.

This may be considered analogous to the silence, solitude and enclosure observed in religious houses.

The office of 'spiritual director' plays a quite important part in contemporary spirituality, especially where women are concerned. The term 'director' has unfortunately superseded the expressive 'spiritual father'.

The director, i.e. the master or teacher in the spiritual life, is 'one to whom a person opens his conscience unreservedly and asks him to direct him along the road to perfection whenever he needs it. This may be done with a superior or with a private individual, in confession or outside it.'[2]

Spiritual friendship—for which writers on the spiritual life say that a great deal of disinterestedness and virtue is required —is another form of relationship between two persons bent on helping each other along the way to perfection.

The director is not, however, indispensable. St Thérèse of

1 J. DE GUIBERT, op. cit., p. 25.
2 LA REGUERA, quoted in J. DE GUIBERT, op. cit., p. 353.

Lisieux had none.[1] All she received in the way of advice was
what she got now and then from her prioress. 'On the rare
occasions when I stayed an hour with her for direction, I was
scolded nearly all the time; and what distressed me most was
that I did not see how to correct my faults, my slowness, for
example, and my lack of vigour at my work.'[2]

(b) Then come exercises 'to reform and perfect our actions'.[3]
First among them is self-examination. This is a process involving application of the mind to the minute details of one's life in
order to obtain self-knowledge. It is an exercise in vigilance
undertaken with a view to discovering sins and imperfections,
obstacles to union with God, and banishing them by an increase
of generosity. The examination may take various forms. It is
general if the different virtues to be practised or defects to be
avoided are all reviewed together, particularly if it bears on a
single point chosen for its special urgency. Writers on spiritual
things recommend self-examination as a means of discovering
the soul's chief defect and the object to which it is most attracted
in the spiritual life. The knowledge in question here is not the
self-knowledge which is immanent in the whole life of any
thoughtful man but the fruit of a definite exercise lasting a
specified time and capable of being repeated more or less often,
usually twice a day, at midday and before going to bed.

The exercise is used for the systematic correction of faults and
acquisition of virtues. It is realistic and not incompatible with a
certain amount of book-keeping. I have often seen squared
paper given to children and to boys between fifteen and eighteen
years of age, with the idea that they should put down the number of their defeats and victories on it and see what balance of
good works they had to their credit. In the *Histoire d'une Ame* we
find it recorded that 'Marie gave her little sisters a string of
beads specially made for them to count the number of times
they practised the different virtues'.[4]

With regard to mortification of the body, the first thing to do

1 *Histoire d'une Ame*, complete ed., Lisieux, n.d., p. 120.
2 *Histoire d'une Ame*, complete ed., Lisieux, n.d., p. 117; cf. *Saint Thérèse of Lisieux*,
   A revised Translation of Her Autobiography, by the Rev. T. N. Taylor, London,
   1927, p. 122.
3 J. DE GUIBERT, *ib.*, p. 26.
4 *Histoire d'une Ame*, Mme. Martin's letter, p. 14; cf. Taylor, p. 38.

is to observe the rules prescribed by modesty and good manners. One classical writer says: 'Anything like flabbiness or effeminacy in matters of bodily posture should be carefully avoided. The body should be kept upright, without strain or affectation; it should not be allowed to slump into a heap or loll to one side or the other. There should not be frequent changes of position. The feet and legs should not be crossed. There should be no sprawling over the bench or prie-Dieu during prayer. Staccato movements and exaggerated gestures should be avoided.'[1] It was said of Cardinal Mercier that he never leaned against the back of a chair. People use such devices because they hope to obtain greater control over their bodies by means of them.

The ascetic shuns comfort. St Vincent Ferrer says: 'Those who would serve God must avoid softness in their bedding, though without exceeding the limits of discretion. The harder your mattress is the more you should like it. Take one or two blankets to protect yourself against the cold, according to the season and the need you feel. Stuff your pillow with straw; have no feather-filled cushions—no luxury.'[2]

When one of the nuns put her sandals on a heater, St Thérèse of Lisieux said to her, 'If I had ventured to do what you have just done, I should have thought I was being very unmortified.' In the same way, she would not allow a novice to fasten up the wide sleeves of her habit with pins to keep the cold out.[3]

With regard to the amenities of life, such as food and sleep, the ascetic takes only what he finds to be essential. He goes well beyond the moderation necessary to all decent living, in that he acts against the pleasure or satisfaction inherent in the exercise of certain bodily functions. Thus St Thérèse of Lisieux was always glad when the food was unpleasant; she would mix bitter herbs with what she ate and when she had bitter medicine to take she sipped it slowly.[4]

Then again, you sometimes find bodily sufferings self-imposed by way of supererogation—pains such as those caused by things like the hair-shirt, iron bracelets or the discipline.

1 A. TANQUEREY, Précis de théologie ascétique et mystique, 4th. ed., Paris, 1924, p. 500.
2 On the Spiritual Life, c4, quoted by H. PETITOT, Introduction à la sainteté, Paris, 1934, p. 23.
3 H. PETITOT, op. cit., pp. 23–24.
4 Histoire d'une Ame, p. 277.

St Madeleine Barat took the discipline as a remedy for im-
patience, and as she said herself, she used to hit as hard as she
could, so much so that she would be left with a nervous trem-
bling for ten minutes afterwards.[1] St Thérèse told her sister
Céline that she took the discipline so as to hurt herself as much
as possible. She used to hit hard and the strokes fell so fast that
they would amount to three hundred and fifty by the time she
had finished the *Miserere*.[2]

The extraordinary achievements of the Curé d'Ars in every
field of asceticism are well-known. He resolved, we are told,
'not to smell flowers, not to drink when parched with thirst, not
to flick away flies, never to complain of anything that interfered
with his comfort, never to lean his elbows on anything when he
was on his knees'.[3]

St Teresa of Avila says that an 'attempt to reconcile body and
soul, so that we may lose neither comfort in this world nor
fruition of God in the world to come . . . will mean advancing at
a hen's pace and will never lead us to spiritual freedom'.[4] She
distinguishes, however, between what is permissible for married
people and what the unmarried should do.

All the senses, speech especially, are subjected to a severe process of re-education along these lines. Newman went for a long
time without playing the violin. St John of the Cross said to his
travelling-companion, 'We are not travelling to see the sights;
we are travelling not to see them.' St Thérèse of Lisieux reproached herself with committing a serious imperfection when
she glanced at a fashion-magazine that had been left open in the
convent common-room. Other instances could be gleaned in
plenty.[5]

It should be observed that this determined fight against sense-
enjoyment is a passing thing. Its object is to restore the perfect
harmony human nature once had. When the spirit has obtained
complete mastery over the flesh, the ascetic may again make use
of the joys of art and sense, as instruments, now at every point

---

1 Mgr BAUNARD, *Vie*, ii, p. 549. See H. PETITOT, *ib.*, pp. 21–22.
2 *Ib.*, p. 21, n.1.
3 *Le Curé d'Ars*, 17th ed., 1904, ii, p. 475, quoted by A. HAMON, *Ascétisme*, in the
   Dict. Apol. Foi catholique, Paris, 1911, i, p. 203.
4 *Life.* c.13, ed. Peers, i, 75.
5 H. PETITOT, *Introduction à la sainteté*, p. 35.

H

responsive to the spirit. In the *Ascent of Mt Carmel*, St John of the Cross stresses the need for thoroughly cleansing the senses of their pleasures. The heat of sensible pleasure and the desire for it must be extinguished, he says, until spiritual freedom is attained and a state of innocence entered upon analogous to the original state of integrity. In that condition a man with senses cleansed and made obedient to the spirit even in their first stirrings towards sensible things will derive great delight from them: he will see them in God, and it is impossible to say how much they will remind him of God.[1] In the same way, Mère Agnes de Jesus says that the asceticism St Thérèse of Lisieux practised became progressively simpler and more moderate, and that she stopped denying herself the pleasures of nature and music.[2]

There is in this a process analogous to the one described by Kierkegaard when he talks about the fullest possible and most stable harmony with existence continually showing through his antagonism to existence. The phase of renunciation in Christian asceticism is there for the sake of the later phase of acceptance. P. Petitot, for example, in all his writings on spiritual things, with great felicity stresses this note of wholeness that is so characteristic of the spiritual life in its perfection and yet so dependent on radical self-denial—and so rarely found. For the transition in question is not the dialectical progression that belongs to thought merely; it is that deeply mysterious thing, a real transformation or rebirth of the personality.

The spiritual masters all say that physical asceticism is by far the least important. They are for ever advising moderation and restraint and recommending that bodily asceticism should be controlled by sound judgment. They are even apprehensive that it may turn out to be a source of pride.

After the vast field constituted by the body and the senses, the classical theory and practice of asceticism deal with the non-rational tendencies. These were divided by the ancients into two

1 Bk. III, C.26; cf. Peers i, 289.
2 See H. Petitot, *La doctrine ascétique et mystique intégrale*, Paris, 1930, i. pp. 90 sqq., and the same writer's *Sainte Thérèse de Lisieux. Une renaissance spirituelle*, Paris, 1925, p. 30 and the whole of the first chapter, which deals with the saint's asceticism. This is a very balanced book and by far the best yet written on St Thérèse; it has not been superseded even by the latest books about her.

classes, the concupiscible passions (passions whose function is enjoyment) and the irascible (passions aroused in overcoming obstacles). Both depend on love.

The task before Christian asceticism in this sphere is to repress the passions with a view to sublimating them; at least it is if sublimation is taken not in the technical Freudian sense but as a 'deliberate, conscious evolution from an originally instinctive movement'.[1] The devices used for educating these tendencies will evidently be of a more inward kind than those used in disciplining the senses. They are often left undefined. Writers on the spiritual life content themselves with saying that the slightest stirrings of the passions or of natural activity must be mortified if they are in the least unruly;[2] or else they recommend that will-power should be brought into play to inhibit the passions—they advise the avoidance of acts, thoughts and gestures likely to foment them. Emotional pressure, too, they say, is to be transferred from the objects of the passions to things of greater worth, which should be kept continually before the mind, and positive acts of virtues contrary to the passions should be made—e.g., courtesy should be shown to people who are found distasteful and indifference to those one is inclined to love too readily.[3]

It should be noted that the great masters are often infinitely more flexible on this point than those who provide mediocre digests of their teaching.[4]

Meditation is recommended as a means of harnessing the passions in the service of the good, because it attempts to substitute affective patterns based on the ideal for those dominated by self-centredness.

There can be no doubt that modern psychology, which has taken this question of the non-rational tendencies as its favourite hunting-ground, could provide the ascetic with useful information on the subject. All the same, it is probably true that something between the various forms of psychology of the unconscious on the one hand and the various kinds of psychology of

1 E. de Greef, op. cit., p. 42.
2 R. Garrigou–Lagrange, op. cit., p. 344.
3 A. Tanquerey, op. cit., pp. 511 sqq.
4 See The Ascent of Mount Carmel, Bk. 1, cc. 6–12.

the ideal on the other—a system of psychology based on com-plement and structure, i.e. one taking full account of every aspect of the human being—alone can provide an adequate foundation for a method of asceticism affecting the whole man.

With regard to mortification of the memory and imagination, the first essential is obviously to banish all images and memories leading to lust, resentment, jealousy, envy, hatred or any other form of evil.

To give way to daydreams is harmful, because it amounts to flight from reality. This tendency to languid self-surrender in daydreaming can be countered by application to the task that duty requires one to do at the moment. Many of the saints possessed a remarkably realistic outlook and made every pos-sible effort to exploit the potentialities of the present. Consider-able problems arise in this connection, particularly as regards the reconciliation of the poet's needs and the artist's with the mortification of the memory and imagination. When the spiritualising process is successful in this field, it may give rise to a special type of beauty. St Augustine calls it spiritual beauty. Examples are not far to seek: St Augustine's *Confessions*, Fra Angelico's frescoes and the poems of St John of the Cross will occur to the mind at once.

Mortification of the memory should also be a remedy for for-getfulness of God. 'Because we forget God, our memories sink as it were in the sea of time and forget the connection of time with eternity and with God's blessings and promises. This defect leads the memory to see everything horizontally, on the axis of time, a fleeting thing whose reality lies only in the present, between the past, which has ceased to exist, and the future, which has not yet come into being.'[1]

Thus the sort of application to present duty which produces sanctity does not imply absorption in the present; it implies that the present should be kept open to the influence of eternity, that moments of time should in that way be transformed into moments of eternity.[2]

In whatever field it operates, asceticism always proceeds in

1 R. GARRIGOU-LAGRANGE, *Les trois âges de la vie intérieure*, 2 vols., Paris, 1938, i, p. 4.
2 KARL RAHNER, *Uber die religiose Weihe, Geist und Leben*, Dec. 1948, pp. 407-408.

the same way, viz. by the elimination of the acts through which the tendency to be mortified could find satisfaction and by the practice of acts contrary to the tendency.

Love is often tinged with selfishness, however slightly. Yet it can be eventually changed into something entirely altruistic. This transformation is one of the psychological phenomena in which the power of asceticism to produce a reversal of motives is most clearly evident.

St Teresa of Avila apologises for talking about spiritual love, which she says is a difficult subject and one beyond her capacities. 'I am not sure that I know when love is spiritual and when there is sensuality mingled with it, or how to begin speaking about it', she says. 'I am like one who hears a person speaking in the distance and . . . cannot distinguish what he is saying.'[1] Leaving aside the warning repeated by all writers on the spiritual life against what are known as particular friendships or friendships based on feeling, we may turn to an expressive passage in the autobiography of St Thérèse of Lisieux where the whole of this purifying and spiritualising process is shown at work on love. 'I remember', the saint says, 'that when I was a postulant I was sometimes so violently tempted to seek my own satisfaction and look for a few crumbs of comfort that I was obliged to walk quickly when I passed your cell [the prioress's] and to hold on to the banister to stop myself from turning back. A thousand and one pretexts for justifying my natural impulses and gratifying them . . . came into my head. But I am glad now, indeed I am, that I denied myself on this score at the outset of my religious life. I possess the reward promised to those who fight bravely already. I no longer feel that I must deny myself the consolations of the heart, for my heart has grown strong in God. . . . Through loving him alone it has gradually expanded until it has reached a point at which it gives those dear to it an affection deeper beyond comparison than anything it could have given if it had clung to a selfish barren attachment.'[2]

St Thérèse condemned herself to real martyrdom in her

1 *Way of Perfection*, c. 6; ed. Peers ii, 27.
2 *Histoire d'une Ame*, p. 182; cf., Taylor, p. 175.

efforts to mortify her naturally loving disposition, so much so
that she gave scandal over it.[1]

I may perhaps be allowed to give a few more quotations.
They will throw the nature of this renunciation into relief
better than any commentary could do and will show that it is
not refusal to love—for the other, the beloved, is never
renounced—but resistance to the natural passion for loving
and being loved.

St Thérèse of Lisieux, then, further says that 'the more we
deprive ourselves of the satisfaction of our natural desires, the
stronger and more disinterested our affection becomes'.[2] The
words she wrote for her profession-day are well-known and
could be paralleled from countless other sources in the literature of the spiritual life. 'May I never seek or find anyone
but you. May creatures be nothing to me and I nothing to
them. May no earthly thing disturb my peace.' And in the
autobiography she goes on to remark how different God's
teaching is from natural feeling. 'Without the help of grace it
would be impossible to put it into practice or even take it in.'[3]

P. de Grandmaison shows a keen psychological sense in his
description of what has become known as his 'great sacrifice'
and his account of the repugnance he felt towards it. It would
indeed be a grievous error to imagine that holy people are
incapable of loving.

'I consent', P. de Grandmaison wrote, 'to the sacrifice,
whether actual or in disposition merely, of all my intellectual
and artistic tastes. . . . I consent to seeing my life reduced to
ashes and all human kindness towards me killed with it.
Consequently I am willing to give up my family and the pleasure
of following the activities of its members with my thoughts and
affection. I am ready too to give up my friends and become
even for the most intimate of them as though I did not exist, and
as far as my feeling are concerned I am ready to act as though
they did not exist for me.' And as to the repugnance he felt
towards this sacrifice, 'I offered this prayer', he says, 'with the

1 See H. PETITOT, *Sainte Thérèse de Lisieux*, p. 240 sqq.
2 *Histoire d'une Ame*, p. 182; cf. Taylor, p. 175.
3 *Ib.*, p. 171; cf. Taylor, p. 167.

reflection that from a purely natural point of view it was chimerical and unreasonable.'[1]

P. Petitot summarises the characteristics of spiritual love as follows:

(1) It is absolutely gratuitous and disinterested, i.e. essentially devoid of self-seeking and with no other motive than love itself and its exclusive willing of the other person's good. Note that there is no question of metaphysics in this or of the famous problem of pure love, *l'amour pur*, the disinterestedness we are concerned with is simply a descriptive psychological characteristic.

(2) Love of this kind does not look for payment in return. St Teresa of Avila says that those who love spiritually scarcely think at all about being loved themselves.[2] 'This distinctive property of spiritual love is diametrically opposed to the deepest instinctive tendencies of human love.'[3] Taking a metaphor from the gospels and speaking of her novices as lambs, St Thérèse of Lisieux declared that her affection for them was so disinterested that she did not even want them to know of it. Through God's grace, she said, she had never tried to draw their hearts to herself.[4]

(3) Spiritual love does not feel the need to express itself by perceptible signs or outward tokens. It has faith. Time cannot daunt its fidelity.

(4) It can be recognised by the entire absence of even the slightest degree of jealousy.

(5) It wants the person loved to have what is good for him. The affection springing from it is exacting, severe and absolutely straightforward.

The idea of spiritual love obviously raises many questions hard to solve even in theory and harder still to deal with in the active field, especially when the object it has to animate is some particularly attractive and unquestionably legitimate human affection.

Where the mind is concerned, it is essential first of all to mortify leanings towards sin, those most often mentioned being

1 J. LEBRETON, *Le P. Leonce de Grandmaison*, Paris, 1932, pp. 127-128.
2 *Way of Perfection*, c. 6; ed. Peers ii, 28.
3 H. PETITOT, *La doctrine ascétique et mystique intégrale*, ii. pp. 56 sqq.
4 *Histoire d'une Ame*, p. 185; cf. Taylor, p. 177.

ignorance, vain curiosity, precipitancy, pride and self-opinion-atedness. The intellectual and moral education to which all this is subjected we shall say nothing about here.

Pride receives special consideration. On the one hand it finds its way into the spiritual life itself, where it takes the form of spiritual pride. St John of the Cross says of beginners that they find a secret source of pride in their own fervour, as they come to take pleasure in their good works and think highly of them-selves.[1] On the other hand, humility acquires ascetic value because of its exceptional importance. It is in fact humility which is the distinctive note in orthodox Christian asceticism. Through humility their lives are pitched in a special key, that of heroism in weakness, which is what makes them so different from the heroes and wise men whose lives express the pagan ideal. Humility is the essential condition of magnanimity in the Christian.

All writers on the spiritual life lay great stress on the necessity of humility and exercise their ingenuity in contriving means for bringing it to birth and fostering it. They advise their readers to keep their past sins in mind and see that their consciences attend to their present failings. These devices are reinforced by external practices; people may have their faults pointed out to them, be corrected in a friendly way by their companions or be humbled in public or in some other visible way. Such practices are still in use in many religious houses, as far as their form at any rate is concerned, if not their spirit.

The kind of asceticism proper to the mind is the surrender of concepts and images for the sake of attaining a less distinct but purer knowledge of God, one more influenced by faith. Mental prayer, which the clergy are bound by canon law to practise every day, seeks union with God through unknowing rather than by the pursuit of knowledge. St John of the Cross says that it is better to be blind and in the dark than to keep one's eyes open to receive the rays of God's light.[2]

A vast field of psychological, metaphysical and theological questions is opened up by all these considerations. We can do no more than glance at it in passing. As we pass from the mortifi-

1 *The Dark Night of the Soul*, Bk. 1, c. 2; Peers i, 352.
2 *The Ascent of Mount Carmel*, Bk. 2, c. 8; ed. Peers i, 97.

cation of the lower faculties to the mortification of the highest, the limitations of our viewpoint in this article become more and more glaringly evident, for in the case of the mind asceticism is identical with the purification accomplished by faith. But faith is much more than a form of asceticism and infinitely more than any device or practice. The theological virtues are what give the spiritual life its unity—but the manifold implications of the theme themselves place it beyond our limited horizon.

Having directed its attack at every part of the human personality, asceticism sets out to kill the root of the disorders that cost it so much hard work; it strives to rid men of self-love and give them love of God instead and love of their neighbour, two kinds of love which are really one and the same.

The purification of the will and the conquest of selfishness depend directly on the progress the soul makes in charity, and the remark we made about faith applies in this case too. Nevertheless, when writers on the spiritual life are speaking from the ascetic standpoint, they do talk about resistance to self-will. Human wills must be made to conform to God's will as it is manifested in the concrete through the duties attached to the various states of life, through superiors and through the ascetic device known as the rule of life. This rule is often drawn up with the approval of the spiritual director, who is considered to represent God. It takes on a social character and acquires official status in the rules of religious institutes—in the regular life.

Considered in this context, obedience is not simply a social factor but an instrument at the service of asceticism, a means of procuring the union of men's wills with God's. Humility is not very different from obedience, and the two together regulate Christian asceticism and are specific features of it. They are, moreover, inconceivable as virtues except on a religious interpretation of the world. William James, it will be remembered, says, 'The secular life of our twentieth century opens with this virtue held in no high esteem. The duty of the individual to determine his own conduct and profit or suffer by the consequences seems, on the contrary, to be one of our best rooted contemporary Protestant ideals, so much so that it is difficult even imaginatively to comprehend how men possessed of an inner life of their own could ever have come to think the

subjection of its will to that of other finite creatures recommend-
able. I confess that to myself it seems something of a mystery.'[1]

We thus come to the end of our skeleton inventory of the
ascetic practices in use today. I repeat once more that all we
have been trying to do in these few pages has been to reflect
current teaching, but the angle of approach adopted necessarily
involves distortion, for asceticism cannot be understood in
isolation; it needs to be seen in its place in the spiritual life as a
whole.

'Its aim is indeed admirable; the real question, therefore, is:
To what extent does it fulfil its aim?' So writes the psychologist,
J. B. Pratt.[2]

Generally speaking, the answer to his question is provided by
the saints and the great men of religion. And yet it looks as
though Christians today feel somewhat ill at ease when confronted with the classical programme of asceticism, even if it is
adapted to fit their particular state of life, whatever it may be.

There seems to be a keen awareness of the danger of formalism inherent in all 'methods'. One of the chief activities of the
present Catholic revival is the search for 'spiritual conditions
which will make possible the formation of a new Christian
"life-style".' What the avant-garde would like to do is to 'reduce
the technique of the spiritual life to its essential constitutive elements, viz. responsiveness to the inspirations of grace—a condition that reveals its existence through the universal rejection
of selfishness in motivation—and responsiveness to reality, a
condition in which the decision as to what to do is made by considering other people's circumstances, rights and wishes and
attending to the laws that govern the development of life and
personality.'[3]

Of course, it would be unwise to reject any method, or at any
rate any tradition of asceticism without weighing it carefully,
for these traditions represent the distillation of a great deal of
wisdom, which becomes available to the beginner through them
and enables him to develop with greater speed and sureness on
his own. What M. Le Senne says of moral principles—that if

1 *The Varieties of Religious Experience*, New York, 1902, p. 310.
2 *The Religious Consciousness*, A Psychological Study, New York, 1921, p. 384.
3 *Jeunesse de l'Eglise*, Cahier I, pp. 46, 44.

they were not there, invention would start at a much lower level in the moral sphere and its efforts not bring it so high[1]—applies to ascetic methods as well. Every new form of spirituality sprang from an original experience, but in most cases no awareness of the experience was possible until it had been measured against the tradition that came before it. A tradition ought to leave room for personal invention and experience. Methods are often too cumbersome and can become something of an obsession. What Jacques Maritain says about the academic in aesthetics could be said with equal force about the substitution of a rigid framework for the living conscience, a phenomenon which has been known to occur in the spiritual life. 'Method and rules', he says, 'regarded as a set of formulae and recipes effective of themselves and mechanically acting as a buttress to keep the mind from collapsing, tend to take the place of *habitus* everywhere in the world today.'[2]

It would be desirable to have greater stress laid on certain aspects of the spiritual life well-known to tradition but not much to the fore these days—such things as judgment by the individual conscience and the fostering of dynamic qualities capable of reacting to an infinite diversity of situations and dealing with them creatively.

The contrast between what Bergson called mere training on the one hand and the mystical approach on the other is doubtless not so absolute as he imagined. There must be observance of the letter if the spirit is to develop along the right lines, but it is equally true that the letter without the spirit bears death within itself. Still, Bergson does bring out the sovereign importance of the personal element. 'How', he asks, 'can a hold be obtained over the will? There are two ways open to those responsible for education. One is by training, in the best sense of the term, the other by mystical action, the expression being taken in this case in the humblest of senses. The first method inculcates a system of morality made up of impersonal habits; the second leads to the imitation of a person and even to spiritual union or more or less complete identification with him.'[3]

1 *Traité de morale générale*, Paris, 1942, p. 523.
2 *Art et scholastique*, 3rd ed., Paris, 1935, p. 67; cf. Eng. tr., London, 1930, p. 41.
3 *Les deux Sources de la morale et de la religion*, 11th ed., Paris, 1932, pp. 98–99; cf. Eng. tr., London, 1935, p. 79.

That is the point. It is only in so far as asceticism becomes a shaping of the self to the likeness of another person, a sharing in the mystery which is Christ, that it draws on its reserves of magnanimity and determines to share to the full in the work of the crucified Redeemer by suffering with him. And then there is that other kind of asceticism, the heroic and absolutely gratuitous quest for suffering which took possession of many of the saints and made them 'mad about the cross'. (cf. 1 Cor. 1: 23.) This tendency, which finds perfect expression in St Teresa of Avila's aspiration, 'either death or suffering', we have left out of account here altogether.

This last consideration is at any rate enough to remind us that however near to perfection a method of asceticism may be brought by the latest discoveries in psychology, it must still take care not to trespass on spheres outside its own domain—for the renunciation presupposed by the life of Christian perfection is radical and goes to awe-inspiring lengths. 'Yes, brethren, freedom claimed you when you were called. Only, do not let this freedom give a foothold to corrupt nature.' (Gal. 5: 13.)

The aim of asceticism is not to produce decent, well-balanced citizens but to make saints, and the means it takes to do will always, unquestionably, be painful, for its business is to keep the *scandalum Crucis* alive.

CHAPTER VII

NOTE ON INDIAN ASCETICISM

By OLIVER LACOMBE

THE practice of asceticism goes back to the earliest days of Indian history. More than one act of 'virtuosity' in asceticism (if the expression is permissible) is mentioned by Greek historians and set down to the credit of ancient India. Sylvain Lévi says[1] that although Alexander's soldiers knew of Diogenes they were none the less surprised to 'meet with the Naked Sages in the streets of the town' [of Taxila]. These conquistadores who had been led so far afield by their desire for booty were taught by the Gymnosophists that the height of happiness was to be found in an inertia and indifference transcending all earthly things. Yet the encounter did not result in conflict. In some cases, even, friendships were formed. One of the Sages, whom the soldiers had nicknamed 'Father Good Day' or *Calanos* (*kallâna* in the Indian tongue, *kalyâna* in Sanscrit, the usual form of greeting), joined the expedition and left India with it. Being overcome by fatigue and old age by the time they reached Susa, of his own accord he mounted a funeral pyre in the presence of the whole army, which was drawn up in ceremonial array to see the novel sight.

Suicide may in fact be considered as the highest form of Indian asceticism, whether it be taken as a voluntary atonement for some particularly serious lapse or as salvation by death, the culmination and consummation of the ascetic's striving for release.

It should however be noted that according to the doctrine of *Karma*, self-chosen death cannot put an end to servitude in the case of the ordinary man, because he has not yet become pure and spiritual. And Buddhist tradition, and with it all the more

1 *L'Inde civilisatrice*, Paris, 1938, p. 45.

balanced and moderate elements in orthodox Indian circles, is against suicide for religious purposes, even where professed ascetics are concerned.

I may perhaps be allowed to deal with the picturesque side of the subject straight away, so as not to have to come back to it later. It is so prominent a thing that I cannot avoid saying a word or two about it.

First there are ascetics who lie on beds studded with sharp spikes, often for years at a time. The reason is that they are imitating the behaviour of a hero in the Mahabharata, who, though pierced by arrows, reclined on them for several days as on a bed, teaching the great doctrine of renunciation the while.

There are others who hold one or both arms up until atrophy sets in or the limbs waste away. When both arms are affected, the ascetic becomes entirely dependent on the people with him, as he cannot even feed himself. A refinement consists of keeping the fist closed, so that the nails grow into the flesh.

Then come practices not quite so cruel as these—standing on one leg, for instance, or again the ascetic device of the five fires: a man takes up his stand between four fires and the sun, which constitutes the fifth.

On roads leading to places of pilgrimage men can sometimes be seen advancing with the utmost slowness towards their journey's end, because at every step they lie down at full length on the ground and repeat ejaculatory prayers. I came across a pilgrim of this kind myself at Mathura.

Fasting, of course, occupies a prominent place in Indian asceticism. It may take all sorts of forms. The best-known is regulated by the phases of the moon: the amount of food is increased when the moon is waxing and decreased when it is waning. These fasts may be extremely severe and very long.

Silence, too, plays a very important part. It may go as far as abstention from speech altogether for several years. A famous *yogi* who died recently in South India, where he had spent all his life, practised it in that way during his training period.

Poverty and chastity are also essential to the classical Indian conception of asceticism.

It is not easy to draw the line between *asceticism* properly so-called and *yoga* considered as a form of discipline aiming at the subjection of the physiological, psychological and spiritual energies of both the microcosm and the macrocosm to the control of the will. Some of the claims of *yoga* can be checked scientifically—the claim to control the movements of the heart by the will, for example, which seems to be able to inhibit them entirely or almost entirely. Movements in the respiratory system can be reduced until they are few and far between, so that people can be buried for a considerable time, provided that the burial ceases at the time they have previously decided upon for the resumption of their normal physiological activity.

This leaning towards asceticism seems to have come not from the Aryan invaders who gave Indian civilisation its form but from the previous layer of population. It nevertheless became a characteristic feature of Indian religion in general. The problem is absolutely vital for Indians. To see that it is you have only to think of the consciously original element in early Buddhism, the thing it deliberately adopted in contra-distinction to the surroundings it developed in. Buddhism claims to be a *via media*, i.e. a mean between two extremes in the Aristotelian sense, a mean between the extreme of easy surrender to sensual impulse and the extreme of violent mortification. Its asceticism is strict but temperate.

Of the Indian terms and ideas most nearly corresponding to what Christians call asceticism, two seem to me to be particularly deserving of attention. They are *tapas* and *prāyaschitta*. *Tapas* comes from the root *tap*, which is also found in Latin in the word *tepor*, but with less intensity in the meaning: where the Latin word means 'tepidity' the Indian means 'heat'. From heat it passes to the idea of pain, perhaps because in the tropics heat is painful. This pain may be self-inflicted, deliberately, for a religious, magical or moral purpose. It may be done for any one of a variety of motives, but they all bring us back to our central theme of penance, austerity and mortification.

The change from the purely physical meanings of brilliance, fire and heat to meanings with at least a moral aura, an atmosphere of repentance and penance,[1] took place at the end of the period of the Rigveda, the oldest of the four Vedas. A little later

---

1 Cf. the term *anu-tapas*, *tapas* following sin, i.e. repentance.

we find the Atharvaveda, which is essentially magical in out-look, regarding *tapas* not as a merely natural phenomenon but as a specially effective ascetic practice. Where the Rigveda says, 'He killed his enemy with an arrow', a physical weapon, the Atharvaveda makes the correction, 'He killed him by his *tapas*', i.e. by his asceticism used magically as an offensive weapon.

If the ascetic is praised so much, it is because he has a proto-type in the Demiurge himself. When the Demiurge tired of his solitude he thought he would create other beings. The thoughts of the Demiurge necessarily take effect, but between his thoughts and the time when they take effect an ascetic effort—*tapas*—has to be made. If he is to produce other beings, the Demiurge must in a way exert himself. He gets hot, he perspires; the waters are born of his sweat and the other creatures are born of the waters. Evidently *tapas* is here very close to *yoga*; it is a kind of 'mastery'. But because it is effort and heat it is virtually pain, and where merely human ascetics are concerned it will actually be pain.

In the hinduism of more recent times Siva, the Great God, is represented as the Prince of Ascetics. That does not prevent him from being Chief Procreator and Chief Artist as well. Like his cosmic dance, his austerities have a twofold significance; he is at once the creator of worlds and their destroyer.

A very ancient passage in the Buddhist scriptures mentions three kinds of people as worthy of condemnation because of their violence. The first are those who are violent towards themselves. The allusion is to adepts of extreme forms of asceticism, and it is significant that the word used is *tapas*. Then come those who hurt others—executioners, butchers, etc. The third class includes those who hurt both themselves and others, i.e. those who perform the great vedantic rites, offer blood-sacrifices and go to excess in mortification. The Buddhist must abstain from all three kinds of violence. He should be self-denying and kindly; his feelings should be 'cool' (the contrast with the etymology of *tapas* is striking), without however exclud-ing 'heat' in zeal or repentance. That could never be anything but praiseworthy, and it is denoted by terms with the same root, *tap*.

As for *prāyaschitta*, 'atoning thought, propitiation',[1] in the

1 This is the translation suggested by L. Renou.

vedantic age it was a ceremony to make amends for mistakes in ritual or deliberate breaches of the rubrics; in the classical age it meant expiation for moral and social crimes. It was thus a religious penalty existing concurrently with the punishments inflicted by the civil law. The guilty were rehabilitated when they had performed their *prāyaschitte*, but there were some sins which could not be atoned for in this life at all. When the *prāyaschitta* was not a ceremony, particularly a ceremonial puri- fication (washing, etc.), it consisted of some practice involving *pain*—which brings us back to the category of *tapas* (fasting in accordance with the phases of the moon is a form of *prāyaschitta*) —or again of a 'good work', alms or something of the sort.

The regular practice of asceticism constitutes a 'state of life' and entails a special canonical status—it is an *āsrama*. 'The word means "affliction" (resulting from religious exercises); hence "the place where these exercises are carried out; hermitage";[1] and "way of life" (with a religious connotation).'[2] The life of an orthodox Hindu, or at any rate of a Brāhman, in theory passes through four successive stages. He should first be a student of Brāhmanism, then head of a household, then a hermit living a secluded life in the forest (the *hylobios* of the Greek writers), and finally an itinerant mendicant monk. In actual fact, most Brāhmans never get beyond the second stage, and of those who do, a considerable number enter the third and fourth stages directly, without having first been married.

Both the hermit of the forest and the itinerant monk practise asceticism; both are *tapasvin*. But while the hermit still belongs to the orthodox social group, is subject to the laws that govern it (especially the caste-regulations), and is bound to perform the ceremonies ensuring its maintenance, the monk has broken once and for all with every kind of social bond and obligation. What- ever the historical origin of these differences may be, there can be no doubt that they eventually came to denote an advance in detachment and freedom of spirit. But it will be well to let the sources speak for themselves.[3]

When his face is covered with wrinkles, when his hair turns grey, when he has seen his son's son, the head of the household

1 The *ashram* so much talked of today will be recognised in this.
2 L. RENOU, *L'Inde classique*, Payot, Paris, 1949, i, 379.
3 The following paragraphs are based on the Visnu-Smrti.

J

ought to go and live in the forest. Before he leaves, he should give his wife into his children's keeping, unless she wants to go with him and share his austere life. If so, they will live together as though they were not married. The sacred fires will be kept burning in the hermitage as before. The domestic ritual will be observed, but with wild fruit and roots instead of the specially-prepared products. The hermit must not give up reciting the Vedas in private. He will dress in animal skins or, if possible, in the bark of trees. He will let his hair, beard and nails grow. His life must be so austere that his body *withers away*—*tapas* again and no mistake. In summer he will expose himself to the five fires. In the rainy season he will sleep in the open. In winter he will wear wet clothes. His diet will be strictly vegetarian.

A man intending to enter on the fourth state of life must first renounce all his possessions. The monk will keep the ritual fires alight in spirit only (in other words, the ceremony ceases to be an external act and becomes nothing more than a spiritual attitude). He will cease to frequent human social groups, for he has deliberately severed himself from society and hence from caste, in spite of the canonical character of his state of life, the instrument of this separation being the very act of renunciation that gives him a claim to special respect. He will eat no food but what he begs from day to day. He will beg courteously but without in the least lowering himself. He will never knock at the door of a house until the master, family and servants have finished their meal—he has a right to nothing but the leavings. If he is rebuffed, he will withdraw without complaining or being annoyed. He will aim at perfect indifference. If someone cut off one of his arms with an axe while someone else rubbed the other with sandalwood ointment, he would neither curse the first person nor bless the second, even in thought. He ought always to be meditating and thinking about the imperfection inherent in temporal existence—its short duration, the impurity of the body, the ravages inflicted on beauty by old age, the suffering born of physical and mental illness and of passion; the sorry state of the embryo, surrounded by darkness and living in a filthy sewer; the horror of birth and birthpangs; the ignorance of the child and its dependence on others; the difficulty the adolescent finds in learning; the unavoidable presence of things and people one detests; separation from things and people one loves; the torments of hell; the sufferings of souls obliged by their past deeds to migrate into the bodies of animals. He must also practise the discipline comprised in *yoga*.

I have already mentioned the ambivalence discernible in Indian asceticism, its ability to take on a magical colouring as well as a moral and spiritual one. The point is worthy of closer attention. On the one hand the practice of asceticism is considered as a means of developing power over nature or the cosmos, in some way proportionate to the amount of will-power brought into play. In its highest forms, *tapas* is all-powerful; like its prototype, the *tapas* that produced the universe, it is irresistible. In this sense, asceticism is focussed on the will to power and has nothing to do with the moral order. But asceticism may also denote something quite different. It will then be said to blot out sin, and it will take us into the moral order to the extent to which the idea of sin is given a moral connotation. Taken in this context, it will be seen as incorporated into a group of virtues all characterised by the same radical detachment, and its function will be to effect a spiritual transformation in the ascetic and prepare him for 'release' or salvation. Hence the behaviour of the Indian monk often shows a mixture of extreme delicacy and colossal indifference to natural or social conventions, because he moves on a plane far above them. If certain classes of *sādhus*, as they are called in India, go about naked[1] (in so far as modern police-regulations allow), the reason is that the state they are in is looked upon as a return to the innocence of the first days of creation and the inalienable possession of liberty. If others carry the determination not to hurt any sensitive creature to a degree scarcely compatible with the conditions of human existence, this is not to be attributed exclusively to the attention traditionally paid by the Indian mentality to the problem of pain.[2] It is due even more to the

1 The *sādhus* are recognisably the gymnosophists of the Greek historians. The Indians call them 'men clothed in space'.
2 As we have seen, Indians have no objection to the pain consequent upon the 'athletic' exercise of the will. But they are horrified by the idea of pain inflicted so that a creature receives it passively. Hence the gradual disappearance of animal sacrifices. Hence also the negative reaction of Indians to the Christian mystery of the *passion*. The sight of blood, too, is a thing they cannot bear, unless they happen to be thrown off their normal balance.

strictly metaphysical concern not to act on any creature *from without*; not to force people over anything, but rather to recover what is properly speaking a divine mode of being and acting, viz. one which is *inside* all that is. In this sense, 'non-violence' is the most positive of dispositions, even though it is at first manifested by 'non-action'.

As I said before, these considerations on Indian asceticism ought logically to be followed by an account of *yoga*; but space does not permit of it.

CHAPTER VIII

OUTLINING A THEOLOGY OF ASCETICISM

By L. B. GEIGER, o.p.

I. The ontological significance of asceticism. 1. Creation. 2. Sin.
3. Redemption. II. The life of love and the psychological impulse
of Christian asceticism. 1. Sensible affectivity and spiritual affectivity. 2. Of interested and disinterested love. 3. True love of self
and its ascetic significance. 4. Asceticism and the truth of love.
III. Practical consequences. 1. Negative practices and positive.
2. Various modes of Christian asceticism. 3. Purity of heart. 4.
Specifying Christian asceticism.

IF it is true that theology is essentially wisdom, we cannot put
asceticism into its theological setting without raising it up
to the level of wisdom, because it is from this point of view
that the theologian studies mankind. Indeed, asceticism, however one may define it, is concerned with that activity by which
man forces himself to build up what he believes to be the perfection of a human ideal. Among all the beings of which we have
direct experience, man alone sets himself to study the problem
of his existence and has done so all through the centuries. And
he alone, once he has found the answer, can freely express it in
real life or can just as freely refuse to do so. Consequently he
alone really builds up his life according to his own choice of a
final aim.

For a Christian, and particularly for the Christian theologian,
this amounts to saying that the problem of asceticism lies within
the broader problem that the medieval masters called man's
turning back to God. In contrast to what the layman may think,
a theological viewpoint of the world is not necessarily a fixed
system, least of all was that the viewpoint of St Thomas Aquinas.
Marked throughout by the history of salvation, confined to the
Holy Scriptures and to a philosophy of neo-platonist inspiration,

that of St Thomas presents the whole of creation as a double movement, coming from God and returning to God. The plan of St Thomas's two great works, the *Summa Theologica* and *Summa contra Gentiles*, is God in himself; creatures coming from God as from their source, that is to say the free creation of a world clearly defined as a whole and in each of its parts by the wisdom of God; and the return of all things to their beginning by the perfect realising of the powers placed in each being by the gift of creation.

Nowadays we like to intensify still more the imposing vision of this returning of all things to God by emphasising the discovery of our own times, the growth of the visible universe in the course of an evolution the stages of which we are always trying to grasp further, and the workings of which we are always trying better to understand. The present structure of the corporeal universe no longer appears to us as the effect of God's sole original ordering, but more as a process, a history. Clear-cut opposition between a stable cosmos on the one hand and a series of human upheavals on the other has diminished. The whole of creation is on the move, and everything can seem to us to be the result of a choice and therefore of a renouncing. To these things nature, in its creative impulse, has been obliged to conform.

These views may be rather broad, but if we want to determine the place of asceticism from a theological point of view, we must consider it from the viewpoint of man's return to God, that is of his effort towards realising fully what his Creator meant him to be.

If we are now defining asceticism not only in a general way as a methodical striving after an ideal, but more precisely from within that effort, either as putting limits to the satisfying of certain tendencies, or as the complete renunciation of some among them, or finally as the acceptance, even the deliberate seeking, of physical or spiritual suffering, the problem before the theologian is just this: why, and to what extent, is such an asceticism required in this movement of returning to God? Why, from the point of view of what God wants him to be, should man practise asceticism at all?

Needless to say, we shall not be able to treat of every aspect involved in this problem. We must content ourselves with the essentials. Given always the narrow connection between the idea relating to the return of the creature towards God and that relating to the opposite movement, as we might say between moral theology and dogmatic theology, we must first of all remember broadly the relations that bind ontologically the creature to his Creator. Afterwards, we shall show how, psychologically, man must bring these relations into play in his conscious life. The exact aims of ascetic effort will disentangle themselves naturally, one hopes, when these two points are examined.

I

1. IN the eyes of a Christian, man is only truly man in so far as he is what God means him to be and so it is important to remind ourselves in a general way of the relations between creature and Creator. The *Credo* professes, to begin with, faith in one God, creator of heaven and earth, of visible and invisible things, and in Jesus Christ the Son of God by whom all things were made. In the prologue of his Gospel St John asserts that all things were made by the Word. This amounts to saying that we do not admit of a bad creative source, antagonistic to the source of all good. Every being, as a being, is good since it is the work of a good God, who created all things through love, with a view to communicating to others his own goodness. For the Christian, then, there does not exist any reality, nor any aspect of reality, that can be bad in itself.

We admit the existence of evil, either in the general sense of the finiteness of beings, each finite being necessarily falling short of whatever is outside of its own determination, or in the more restricted sense of natural weakness and corruptibility, or finally in its proper sense, the privation of something that is due to such a being to ensure its integrity of structure or development. This last form of evil, which constitutes evil properly so called, can be sub-divided in its turn into physical evil, the effect of physical causes, and moral evil deliberately chosen by the subject who is capable of freely growing in the way of perfection or of swerving from it. Suffering and sorrow are evil on the one hand by their psychological content which puts a check on the state of goodness and the feeling of harmony to which we are consciously drawn, or on the other hand because they make us aware of the existence of one or other forms of objective evil.

What is true of every creature is particularly so of man. He also is good in his entire being. As far as his being is concerned simply as being, nothing in him can be qualified as evil, neither in his structure nor in his tendencies. Made to the likeness of God, it is from God that he holds his being, his life, his knowledge. All his natural tendencies, as such, are good, and betoken for him a relative and partial, but none the less real, well being. To admit a tendency that is naturally bad in itself essentially and not merely by an accidental disposition would be to do injury to the goodness or the power of the very Author of all nature.

Only, if man's being is good just like that of every other creature, so will he be affected, like every other creature, by the different forms of evil that we have described above. Finite in his being, subject to corruption and death, he may also be deprived of the more or less numerous elements that should normally safeguard the integrity of being and of his happiness. From his very consciousness of them these different forms of evil take on for him a uniquely grave character. They are laden, one might say, with the additional evil of propounding the problem of evil. Add to this, from the very weakness of being a mere creature, man can be tainted with evil even in his liberty, freely choosing, whether from frailty or malice, to act contrary to his own true good. Such is the tragic privilege of a creature who is also spirit; he alone is capable of grasping evil in itself, he is the one to suffer by it explicitly, and yet he will choose it as the object of his actions.

From the point of view of asceticism, the brief summing up of these essential facts proves from now on that Christianity can never rest in any way upon a dualism either of human nature or of nature in general. However satisfying to our imagination it may be, we must give up the idea that there are beings that are evil or tainted in themselves which it would suffice for us henceforward to avoid in order to keep morally good and pure. Our renouncing of any creature or of any form of activity can never be based upon the assumption that any being of its own nature can infect us with evil like leprosy. 'God saw what he had made and he saw that it was very good.' All Christian consideration of asceticism must begin by facing this essential truth.

A deep-seated optimism must thus run through all Christian conception of creation. Asceticism, in so far as it is negative, can never be an end in itself. It only enters into the question from the fact of the very limitations of the finite creature and its consequent needs, whatever they may be, of which we shall speak later. Man, as a finite being, cannot be everything. He cannot even, without contradiction, develop simultaneously all the powers he possesses. He must choose among his riches and choosing always involves a refusal. The budding powers that he calls into development stifle those that he cannot nourish. Even among those that he cultivates there is bound to be inequality reducing some of them to a subordinate role. Thus every effort of man over himself, or in the world, is accompanied, as by its shadow, by a manfully accepted renunciation. The acceptance of suffering properly so called, of risk, of heart-breaks and failures of all kinds, although not exactly part of asceticism as understood in its exact meaning, can and should be seen in the light of the requirements of human development making its way in a world that is material, fragile, subject to law and necessity, following out designs that are not altogether under man's control.

Henceforward, and before we sound the depths of the truly Christian demands of asceticism, we must notice that this asceticism involves very different methods and ideas according to what we conceive to be man's vocation even on purely philosophical grounds. The asceticism of *Homo oeconomicus* will not be the same as that of a *gentleman* (Fr. *Honnête homme*). That of a *savant* will not be the same as that of Aristotle's *prudent man*, which again will differ from the sage of Plato or Plotinus. In those first cases it is a simply rational thing, produced by an exact adjusting of means to an end worthy of man. In the last case it will become mystical and then it may reach excesses and follies, which become inevitable, almost normal, through the seeking of contact with the Absolute where lies the true development of human vocation. Under the appearances of denial or renunciation carried to extremes, asceticism will still serve a positive purpose since it is in and through a purifying of all inferior elements, that we intend to set free, that is to restore to its perfect integrity, that spiritual foundation upon which all man's dignity rests.

2. Our Christian faith teaches us that man's true greatness, made as he is to the image of God, consists not only in the possibility that is offered him of getting into touch with God at the beginning and the end of his creation, but even more *immediately* through an exchange of personal relations in faith and charity. Of the earthly tasks confided to man, nothing has been taken back. 'God has given the earth to the sons of men.' He commanded them to grow and multiply. He placed on their brow the mark of intelligence, the mainspring of all their conquests. But human activity falls short of its true dimensions unless it reaches up ultimately to him through whom all the things upon which it is exercised exist, and from whom its strength is drawn. But being of necessity intelligent, that is to say inspired more or less explicitly by a definite outlook on the ordering of things, man's activity can never remain in the world like an uncrowned monument. It multiplies there, as a lawless and therefore noxious proliferation, inner cells of a living organism, each time that it omits or refuses to reach completion by a loving adherence to the Creator who is Love. For the love of God is not merely a matter of our emotions or of our imagination, in a word a subjective thing; it concerns the very existence of this world of spirits whose axis it defines. To interfere with this love is in the true sense of the word to deprive the spirit world of its axis, and with it the whole of creation in so far as the solidarity of all its parts is concerned.

Again, faith teaches us that it is precisely in this highest point of the spirit life, in its attitude to God, that the gravest disorder, evil in its most virulent form, can enter. Neither does this evil merely affect some finite being, but it affects the relations of this being at its very core. The order that reigned in a world that was essentially good, even though affected by the different forms of evil described above, was overthrown not through some catastrophe due to blind forces but by this particular and radical evil, a free choice made by intelligent creatures of insubordination to their creator. Here disorder becomes complete, anti-order which attacks the created being in the very thing that causes it to be, its bond of dependence upon God. Evil, which, ontologically speaking, can never be anything but a privation of being, here takes on a form that is in some sort positive since it is the object of a choice. It penetrates as far into one's being as possible, and in default of positively affecting the very being itself, it reaches to the activity of the spiritual being, who is capable of grasping being and of discerning its meaning and movement from its very beginning, so as to snatch it, if that were possible, from its natural gravitation. It is an affront to God himself. It is no longer physical but moral. It is called sin, and from that we can grasp all its cosmic significance.

The angels' sin and man's sin is one solidarity, since according to the scripture it was at the instigation of the devil that man took up the way of insubordination and defiance against the goodness of God. These have disorganised a universe. Refusing to go in the direction of all things returning to their source, creatures have pretended and still pretend to make self their destiny and that of the universe. Instead of the convergence of all trajectories towards one focus, we have an indefinite number of orbits which necessarily collide with each other, obliged to draw along with them as many beings as possible so as to constitute at least an appearance of system, and fatally colliding with the trajectories of those who are set towards or returning towards their true centre. The unity of the universe has been broken and will be broken to the end of time, not merely because an evil principle has been at work but because creatures that were created good have freely chosen to be active centres of disorder, losing by their sin all the preternatural privileges which would have neutralised the effect of the relative evil inherent in the material world. Even should it happen, as it does in the case of man himself, that this disorder is not desired for its own sake nor in all its full extent, because of some portion of good, of happiness, or of anticipated satisfaction being the chief thing consciously aimed at, the effect is the same. Within man and outside of man it attains to proportions that are a veritable mystery of iniquity. Yet here again, it is not a matter of things evil by nature, but of beings that have become evil by their sinful acts, of offences against the goodness and majesty of God, of disorders in relation to the Principle of all things and which sow disorder throughout the universe.

The result, therefore, for our problem of asceticism is that man's effort towards his genuine development can no longer be presented merely as constructive. It is no longer a conquest, but rather a re-conquest, not merely a growth but a recovery, not merely an education but a rectifying. Asceticism will aim not only at avoiding superfluities but still more at getting rid of the poisons that are infesting the spiritual organism. It will not only mean the confident acceptance of trials and sufferings but even reparation and expiation. Sin leaves its traces under the form of inclinations to evil, the dulling of the moral judgment. Asceticism aims at smoothing out these creases, these deviating syntheses that are hard to remove. Even the attractiveness of creatures is no longer remote. Compromised by the unlawful use man has made of them, they take on more or less the appearance of accomplices from whom it may be necessary to defend oneself more rigorously, not because they are evil in themselves but because, as man has made an ill use of them, he may need to avoid them more carefully, just as a sick organism must avoid certain foodstuffs that a healthy body can easily assimilate. In a word, man no longer stands before God as his creature and his child but as a sinner and a penitent.

3. However, in this struggle for purification, expiation and reparation, which are as far beyond human strength as the holiness of God is above heaven and earth, the Christian knows that he is not alone. The history of the world has been reversed once more by a new intervention of the love of God. Into this world under the dominion of evil forces, where man was floundering powerless, God himself came to take flesh, to suffer, to die, but also to rise from the dead.

In the person of Jesus of Nazareth, in whom human and divine natures were united, one man of perfect and infinite holiness, that is to say entirely rectified as to this order of returning to God and able to accomplish it beyond all measure by his dignity of Son of God, came and took his place in our history, in our struggles, in our misery. This misery he entirely accepted save only sin, the source of our real wretchedness. He came precisely to conquer both sin and misery together: sin by expiating it with his love, misery by making it serve the love that abolished the sin. Death and suffering, the fruits of sin, are now snatched from the tree that bore them. In Christ's hands, grafted as you might say on to the tree of the Cross, they are transformed into the fruits of life, into more brilliant signs of a purer love. Love always knows how to quicken with its own life trial, suffering and even death, and how to draw from what is worthless something from which is born the highest value, that is to say love itself. Christ alone, by the eminent dignity of his person and the absolute purity of his life, could offer to God with the certainty of acceptance a love capable of drawing all things along with it, even evil and death, so as to draw from all this an unquestionable proof of its warmth and its sincerity before his Father and before men.

Thus the Cross of Christ becomes the symbol of a new wisdom in the eyes of a Christian. New, not in the sense that God would not have been Love in his essence and in all his works, but in the sense that on the Cross his love was revealed to us in letters of fire and blood perceptible to the least observant eyes. The love of God hidden, in a sense, in his works, in creation, even in the Old Testament, bursts upon our world and into our history. What St Paul says of the word of God addressed in times past to our fathers by the prophets, revealed in these later times by the very Son of God, can also be said of Love. That too has been finally put before us as clearly as possible in the love of Jesus and notably of Jesus Crucified.

Man's return to God, as the Christian ultimately sees it, is settled then on the one hand by exigencies that might be termed metaphysical, inherent in the relations of creature and Creator, and on the other hand by the historical conditions of a drama being acted between the love of God, always ready to renew or increase its gifts, and man's love which is always slipping away, these two being not side by side but intimately mingled, this Love of God being itself creative Love as it is the mainspring of the Incarnation and Redemption. Created to God's image, man should be able to realise, if he is to be truly himself and as God wished him to be, the perfection of love in its most complete form before God, before his brethren, before the whole of creation. In the world as it is, corrupted by sin, but redeemed and sanctified by the Son of God made man, man's effort is mostly shown in suffering, always in the struggle not only against the evil in finite things, but still more against the forces of evil in himself and outside of himself. For him Christ is at once the source of life and the model. By his greatness and his lowliness, by accepting all the real conditions of our existence except sin, he ensures the perfect return of the entire creation towards God, and he shows to us all what love is, the true human greatness that could not be shaken by suffering, or hatred, or bitter death, or even that apparent dereliction in which God seemed to leave his Son at the supreme moment of his agony.

Christian asceticism will then perforce comprise, besides the general exigencies of a moral life that is upright or well-controlled in human tasks, some seekings, even excesses, that can only be understood in the light of a love whose power of growth, in the face of absolute Love itself, is unlimited. Consequently this love is capable of consuming all finite love, is anxious to prove its sincerity, its purity and its unlimited keenness by the voluntary acceptance, in conformity with God's will, of things that have no value in themselves—privations, sufferings, death, after the example of Christ who gave the greatest proof of love which is to give one's life for those one loves, turning into the service of this love all evil things, the just consequences of sin which is fundamentally a refusing of love. Only the man who cannot understand this urgency and this logic, we might call it, of love in its highest forms, can misunderstand the creative value of Christian asceticism and see in it nothing but negation or self-destruction.

II

Such then is the objective order in which the Christian's destiny is placed and with it the problem of asceticism. Were man a simple being we might be satisfied with this. Were he merely animal he would follow out his destiny no more affected by this drama than any monkey or cat. Were he pure spirit he would necessarily meet with it always in the deepest centre of his soul or in the clearest summit of his vision. Man, however, is complex. Perhaps he knows more often than we suspect it at what level of his being his life is being lived. Rarely can one guess it by the words he makes use of. Man is complex, his words are simple but with a simplicity which is the outcome of poverty, especially so in the domain of his emotional life. We must then complete our first statement by some details concerning the forms of syntheses likely to be produced between the objective truth that we have just expounded and whatever may be the condition of the affective life of the subject.

1. Moralists and spiritual authors have always emphasised the necessity of distinguishing two major forms of our affective activity: sensible affectivity and spiritual affectivity. Of late years discussions have come up on the subject of another distinction, that of *eros* and *agape*. Without entering into these controversies in detail, we shall content ourselves here with a reminder of St Thomas' doctrine on the different aspects of our affective life.

First of all, take sensible affectivity and spiritual affectivity. For our problem of asceticism the following are the important points: sensible affectivity, which has for its subject our powers of sensibility and for its object sensible goods, is essentially known by its concrete character. Hence it is concerned with very definite things. We see it in its pure state in animals whose species we can determine as much by their organic structure as by the objects which make up the whole world of their interests. These last define so narrowly the range of the animals' movements that the deliberately conditioned reflex, that is to say the association of objects indifferent in themselves with the primary objects, is our sole means of extending their circle for our own profit.

More or less precise knowledge of things is of no value in itself. It functions chiefly as a signal of the object's presence releasing in its turn the affective reaction if there is one.

At this level it is almost an abuse to speak of egoism or altruism, categories that can only hold good for spiritual affectivity. Here it is only a case of pleasure or displeasure. Things are good or bad because and only because of the reaction they provoke. The truth is that this life of affective sensibility (the passions of moral theology, not to be confounded with passions in the modern sense of the word) is morally an indifferent thing. It constitutes the matter of our moral life. It may be more or less easy to work upon. In itself it is antecedent to morality.

Spiritual affectivity, often called intellectual or rational affectivity, has an essentially different object. Instead of being formally led by signs of pleasure or displeasure, it follows upon our judgment of things as they are in themselves. Of course we shall never altogether avoid the reactions of our affective sensibility. For man, on his voyage through life, they are like the different coloured lights or luminous dials that a pilot never loses sight of, knowing and understanding their directions and instructions. It is easy to foresee what would become of a navigator who, instead of making use of his brilliant-looking instruments, saw nothing in them but pretty toys, created to delight the eyes, mysterious and subtle. In the same way man, by his education and personal experience, should learn to judge of, and interpret objectively, the more or less durable flashes of light that pass through his consciousness. He cannot prevent them and has no need to prevent them. Only he must not let his judgment or his actions be determined exclusively by these allurements. He must rise to the consideration of their objective worth. It is on this condition alone that he proves himself a man, that he can reach to a spiritual affectivity which no longer judges of the goodness of things simply by the pleasure that they provoke or promise, but which on the contrary weighs the pleasure, if there is any, against the objective value that his intelligence recognises.

All the same this does not mean that our spiritual affectivity is necessarily correct. It always comprises a judgment of the objective nature of the goods that we are proposing to make use of. And just as corporal pleasure and all that facilitates it, riches or power, are good things according to their standard, we may judge them to be the chief and all-sufficing motives for our action. It is a question of judgment. It is our judgment that secretly moves us to act. Pleasure, for example, only acts as a reflex stimulant. Man has lifted it up to the level of something of value. We have here an activity that is proper to man but falsified and therefore bad, since the real judgment, instead of being entirely objective as is its nature, has deflected its course towards sensible affectivity, transforming that into the whole truth instead of a relative or partial one. It is in this monstrous synthesis between a situation objective in itself and a lower determinism, a deliberately accepted synthesis, that the moral fault consists. And thence flow its harmful effects. As a living synthesis it creates a certain unity in our psychological life but only in distorting it.

Spiritual affectivity is not quite fully itself unless it is entirely objective and true, that is to say it must be willing to model the judgments, which it cannot help forming, upon true relative values. From this we see that spiritual affectivity must of its very nature call for an asceticism in the form of a continual effort to direct one's life not merely according to the pull of habits or sensible inclinations, but with clear judgment that faces up to truth. This effort acts in the first place in some way upon the person concerned, keeping him awake, on the spot, watchful, like a sentinel or a watchman in an observation post. It does not act against the tendencies of the senses in themselves. That would be unproductive because impossible, and impossible because contrary to nature. But it aims at keeping these attractions in order by an entire grading of values and so giving them or refusing them such satisfaction as is advisable.

It seems to me that the whole essence of asceticism, and of whatever may be its varying methods, consists in this effort of absolute truth, a positive effort which of necessity expresses itself by putting in its place, controlling, subordinating, the sensible affectivity and its reactions. From its humblest forms of fidelity to duty up to its most sublime transformations through God's will, in the lives of the saints, asceticism touches the very heart of our life of spiritual affectivity. And if it is impossible to standardise life on the basis of instincts, since that would[12] necessarily stifle our truer life, real spiritual affectivity can and should take on the guidance of the life of sensible affectivity so as to rectify slight deviations and to show up some attractions as blunders. But we must steadfastly desire and pursue this integration under pain of undoing the purpose for which we gave it its authority and efficacy.

We have had to insist to some slight extent upon this role of truth, the light of spiritual affectivity, because from it will flow .

K

many conclusions for the solving of our problem. We have already emphasised the close relationship between truth and the very essence of asceticism which is *effort*, in the exact moral sense of the word and not to be confused with an intense expenditure of energy. It needs an effort to be willing to be guided by true values, both because this is not natural to us and will not function by routine and because, by reason of the disorder of our nature, our weakest self has become the predominant one, and especially in view of the downward trend of our natural instincts. The deliberate re-directing of our lives into the truth constitutes the essence of morality; hence we see how closely asceticism and morality are linked together. Again, this is not necessarily in the sense of repressing our affective tendencies, still less of an undiscerning repression, but chiefly in the sense of a subordination of these things to a life that is enlightened more and more, and in everything, by the light of truth. It is not a case of being aggressive against self which would not raise us above instinct level, but of a conversion of our entire being to a life lived according to truth.

2. In the problem of asceticism there is another difficulty which this very character of objectivity enables us to clarify. This difficulty comes from the opposition between interested love and disinterested love. First of all let us state that interested love is generally held to be a love that has for its aim the subject himself or his own advantage, even if it has some apparent movement towards others. On the contrary we call disinterested the love that has no other aim than the benefit of others. It comes out of the subject and makes the subject come out of himself to reach out to the object loved and let himself be absorbed by it. The one is centripedal and the other centrifugal. It is not difficult to see how these descriptions and these metaphors must remain confused and even unintelligible unless one can make a fundamental distinction between these two loves. Indeed, if love were substantially the same in both cases one could not see why or how a change of object—self, others or in a different circuit: towards self or towards others—could change the value of the love.

In reality, in St Thomas's eyes, who in this connection merely comments on the evangelical precept of charity, the important distinction is not solely one of object or sense of direction. More precisely, these distinctions should indicate a modifying or a more essential difference in the structure of the love itself, false love on the one hand and true love on the other. Already from the mere fact that love, on spiritual grounds, always follows upon a judgment which whether true or false, intends to decide the objective value, according to this standard there is produced a love that is itself objective. Affectivity that is purely sensible, such as exists in animals, is no doubt entirely wrapped up in its own subjectiveness and for the most part confusedly. Through the judgment I become aware of what a certain object is in itself and what its worth, and immediately to the feeling of pleasure, if such exists, is added an affective adherence to the object itself. It is in this sense that it can be said that all human love comprises more or less explicitly a certain homage. Sensible affectivity is a slave to its own subjectiveness. In a sense, however unfittingly, it is always self-love of a most absolute kind. Only love enlightened by objectivity can break through this circle and go out from the subject towards the object itself. In human affectivity, in so far as it is human, there is always some portion of objectivity.

Interested love and disinterested love, then, are not opposed to each other in the same way as instinct and superior affectivity. They are opposed like a love that, objective by nature, sometimes stops short at an object or at its goodness or sometimes turns back to self using the goods of others to its own advantage. Interested love is not morally a bad thing in itself, it only turns to egoism when the subject makes itself the last centre of *all* its loves, reducing *everything*, explicitly, to the role of a means ordained to its true or false pleasure or power.

For the problem of asceticism it is then necessary to make a careful distinction between egoism and interested love on the one hand and self-love and love for self on the other hand. Interested love can be legitimate if, objectively, it is concerned precisely with things inferior to ourselves or meant for our service. Interested love can therefore be a virtuous thing. It might become a necessity and its contrary might be a sin. A human being who would let himself die of hunger to avoid interested love in respect of creatures who should constitute his food would make a fine legendary figure, should he be sincere. One would hesitate, though, to recognise the moral truth of his action. On the contrary, egoism is a perversion. For the egoist nothing else exists but good things that are useful to himself though under various aspects. Asceticism should make us radically avoid egoism. It cannot make us avoid all interested love. For that we should have to be transformed into Absolute Goodness, which would be somewhat difficult. Perhaps, however, we should say that if asceticism cannot, and should not, make us completely avoid all interested love in its right place, it should all the same surround it always, and more and more explicitly, with that portion of objective love, of affective homage that we have described above and which is fundamentally nothing more than the acknowledgment of the gratuitousness of all well being and of all gifts, a gratuitousness that gives birth to gratitude. St Francis' canticle of created things, prayers before and after meals, a certain self-mastery, can well express this sort of discreet determination to maintain, even in the use of good things for our own legitimate satisfaction, the whole horizon of truth and therefore of objectivity where, as good things for our own use, all things appear even more clearly to be, like ourselves, creatures and works of the Goodness of God.

3. If in exterior goods we are to distinguish between interested love and egoism, in the things that concern ourselves we must distinguish between *love for self* and *love of self*. Love for self is nothing else but egoism. It consists, as we have said, in setting up oneself, knowingly, as the ultimate good, so as to subordinate everything either to one's own pleasure, or power, or glory and so on. For a finite being this is obviously a perversion. Doubly so in fact: because it attributes to a creature what belongs to Absolute Goodness and because it constitutes, if it is deliberate, an abuse of our power to judge objectively. Love of self on the contrary is nothing else than wanting self to be what it is in truth. That means that it is only intelligible in the case of an entirely rectified objectivity such as we have described above. It constitutes, as expressed on the plane of true consciousness, a tendency towards one's being which is engraved upon every being and which can never be eradicated without destroying being itself. This love of self, far from filling with oneself the

whole horizon of one's love, approaches self from the general
horizon of truth. It only constitutes one particular case of objective love and one really wonders why the subject himself should
be the only thing excluded in an objective love which claims to
cling to the true value of all good. One admits that it is difficult
to live this sort of love. All the same, that is no reason why it
should be confused with its exact opposite which is egoism or love
for self that both should be condemned to the same anathemas.

We must even go further and, at the risk of scandalising many
pious souls, declare with St Thomas that love of self—not love
for self—is the foremost of all loves and the condition of all the
others. Yet nothing is more obvious. To be able to love, even
with the most interested of loves, we must be, and therefore we
must will to be if we want to love or are to be able to love, and
we want to be with the same determination that urges us to love.
This means that any other love presupposes love of self. And on
the part of the subject himself, love implies not only love of his
own being but also love of all its developments, all its acquisitions, all its enrichments which will enable him the better to
use and the better to manifest his own love. The kind of scandal
often taken to this thesis—we see it in the works of Nygren and
the discussions provoked by these works—often arises not only
from the fact that people have never taken into account the
difference between a passive love, polarised by the sole pleasure
experienced in connection with its object, and a love enlightened
by truth and therefore entirely objective in itself in whatever
may be its object, even though that be the subject himself, but
also because love of self and love of others have been separated
to make them seem to act at two moments of time chronologically independent of each other. We might think it was necessary
to love ourselves first of all, after the manner of little autocrats,
to flatter ourselves, to develop ourselves and then, at some other
time, to consider sharing this accumulated treasure with others.
This would obviously mean propounding in the beginning a
love perfectly egoistical in its psychological structure and whatever may be its ultimate intentions, so as to bring out of it, at
some later time, a so-called disinterested love which could
include all self-renunciations, all self-dispossessions for the benefit of the beloved object.

St Thomas's thesis is infinitely more simple and altogether more sound. To love oneself should mean to love oneself in as much as one is in truth. This then means that, from the very beginning, from the first movement of this love of self, the subject understands himself as he is, that is to say, quite otherwise than under the guise of an autocrat. We know that, in truth, we are of God and for God, we are of Christ and his Church and we exist for them, we are of a certain family, a city, a country and we exist for them. These are necessary relationships, graven upon our very being, of varying degrees of depth and necessity, but which we can never entirely ignore under pain of evading the order of truth and falling back into that of imagination or error. The love of self that we are putting at the basis of all other loves, unites therefore, without ever being able really to separate them, all these benefits for which we were made either with a view to contemplating and reverencing them or in order to improve them by our own efforts. Love of self, turning upon a subject whose whole being is referred to the well-being to which he is being directed, or even more or less subjected, cannot help but drive the subject towards these benefits. This means psychologically that there are no other objects towards which the subject is ordained. Love of self is not first of all psychological, an egoism that later will be converted into altruism. It is rather an ontological condition, an implicit fundamental idea that leaves the subject entirely receptive, occupied with God and with his will signified by his Word, but also occupied with his creation and events that take place in it, even with himself in the exact and necessary measure in which the existence of the subject and his complete development are indispensable conditions of the existence and development of his love.

This kind of love of self constitutes the most radical form of self-forgetfulness. For self ceases to exist as autonomous greatness, as much in the role of an idol to be nourished and flattered as in that of an enemy against which is let loose an aggressiveness which we can often suspect of being merely a defence against a false self-worship that is repressed but not destroyed. We are not so important as to merit either such attentions or such hatred. To put self in its place which is that of an unprofitable servant, always to recognise that one is not the only pebble on the beach, is the genuine form of self-forgetfulness in the authentic love of self. And the authentic love of self, in the case of a being who knows himself to be made essentially for authentic love, is finally nothing else but aiming at authentic love, pure and simple.

4. The summing up of these few ideas concerning sensible love and spiritual love, interested love or disinterested love, enables us to conclude our exposition by showing how from the meeting between objective order defined above and a fittingly subjective attitude, an authentic practice of Christian asceticism should be born. First of all the objective order itself is seen in a new light. The Christian can get an inkling in what sense God speaks to him of his love, of how this love is necessarily disinterested while being at the same time love of self, and that it has no connection with a transcending egoism, and yet is a love of all things for oneself. For the love of God is love in truth, totally and absolutely, necessarily so of one who is truly supremely lovable, that is God himself, having nothing in it that resembles the self-satisfaction that certain idols convey. And the love of God is love for all things for his sake, not so as to imprint something upon them but to acknowledge in them all that they possess and because for them to tend towards God is nothing more than becoming more fully what they are by God's creative love.

Henceforth the Christian can grasp the greatness of charity, that love of friendship to which God is calling him. The Christian is invited to love not only absolute unseen kindness and goodness but love itself. His heart, animated with this love which is pure because it is pure offering and pure homage, meets the very heart of God, if one can so express it, and his love of which the negative word *disinterestedness*, seeming to put a brake upon the initial egoism, very inadequately conveys this wholesale gratuity. Hence charity, by its very nature, of a purely objective love for love that is absolute and entirely gratuitous, tends necessarily towards the plenitude of its activity. Plenitude here can mean nothing less than to love with *all* one's heart, *all* one's strength, that means to say to recall *all* our love from *all* other creatures where it has been dispersed, to offer it *wholly* to him who is *all* love, the source of all good and of all love and of charity itself. God has the right, and he uses it, to call certain souls to express even blindly this unique and transcending character of the love of God. Is it surprising, then, that he strips them to an extent that no created usefulness could justify, that he leads them not only to the limits of destitution, but even to torments of body and soul, certain as he is of transforming these in the hands of his friends, like the alms of St Elizabeth, into flowers and fruits?

The deaths of martyrs, the lives of hermits, monastic life with its three vows of poverty, chastity and obedience, can only be really understood in the light of this pursuit of perfect charity. What we call renunciation, mortification, annihilation, even in the extreme forms that we see in the lives of the saints, is always grounded upon some positive impetus. The soul sells everything, gives away everything, not because it sees evil in it but to purchase the precious pearl which takes the place of all other riches. It suffers everything not because suffering is a good thing in itself, but because the very absence of all that is valuable allows it to pursue and attain with greater purity to the love of God which, in suffering and through suffering, claims the adherence of the heart, after the example of Christ who willed to be obedient unto death on the Cross.

Sin itself, conquered by Christ on the Cross, should never be considered outside of this perspective of charity. From us it calls first of all for reparation in union with Christ and then for vigilant measures to be taken against its recurrence. But it is in so far as it constitutes an offence against the love of God that the Christian should always regret it and avoid it. Its true nature, besides, is only seen in the light of charity, even though the Church does not hesitate to recognise its necessity in her Liturgy, as if our going astray had been imperative so that God could make a more brilliant manifestation of his mercy in order to save us. What the harmony and peace of the earthly Paradise could not reveal to our first parents, the bleeding drama of Calvary cries out to us in such clear terms that it becomes almost impossible not to understand them. Christian asceticism, whatever may be its motives, seen in the light of charity which is man's highest perfection is, then, invested with a positive creative character, creative precisely of that perfection of man where, face to face with absolute love, which is entirely gratuitous but so often misunderstood and offended, the soul becomes finally, by extremes of deprivation and filial acceptance of all God's will, nothing more than pure response to love. The negative aspect of Christian asceticism, even though it may take on forms that seem exaggerated and paradoxical, is put at the service of a positive impetus: not to have, not to be this or that, in order to be, and to be as fully as possible, the thing that alone deserves definitely to be called being. But since the aim of this impetus is nothing else but objective and disinterested love in its most complete form, it is obvious that this impetus will not recoil upon a subject who is shut up in himself in a false self-sufficiency. It aims at the subject's development but with a view to opening it up and keeping it as entirely receptive as possible towards the objective of well-being and of love. And this in such a way that its positive element itself takes on, as we have said above concerning objective love in general, a meaning of spoliation and asceticism, of effort and of creativeness, of which the negative aspects though more noticeable are, when all is said and done, but the means. Objective love alone, which delivers up its possessor to God and to all his designs, represents then positive asceticism, which does positively purify and liberate, and which gives an ascetic value to all the practices which in the ordinary way alone bear the name of asceticism.

III

FROM this positive character of charity which is ascetic and purifying, there flow two consequences that we must develop briefly in our conclusion. The first is that negative practices are not the only means of attaining charity. The second, resulting from the first, concerns the divers forms of asceticism functioning in different states of the Christian life.

1. Of course, the negative practices of asceticism constitute a necessary element of every authentic Christian life. The Gospel teaches us that in order to follow Christ we must carry his Cross, and carry it every day. But the Gospel and also the Epistles teach us that in the end the Christian, thanks to the renunciations he has faithfully practised, should come to the

purified and rectified use of all good things created by God and put at man's disposal. Were it otherwise we should arrive at the paradox of a life that would only be Christian and good by fleeing from creatures and that it could not be so in the necessary use of these same created things or in its dealings with men. Now, if it is true that all things that exist proceed from creative love, the ideal of the Christian life should finally result in purity of heart, a simplicity that knows how to preserve charity in everything, a love that accepts everything from God and gives thanks for everything through Jesus Christ. Such purity as this seems hardly attainable for our sin-stained souls, except in terms of renunciation. He alone who, for the love of God, knows how to consent to all deprivations and to accept all trials, can be capable of using the good things of God's creation with a pure heart. And this not primarily to seek pleasure in them, which would throw him back into egoism, but to use them in the service of God and his brethren.

Here again a certain form of love, a certain way of using created things and loving them, shows a positive effort of privation, by the orientation that it impresses upon our hearts towards promoting good, and not chiefly towards enjoying the pleasures and satisfactions that we can get out of them. This is an objective attitude which, from its summit where it aims at God himself, comes down upon all other beings who have a right to expect from us help of all kinds. This continual practice of disinterested love constitutes one of the most important forms of asceticism. It is at the same time the expression and manifestation of a purified love and the means of increasing it. If asceticism had no other aim but that of developing and manifesting the energy of our will, our penances could never be sufficiently violent and they would be fundamentally the only things capable of attaining our end. The end of Christian asceticism being the perfection of love, and God being the source of all good things and of all legitimate love, negative practices, however important they may be, can never be the only or even the principal reaction of a Christian in the face of finite well-being and finite love. Only positive practice and love itself remain essentially ascetic because they are contained in the centre of charity, that love which draws us always towards good in itself, which we respect or which we try with all our strength to maintain or if necessary to bring into being. And since this rectified love, enlightened by truth, is nothing else fundamentally but the moral life in its essence, we see that Christian asceticism, while it is unintelligible without the love of God to which it is finally tending, is no less so without a moral life that is as well developed as possible under every aspect.

2. This primary conclusion explains also why Christian asceticism can never be conceived as always uniform. Very often authors who treat of it only see it in connection with that form of the Christian life which is religious life, of which the exclusive aim is perfect charity. Negative means are therefore given the first place and asceticism becomes merely another name for mortification and renunciation. On the contrary, if we observe that charity not only constitutes an end apart from asceticism, but is actually in a positive way asceticism itself, that is to say positive purity of heart, we see that ascetic practices should follow on the different states of charity, or rather more exactly the states of life in which charity is exercised and developed. Now, if God does call certain souls to make perfect charity the exclusive aim of their lives, apart from all other secondary aims, he also demands from Christians the assurance, by charity, of the indispensable functions of family life, citizenship and cultural developments of every kind. We might call this involved charity (*engagée*) if you will, as opposed to that charity which is free (*degagée*) in the pure state that characterises certain forms of religious life.

If asceticism were entirely reserved to practices of renunciation, the condition of a lay-Christian would be most paradoxical, indeed perilous, were asceticism indispensable to genuine Christian life. But if asceticism in its positive form be graven upon the very heart of Christian perfection we can see that not only is it compatible with every state of life—saints show this by their diversity—but as a consequence it calls out all the developments, all the acquisitions required for the Christian's temporal duties. Difficulties crop up here partly because, to a life of charity directed towards God, we must join at the same time our professional life which is not always easy to link with the former. And if asceticism is mostly renunciation and mortification our whole professional life risks lying outside its radius.

Of course, renunciation and mortification have their place in all Christian life. But since asceticism should, finally, lead to absolute purity of heart, everything that leads there merits the name of asceticism and still more so whenever the link with that purity of heart is drawn more closely. If renunciation and mortification are sure means, in the sense that we have described and that all Christian tradition has always recommended, then the right use of the good things of this world, creation in all its forms, self-development for the service of those one loves or of those for whom one is working, constitute the unquestionable means of genuine asceticism.

3. The doctrine that clarifies everything here is that all good partakes of the Absolute Good, all love of the Absolute Love. St Thomas, in a text that deserves to be better known, does not hesitate to affirm that charity, just as it can comprehend in its object all good things, since these proceed from God and return to him, can also animate all loves since these also proceed from the love of God. If in the matter of God himself, the true way of loving is by abandoning everything so as to manifest the all-sufficingness of the love of God in the entire recollection of our heart, in the matter of creatures, especially of our fellow-men, this same love of disinterested and pure charity should urge us to *be* all that is possible, to *acquire* all that is possible, so as to give better and to serve better. Asceticism is proved precisely in giving, in that drive towards the spreading of good, if that is our vocation from God. Neither need we fear that the requirements of renunciation properly so called will be ignored. Renunciation will be found under many guises, inherent as it is in every human vocation. But it should be seen more positively in the very heart of that asceticism which the practice of all the requirements of the duty of one's state, in the service of others and where God has placed us, really constitutes.

Whatever may be his condition, man is called to one essentially positive vocation, to attain to the perfection of charity, charity for God and for his brethren comprised in one single commandment. This perfection of charity represents in itself the purest form of self-deprivation and despoiling carried even to the depths of the heart. It is both love and asceticism at once. It gives meaning to all forms of renunciation and mortification, which are in a way but the hollow underside of its positive spoliation. It calls for these things even more because the heart knows itself to be sinful and indebted to Christ who, being innocent himself, suffered for our salvation. But it is also expressed in the purity of our use and love of all that God has created in his love, the existence and increase of which he has made to be partly dependent upon our own efforts and our own love.

In other words, if we want to put asceticism in its negative form with its correct theological setting, not only must we link it closely with this positive aim, the perfection of love, show its relationship to the objective order of the Christian view of the world, but we must also clearly show this positive asceticism at the centre of love itself. This positive asceticism is a radical but creative spoliation, nothing other than the objectivity of spiritual love when it is enlightened by a true estimate of what goodness is, by being present in all goodness, by movement towards goodness and not merely a more or less intense state of our sensible affectivity. St Thomas's moral intellectualism takes on here its authentic significance. It at once reveals its practical fecundity.

In such a perspective as this, asceticism no longer acts at the level of our instincts by the simple mechanism of repressing, forcing under, or inhibition. Still less will it proceed from a morbid taste for suffering, from pusillanimity, from a tendency to defeatism, or from an unhealthy inferiority complex. It is first and foremost a conversion of heart to a love whose positive demands draw out or enlighten asceticism in its negative form by giving it authentic significance and exact limits. Much more than this, if it is charity that alone, by the conversion of heart that it comprises, confers upon negative asceticism its virtuous value, that is to say asceticism pure and simple, we may well conclude that asceticism is first of all a positive thing which flows out into practices of negative asceticism which it inspires and upon which it subsists.

Finally, then, purity of heart is the only thing of true value, even from an ascetical point of view. This is the treasure hidden in a field. It marks the acquisition of a positive demeanour of which the negative formulas are but an inadequate and clumsy expression. It establishes the soul in a permanent state of asceticism which it should never abandon, even when it has to accept an interested love, since even this for the Christian can never be a seeking of pleasure for its own sake, but a responding, in the truth, to a true ordering of things. It is possible then to acquire this purity of heart and to practise it by acts other than those of negative asceticism. It would, then, be an error to think that it could be found nowhere else. It should include Christian joy as well as tears, the silence of the contemplative as well as the labours of the apostle, the hiddenness of a novice as well as the boldest deeds of the man of action. By a paradox, which is only an apparent one, the excessive insistence on negative asceticism alone, without joining it on to interior positive asceticism, weakens its own significance. We must limit it to certain moments, certain actions, certain aspects of the Christian life. We carry this negative asceticism to the door of the sanctuary if need be, led by positive asceticism, whose slave it is, so as to form within the soul true purity of love rather than any virtue of fortitude or penance.

4. We need hardly insist, in conclusion, upon the features that distinguish Christian asceticism, thus understood in its inspiration and in its aims, from other forms of asceticism, although it does comprise some of their elements. It is distinct from the asceticism that comes from terror of evil powers whose action it tries to prevent or whose anger it tries to appease. It is distinct from the asceticism that aims solely at procuring a ritual purity by separating the pure from the impure. It is distinct from the asceticism that separates the superior powers from the inferior powers within ourselves, in order to make them more efficient in producing various forms of ecstasy or to increase thereby wonderful powers over men and things. Although it comprises a creaturely attitude, a consciousness of and a regret for sin, we must beware of confusing it with the forms of asceticism which spring from the encounter between the religious world imperfectly understood, and the more or less instinctive feelings of fear, terror, personal advantage, rapturous excitement, or guilt. In the same way we must distinguish between all religiously inspired asceticism and that practised for reasons of hygiene, or

of sporting or technical efficiency. Finally, it is important to keep a clear distinction between ascetical practices and other forms of religious sacrifice whose aim is to express chiefly an attitude of adoration and dependence upon the Creator and Master of all things.

In spite of all this it is useful to remind ourselves that man does not at once reach the finished and purified state of his relations with God, such as we have been defining in the course of this exposition. Stages that show psychological growth, difference in temperament and mentalities have their repercussions on religious life. Asceticism should, then, diversify its methods and its immediate aims. Without losing sight of its ultimate purpose it should insist first of all on whether its motives are moral or social. Only in this sense could one have proposed the identification of asceticism with the obvious requirements of the duties of our state of life. It is, moreover, almost inevitable that factors of sensible affectivity should mix themselves up with more exalted motives. Man is not pure spirit and his psychology remains complex. The great thing is to keep a just balance. Obviously we must take into account all our pathological formations because their apparent likeness to genuine manifestations of asceticism can mislead some people and induce others to give up asceticism altogether. The essential thing, it seems, is never to lose sight of the positive aim of asceticism, to lead the subject progressively to the objectivity of love, especially to train his love of self so as to make of it, in conformity with God's will, the determining factor in its own usefulness in the service of his fellow-men, naturally and supernaturally. Being more rational and more moral, asceticism finally becomes theological, in so far as the horizon of Christian perfection reveals itself more completely and according to each one's vocation the initiative of which belongs to God.

All this considered, we must yet remember that asceticism remains one means among others, that it varies from one state to another, that therefore it would be a blunder to drag it from its context to transfer it to some other where it does not belong, but also that we must learn how to make methods of negative asceticism yield to others if necessary and that there can be indiscretion and foolishness in clinging to them blindly. In fine,

Christian perfection consists in that liberty of the children of God who really know when to rejoice, when to deny themselves, how to accept the love of their Father and in this love all gifts and all crosses and how to give thanks everywhere and always through Jesus Christ.

Chapter IX

ASCETICISM AND MORAL UNITY

By L. B. GEIGER, o.p.

IN order to define the moral significance of asceticism it is important to take into account one essential aspect of the moral life, that is its unity. This is expressed by the classic thesis on the connection between virtues, at least since the time of St Thomas.

Seen from the outside, in fact, moral life appears as a studied behaviour comprising a combination of more or less stable habits, the effect either of a training undergone or of a practice that the subject has imposed upon himself. It is at the service of these habits and this training, it seems, that asceticism comes in. It marks as it were the negative side of the directing or canalising of the person's energies. Given the limited assets of energy at a human being's disposal, every choice of his, whether as a passing action or as a fixed habit, exacts some renunciation even if it is only in the form of putting limits to pleasures and satisfactions, a form in which man has always found suffering lurking at the very heart of pleasure.

In a human life that is normal and therefore free from any pathological searching for suffering or self-denial, asceticism will step in quite reasonably as the negative side of the positive measuring out and limiting of one's energies in some directions so as to have the full use of one's strength in the area of activity that the individual has chosen or which has been forced upon him by society. To refuse to satisfy some desire, to know how to take upon oneself some exertion or certain sufferings, is to oppose against psychic energy an effectual barrage capable of resisting any inordinate urge from within and re-directing it in the way desired, and also any pressure from without, maintaining against both a fixed chosen purpose. Moral life itself is only

L

distinguished from a life of following out one's own inclinations in the way that wild vegetation differs from cultivated land. To speak in the language of psychological treatises, on the one hand we have *instinctive tendencies*, on the other *higher tendencies*, the same as the former but raised to a *personal* and *social* level. The important thing surely is to find out for what purpose the subject is cultivating and organising his energy. It all amounts to a question of dynamism, to a problem of equilibrium and the using of psychic energies in which asceticism plays the part of the machinery that blocks and bridles, to which we have recourse in order to master and regulate the discharge of the wellsprings of energy. The handling of such a machinery can be a delicate task and may give rise to blunders at the expense of the subject's equilibrium.

Now, on the other hand, as long as we do not leave—consciously, at least—the plane of natural tendencies, this regulating activity can be exercised entirely in respect of one or other tendency, ignoring all the rest. A certain form of energy will be bridled and so another profits by it. Then this other risks being hypertrophied. But, supposing a certain amount of order is established, even so the subject is still at instinct level. He will be a tamed animal whose whole behaviour, even including the organising of natural propensities, will yet remain, in itself, outside the moral order properly so called. To be precise, we might say that it coincides materially with moral life but that it lacks the essential, formal aspect which would carry it over the threshold of the moral domain.

To be called moral, in fact, an act must not only comply in its natural structure with the requirements of a code or of a catalogue of virtues. It does not even suffice that our reason undertakes to organise our inclinations among themselves, merely on their own plane, making a choice among them, favouring one and checking another with the sole purpose of letting that one triumph which is the most precious in the subject's eyes. The action, materially good, must have been directed by an upright will—that is to say, by a will animated by the objective love of moral good in the right ordering of human life and the true aims of human activity, besides being enlightened, as far as possible, by the concrete rightness of the proposed action in the actual circumstances in which the individual is placed. This brings us back to the statement that over and above the natural tendencies and their dynamism on the one hand, and of the reason that simply undertakes to organise these tendencies on their own level, a new factor must intervene which is this other love by which a man directs himself first of all according to the true order of his destiny, thereafter levelling up his instinctive tendencies to the centre of this truth.

The major conclusion that emanates from the above is that moral life is one in its principle, complete in its aspiration. In fact if an action is only morally good because it proceeds from the desire for the objective order of morality, it is merely expressing, on some specified point, a more general basic attitude without which it would not belong to the moral order at all. And since this attitude is nothing more than the objective will towards the moral order loved for its own sake, we cannot claim that an act is truly moral on some specified point in respect of some specified object without having first of all achieved this total interior conversion, at least implicitly. This conversion, drawing us away from the purely instinctive plane, even though it be rationally organised at its own level, would raise us up at once in all essential things to another order, that of true human destiny determined upon and loved for its own sake.

It was in relying on this conception of morality that St Thomas, one of the first to do so, taught that all the natural virtues were connected under prudence, prudence being precisely the virtue that rules our conduct objectively in the seeking and the estimating of means, after the will has already been put right as to its deepest impulse, through love of the whole moral issue.

It follows, then, that we cannot acquire one moral virtue without acquiring them all, not of course in their perfection but at least in the bud, since genuine morality is inseparable from the objective will towards all good. This last is total, that is to say it embodies in its will the whole domain of morality even where it is not acting.

Different moral virtues are, then, but the expression of this fundamental and total resolution in the different domains where man's free activity can be exercised, and its being applied to man's various powers, notably in all the combination of dynamisms that constitute his affective life. There is no such thing as an isolated virtue, that is to say willed by itself to the exclusion of even one of the others.

It is important, then, to distinguish clearly between the *natural inclination*, a certain *natural taste*, for such or such behaviour, which can materially be described as good, such as gentleness, kindness, courage or justice, the *acquired habit* of such behaviour either out of a natural disposition or from social conformity or training, etc., and the *moral virtue* properly so called which, though it can and ought to make use of the above forms of natural goodness or good habits acquired for example by education, only exists if the subject performs well (morally) actions that are good materially. We know too well how frequently these two domains are confused. We mistake for true morality a good education, that is to say a behaviour which conforms to a certain sphere and its conceptions, even though the heart may play no part in it and the soul is left shut against the true requirements of morality. And routine, in the moral domain, as in other similar domains, is nothing else but an entirely material fidelity to certain prescriptions, certain ways of acting when the living presence of goodness loved for its own sake in its reality has become extinguished in the soul together with that wholesome uneasiness which prevents the soul from ever forgetting the abyss which separates what it is from what it ought to be.

However that may be, it is obvious that, if asceticism is to have moral value, it must proceed from the same moral will. It is therefore one, like this will itself, and complete in its resolution.

First of all, asceticism is to proceed from the moral will itself. It is ordained to this will and subject to it. It has no moral value except by the will and through the will. Apart from this will it may be accepted for useful, praiseworthy ends, such as a better professional efficiency, complete mastery of one's inclinations in the service of some task whatever it may be, but it may also be found at the service of ends that are morally bad, such as the more lively satisfaction of some propensity to which the subject clings more particularly or from which he expects pleasures that he willingly seeks.

Organically linked to the moral will, asceticism is by this fact one in its principle and in its sum total like morality itself. It comprises the acceptance of, and the positive will for, all renouncing of inordinate satisfactions, that is to say both those that are outside the rule of morality as well as troubles, sufferings, penances, macerations which, in a fallen nature like ours, are required by an effort of amendment or purification that a more and more exacting moral foundation may carry in its train. It cannot consist simply in frustrating one propensity for the sake of another which has become predominant. It is not concerned with a displacing of energy from one point to another with all the dangers of breaking up the equilibrium which that might involve. Again, it is not concerned with outside pressure brought to bear upon our inclinations, so as to comply with social requirements, for this would not come spontaneously from the subject. The ascetic effort being only a free acceptance of all renunciations and all privations in the pursuit of a moral ideal freely willed by the subject, because that is the proper aim of an objective love which is as real in us as our instinctive propensities, asceticism itself has all the marks of free choice. If there is conflict, it is not between ourselves and something other than ourselves, between life and the enemies of life, but between two levels of life, both of them rooted in our complex nature, animal and spiritual, and which must be brought into harmony, inspiring, ruling, animating all our behaviour by the objective desire for morality. This should not destroy our tendencies, under the false pretext that they are bad in themselves, but should direct them by submitting them to the guidance of our prudence. The *Yes* and the *No* should proceed from the same source; to be more exact, the *Yes* that we say to the positive work of moral constructiveness comprises the *Yes* that we ought to say to the ascetic effort, both together expressing the whole domain of moral effort in its unity and its completeness.

CHAPTER X

COLLECTIVE DIMENSIONS OF ASCETICISM

By M. D. CHENU, o.p.

1. Does asceticism possess a collective dimension? 2. Sociological data. 3. Sociological laws.

THIS title is much too ambitious; and, if it expresses the lively curiosity that a fine problem rouses it also covers the embarrassment one feels in determining not only its component parts but also its exact meaning in a complex state where some dissimilar questions are blended: asceticism practised in common, asceticism settled by the combined intentions of a group, asceticism incorporated in the rule adopted by a community.

To give body to what one feels is the truth, in religious history, about a certain general character of practices of asceticism, we should have to follow out a sociological investigation that has never been expressly undertaken by either historians or spiritual writers. Some sensational and abnormal episodes, in which the collective element went beyond personal intentions and involved private behaviour, were the only things that sufficiently roused their attention to warn us against excessive individualism in estimating penitential values: the famous episode of the flagellants at the close of the middle ages with their infectious processions, certainly reveals a morbid phenomenon in which an epidemic is the ruin of true and healthy penance; but there, as in other cases, examining monstrous cases helps towards discovering the normal elements.

This is not the place to agitate for the investigation for its own sake of these normal or abnormal phenomena from which we should proceed to a lengthy sociological induction. We shall merely confine ourselves to a few given summaries to which we shall apply sociological categories in order to discover their intrinsic value. This is a somewhat artificial procedure the limitations of which we admit in advance, but which, when used prudently, will be legitimate and efficient.

1. *A priori*, it seems that the consideration of collective 'dimensions' (since we have used that simile) of asceticism is of great significance. In every domain, since sociology became organised, new perspectives have been opened in man's knowledge, and the excesses to which men have let themselves be drawn do not compromise the method or its results.

But in the present case, we cannot help being forewarned against the intrusion of adventitious data in a behaviour whose truth or healthiness, a Christian truth and a psychological sanity, are only assured in a strictly personal relationship with God. Has not the public régime of sacramental penance become developed in the Church to the most strictly secret individualism?

This is true, and it is only as a preliminary precaution that we first of all put forward, as a supreme and complete criterion, the spiritual privacy of a soul that turns back upon itself so as to recover or to secure union with God. *Noverim te, noverim me*: that is the last word in the penitential life as in the contemplative life. Asceticism, when it becomes decisive, is strictly personal, and it has no meaning except in so far as it converges upon personal actions. It is a case of freeing the soul to be occupied with God, with prayer, with contemplation, ultimately with the apostolate as an eminent act of brotherly love. To free the soul: it is then at the very crux of the personal life that asceticism works, is practised, comes to perfection.

Personal it should be, both in its commonplace practice as in its demonstrations, if I may so express it; in current practice, day by day, so as not to be corroded by that impersonalised rust, a collective unconsciousness; in its demonstrations, in order that it may be very closely directed by a strictly personal vocation, such as the asceticism of St Benedict Labre. Do not set yourself up, even out of fervour, as an imitator of this magnanimous beggar; for you it would be a disease to 'copy' him. And we well know how the instituting of a system of penance by a founder can present a difficult state of affairs for the Order he

has founded, in which the imaginative mirage cannot spiritual-
ise a round of hardship and poverty.

Still more in its intention, in the idea that inspires and
measures it out, must asceticism be personal. It is controlled in
that case by the supreme value of the vocation, a personal thing
in the very bosom of its institutional or vital setting, and therefore, on the underside, by the constant psychological incidence
of the subject. Its aim is to regulate exactly the psychic and
virtuous organism of an individual to further that incommunic-
able and interior call to perfection and love.

Finally in its effects it is personal: on the plane of natural
asceticism, since it is diffused physiologically and psychologically in an individual system; and also on the supernatural
plane, which that nature assumes. The merits that I acquire are
not transferable; it is only by a metaphorical extension that I
can do penance *for* my neighbour.

Can we never, then, put these collective contexts together,
except as amorphous and trivial elements? The facts make it
imperative that we should take them into consideration.

There are some indications, and to follow these will take us
far. The historian notices that ascetical practices have varied
according to the times, and are therefore ordered objectively as
from outside, and not according to the subject's inspiration
alone. There was a time, in the middle ages, when fervent individuals, men and women, mostly women, in order to be occupied with prayer (and sometimes with a sort of preaching by
testifying), walled themselves up at the gates of a town, in a
narrow cell of a few square yards.

We can determine chronologically the area of this manner—I
was going to put that into the feminine—of penitential life.
Outside of those times, such-and-such a fanatic imitated' this
original attitude; but then it was a morbid phenomenon or very
nearly so; whilst formerly it had been, in a certain period of
Christianity, a perfectly healthy enterprise in contexts that were
materially and spiritually in keeping with it.

To take another case—the practice of taking the discipline.
We can trace its origin, its diffusion, its stages, its becoming
institutional, its causes. St Peter Damian credits it to the West,
it characterises the Christian customs of the thirteenth century,

it fixes itself even within the framework of the monastic liturgy, it is part of the rule with Friars Preachers who love it of all things, it is contagious and will have its upheavals, it becomes spiritual and becomes personal, yet always retains certain features of a children's chastisement, grown-up children; a day will come when, as a ritual, it will be exposed as a ridiculous symbol, and its stress and its true fervour will return to individual initiative. From beginning to end, its evolution is linked up with collective elements.

Evolution of asceticism with reference to places: there are 'regions' of penitential life. The Irish have a great monopoly of this kind, from ice-baths to 'purgatories'. The East has its Stylites. These are extreme cases and yet revealing, and they encourage us to widen the field of extra-personal influences.

Even when a penance seems to be materially the same, it is bound up with environments, with mentalities, with aspirations, with some particular view of the world and of Christianity within the world. Eremitical life, whose whole rigidity seems to lead to an unvarying type, is utterly different in the case of the Fathers of the Desert and that of Père de Foucauld, at the two extremities of the history of Christendom. Nay more, from them alone, in the solitude of the same desert, we might define two Christianities. The unforeseen and magnificent contagion of the 'solitude' of Père de Foucauld is at work gaining Christians of both sexes from our city workers, and their testimony of coming simply, without proselytism, into an ingenuous common destiny, will doubtless come to define the spirituality of the twentieth century. Ascetically, it is the very opposite of the Fathers of the Desert. And all this has followed from this eccentric man of extremes, discouraging in his repeated failures. This is a collective dimension of penance, strangely set in a type of contagious living.

There are variations of quality, of course, that is to say in spirit, therefore in the personal spheres of love. But to be precise, do we not see, in our analyses, this general reaction today sometimes to an excessive and senseless extent, in certain spheres of Catholic Action, against 'penitential observances' out of date in way, artificial in our famished and concentrated world, in favour of real, vital constructive asceticism, the mother in the home, the working man kept at the grindstone, who have fixed Christ in their lives and fill up, in the world of 1950, what was wanting to his Passion? It is a cause periodically taken up again in the Church as it was formerly with the Prophets of the Old Testament, against ritualised practices in which social pressure, however devout, has de-personalised, de-vitalised a régime where love should be constantly renewing the spontaneity. It is a collective phenomenon, which reaches the very heart of our contemporary asceticism, in one unquestionable solidarity, both spiritual and constitutional. There as elsewhere we have the true dialectics of person and community.

2. Let us try to summarise the elements, or rather the aspects of this collectivism, if one may so express it.

The first and rudimentary observation: penitential asceticism is often practised in common. A commonplace fact, just as it is commonplace to eat in common; but its significance passes beyond the materialness of fact. My senior, my neighbour, has done such-and-such a thing: fasting, going without, poverty, silence, gestures of grief; I copy him, instinctively or upon reflection; therefore I am linked up with him, and the chain continues. We resemble each other and we assemble together; cordial agreement, in which perhaps my spiritual life will gain confidence. Examples abound. And the simple repetition already presents a great collective power.

The second datum: ascetical practice becomes legalised in an institution, in a 'customs book' or in a law, with the sociological hardening that results. Two major cases in Christian history: the first, general and permanent, is that of the penitential laws of monastic orders, copied moreover by more recent congregations, clerical or lay. These are the organised and stabilised penitential 'observances' of which the individual, from the fact of his having entered the Order, endorses the pre-established régime, including faults, very characteristically since they are defined as common even in the case of actions that are strictly personal.

First custom, then law, have fixed an experience that has established itself as of high quality; ascetical practice has found its status in an organic cohesion, which mysticism invigorates, devotion nourishes and tradition protects. By this very generalisation it finds its guarantees of discretion, equilibrium, firmness; and individuals are little by little integrated into this living organism. Think of the value and the role of the rule of St Benedict in Western asceticism as against oriental asceticisms.

Then penance also takes on an 'objective' character: it is no longer instigated by specified inspirations, called for and measured out by personal needs; it is ordered by the group and for its collectively appreciated ends. Indeed, I have entered into this group and my vocation is achieved in union with its commands; but the legal objectivity of the penitential life tends to de-personalise its exercise, especially where ritual solemnities and rubrics are added. A sociological phenomenon of extreme importance in its ambiguity. All conventuals know into what a degree of insignificance the weekly chapter of faults can fall which can scarcely be reanimated by sham artifices and which on the contrary will find again its first impulse and efficiency in popular Christian communities or in road chapters. The ritual has been fatal. For the sociologist, matter will be furnished which will be both admirable and distressing in the history of the rules of poverty in the Church: a rule of poverty, whether mendicant or not, observed 'objectively' in the midst of comforts and securities which have nothing evangelical about them. And on the other hand, was not a priest-worker living as a proletarian recently accused by his Superior of not observing the laws of 'poverty' specified in the spiritual 'rule'?

It was the copious matter of classic criticism of observances that brought forth an Erasmus and a Luther; the fact that they went to unjust excesses must not conceal the almost automatic danger of this legal debility, in which formalism takes away the personal element from the old spontaneous fervour, or even exalts the abject prescriptions of Novitiate customs to the detriment of the elementary laws of natural morality.

Another case of legalised asceticism which has disappeared today, but which had formerly a curious vogue in the middle ages in certain areas and which presented the particular interest of being linked with the sacramental order: this is a question of fixed penance, that is to say of a régime in which the penalty for sins is established in advance in a scale of public penitential acts. If someone had struck his brother, he must fast for three days . . . if someone had deprived his neighbour of the use of one of his limbs, he must do penance on bread and water for three years . . . if someone had committed adultery he would do penance for three years, etc. . . . A régime, then, of penal statute, in which, in the clamping together of the internal tribunal and the external tribunal, the collective penalty and the common policy, in a society that was rough and brutal, went beyond the personal improvement of the subject. Penance was first and foremost a punishment.

Over against this penitential legalism there has risen up in the Church, and periodically with intensity, outbreaks of asceticism emanating from communities of mystics expressing the deepest instinct of Christian grace: the third sociological datum. The primitive Church furnishes us with the prototype which remains as a mirage for all generations stirred to an evangelical awakening. In groups that are sociologically and hierarchically rudimentary, the community instinct expresses itself in the matter of penance with the fervour of biological determinism, and the 'brotherhood' take into their charge mystically, over and above any legalism, the weight of penance called forth by faults committed. A very delicate common fund, and easily upset, unless it is balanced by the uncompromising personal element of the secret relations of the soul with God. We remarked just now that the outworn monastic chapter of faults would be revived and regain its worth in the evangelical communities among the people: the moving *Confiteor* of the beginning of Mass in the Mission de Paris. Some ingenuous realism in the practice of poverty by which lodgings in common, food in common, meagre leisure spent in common represents, outside of all legalism and charges, the surest understanding of the law of the spirit and of love. To take an objective line will become necessary some day, with the passing of communal forms to social forms; for the moment we have reached an asceticism in which the mingling of souls guarantees personal balance.

3. Simple imitation, general law, communal mysticism; these three types of collective dimension present very different developments and methods.

Imitation can go, psychologically, to the limits of constraint, through inter-personal contagion. We well know what pressure, in other domains of collective life, publicity and propaganda can ensure, whilst appearing to respect one's liberty. But in the end imitation acts under personal consent; it is not the group, nor its rules, that take command, but each one's own fervour. Again, even here there is something sociological. There is the role of example, say the moralists in their secular platitudes; role of imitation, analyse the sociologists such as Gabriel Tarde, master of the subject. That is primary sociology, if one may say so, in this sense that, speaking in the abstract, the network of influence is inter-personal and not communal; but the social pressure is real and comprises certain standards of morality. The prestige of a Nero, the taste for performing, among other things, are the factors that are psychologically efficient and to be taken into account in estimating morals; conformism plays a part, too, and already we are at the source of 'traditions' that are to weigh upon personal destinies or upon the life of groups of people.

Second sociological law, corporate solidarity, which appears with institutionalised penance. The initiative comes from authority, an anonymous general law or legal authority. The penitential régime is no longer solely, nor perhaps firstly, a means of personal sanctification, but part of the framework of the institution, the bulwark of its established order, the miserable symbol of its survival if, in the unconscious vision of the group, these ascetic methods have ended by stopping the dynamic perspective of the original aims. Penitential law is no longer merely moral, it has become social.

Fervour then clings corporately, loyally, to these group rituals. There may be no personal desire for these practices any longer, we remain faithful to them—and rightly faithful—through docility; moreover we love them as collective representative assets. As a Dominican I cling to such-and-such an austerity that my seniors have practised; as a Franciscan I observe literally the old symbolic gestures of poverty that the modern round of life would eliminate, but which within the conventual life create the right atmosphere.

Another effect: attachment to detail. In the hammering of daily life, the great laws of life (moral, natural or mystical) remain remote and almost airy, transcending rites and customs;

on the contrary, details become legalised, ritualised, furnishing the tissue of common life, becoming the susceptible criterion of the law, reassuring consciences, including that of the superior who satisfies his own sense of duty by adjusting his own orders to the law. We know the commonplace of Novice Masters on detailed obedience. Useless to see in it—as a sociological truth—the value, but also the limits and sometimes the error against the supreme law of the spirit. Dialectics again of the society and the person.

Third law then, the law of the spirit: the law of mystical solidarity, rooted in this common power whose mainsprings and qualities we have listed in the preceding paragraph. Here the Christian doctrine of the Church the Body of Christ furnishes the sociologist with privileged matter of which the deep density in 'mystery' leads to wonderful communal consequences, visible and invisible. We have noticed that all evangelical awakenings have been marked by it, and doubtless in their very delicate poise, this is the criterion of their truth and soundness. The afflictive privations of asceticism are practised with the spontaneity of an organism which has not so far reflected on the rules of its life, but which applies them instinctively as means to an end. Privileged moments, in which theologians see the source in the charisma and the gifts of the Holy Spirit, *collective* charisma at the service of the Community, *personal* gifts through which is accomplished the theological life of the soul.

In this common régime which develops in a society of persons, the turnover of merits—always personal things—expresses in terms of a society the mystical community. It is there that penitential life finds its lofty inspiration, in the power of the group as well as in respect of personal predestination.

To loosen the somewhat stiff setting in which we have analysed the collective aspects of asceticism, we must elaborate our investigations and notice the effects of this socialisation at close quarters. These effects are ambiguous since it can provoke either a kind of excitement or on the contrary the flattest of formalism, since it assures equilibrium, even in the paradox of the solitary life and yet can also lend itself to unconscious and contagious disorders. The history of religious groups in the Church (not to speak of non-Christian religions) furnishes rich material to the moral theologian who is sensible of the collective character of the most spiritual and therefore the most personal of human achievements.

Nature and grace come into play here in reinforced agreement, since man is *by nature* social, and divine life is only given us in the Mystical Body of Christ, wherever is accomplished by ascetical penance the mystery of his death and his resurrection.

Asceticism should be considered, maintained and practised in the setting of the whole conception of the Christian world. The twentieth century of Christianity gives us a lesson in this, with all the force of evangelism, as well as with the stirring realism of an inescapable socialisation.

CHAPTER XI

THE MODERN MENTALITY

By H. MULLER

1. The revolution in population. 2. The industrial revolution.
3. The gradual disappearance of illiteracy.

THE task of describing the man of today is one in which
sins of omission are inevitable. As it is also difficult to
define, I will first try and show how I regard it myself.
In a sense, there is no such person as the man of today. The
'day' to which a man belongs depends on the man himself:
everybody knows what we mean when we say of a person, 'That
man has stepped straight out of the twelfth century.' Many
people alive today are not living in the same age as we are.

In any case, there are whole races of people (three quarters
of the human race, numerically speaking) whom we do not regard as belonging to the same age as ourselves. The 'man of
today' is thus a species of *homo occidentalis*. And that concept too
is an extremely flexible thing. If the last war did not bring the
nations permanently closer to one another, it did at least jumble
them up together for a time. It taught us that the Germans are
not like the French, that North Africans are different from South
Africans, and so forth.

At first, then, I saw my subject receding before me. The only
way I can attach any meaning to the term 'man of today' is by
contrasting the man of today with the men of other ages. Men
have not remained stationary from the medieval period to the
present day; to some extent there has been development. The
course this development has followed is the thing we must keep
before our eyes as we try to paint the portrait of the man of
today.

In certain exceptional cases, the development can be watched as it occurs. We can actually see primitive people becoming modern. A sort of cleavage takes place in them, as in the case, for example, of Kabyls who leave North Africa and come to France, where they absorb the influence of French civilisation and eventually settle down.[1]

For the sake of clarity, I will arrange my observations on this aspect of human development under three headings. The method has the great drawback of making things look too cut and dried. The way it sets out the facts gives the impression that it is trying to explain them. I beg the reader not to take it like that but to regard it as a mere device for arranging the facts on paper and nothing more.

The three headings are: the revolution in population; the industrial revolution (about which I have little to say, as the

---

[1] The change can be observed all the better in that it is reversible, though the fact is sometimes overlooked. That such is, however, the case can be seen when both 'primitives' become modern and moderns turn primitive.

I may perhaps be allowed to tell a couple of stories by way of illustration. I once met a Kabyl in a village near Michelet. He spoke French extremely well, his English was better than mine, his German, Italian and Spanish were not at all bad. He had spent thirty years with the Compagnie Générale Transatlantique as a pot-boy and for a time had been a bar-tender in New York. He had lived in the comfortable conditions of modern civilisation and to all appearances had been perfectly acclimatised. Then one fine day he found he had saved enough money to make the dream of his life come true. Back he went to the village he had come from and there, in the one room which is all that a Kabyl house consists of, he lived with the goats and sheep that do duty as central heating. He was perfectly happy.

You may say that in his case the modernity was only a veneer and that he remained essentially primitive. But I have seen another phenomenon too, one that we are inclined to regard as pitiful, although I do not know why we should: we are rather superficial about it, really. French girls sometimes marry Kabyls who come to Paris to work in factories like the Renault or the Citroen works. I have known cases where the Kabyl had one day said to his wife, 'You know, I'll never have any prospects in Paris. In Kabylia I've property of my own. I'm sure of a house. Suppose I took you back with me.' And the girl has agreed to go. It was true that he had property—he would have a share in the family house, the one room I have just described, and he would own a field: considering the Kabyl laws of inheritance, it might in some cases amount to a mere eighth or even a sixteenth of an olive-grove. From what I am told by people in the civil service out there, it seems that the girls usually get something of a shock. A good deal of the immigration comes to nothing: in two years, 80 per cent had abandoned their husbands and returned to Paris. But even if we accept these figures, which I have not been able to verify, we are still faced with the fact that there are 20 per cent who stay. I have seen some of them myself. They become just like Kabyl women and the children are typical little Kabyls.

This 'regressive' evolution is very rarely seen, because the conditions essential to reversibility are very rarely fulfilled; but it does occur and it happens even to people living the life of present-day Paris or the suburbs.

M

subject has so often been dealt with before); and the gradual disappearance of illiteracy.

1. Between 1800 and 1900 the population of some countries increased by 100 per cent, as in France, while in other countries, e.g. in certain parts of Europe and America, it increased by 500 per cent. Figures are available from which the increase can be estimated mathematically: in France, England, Germany and America, the population has increased from something like 40 or 50 inhabitants per square mile to about 210, 260, 310 and 520 per square mile respectively.

This increase in the density of the population has involved on the one hand a general increase in numbers and on the other the creation of large urban centres. The two phenomena are parallel but nevertheless slightly different.

The increase is probably due to improvement in living-conditions and hygiene: it has been produced by a lowering of the death-rate, especially among children and young adults—i.e. the revolution in population rests on an increase in the average length of human life.[1]

Another feature, paradoxical though it may seem, is that the increase in population has been paralleled by a decrease in the birth-rate.

A glance will be sufficient to show—though there are exceptions: the reader will no doubt be able to think of scores—that the western civilisation which we are hoping will give us a clue to the features of the man of today, covers all the countries where the population has increased in density because of the increased length of human life.[2]

Deliberately putting the matter in the strongest possible terms, one might say that fundamentally the civilisation of the west is the civilisation of birth-control.

Not much has been written, as far as I can see—unless it just is that I have failed to light on what there is—about the psychological side of the growth in population and the entirely new

1 Increase in the length of human life has meant a notable increase in the number of people living to a very advanced age. There are not many more centenarians now than there were before, but there are many more people aged sixty and over.

2 In general, the countries behind the iron curtain have not yet experienced the nineteenth-century revolution in population, i.e. they still have a high birth-rate and a high death-rate.

living-conditions imposed on men in consequence. And yet
there are factors, it seems to me, that can now be discerned. I
will pick out three of them.

The first is consideration for children. Those whose memories
of their schooldays are as recent as mine may remember how
when they read Montaigne the master would draw attention to
the way Montaigne talked of his children—he had lost two or
three when they were very small: he had forgotten how many.

In spite of the high birth-rate, the population of France in
fact remained stationary until the beginning of the nineteenth
century. That was only to be expected: children were meant to
die.[1]

But in the civilisations we now see about us, the child rules
supreme. People talk about nothing else. Those whose business
it is to examine students in welfare-work or nursing will tell you
that when they ask a question about some point of social or
mental hygiene, the candidates invariably begin their answers
by talking about the health of the child, as though the grown-up
did not come into the picture at all.[2] The child has become king
of society. If the death of a child has become such a harrowing
affair the reason is that we have lost the habit of seeing children
die.

The second factor is old age. In former times, age was
genuinely respected. We still do pay it lip-service. In an anthol-
ogy compiled by a friend of mine, I find the saying, 'We ought
to respect the old. Respect is all they deserve'! A very real
change is epitomised, symbolically, in those words.

Old age used to entitle a man to respect. At Venice, it was of

1 A few instances will serve to illustrate this attitude. I am told by specialists
in children's diseases, people with wide experience of the Parisian hospitals,
that in families which have recently emigrated from Central Europe, a child's
death releases very little emotion. The parents are fond of their children but
they consider it quite natural that they should die.
    A friend of mine who had lived for a long time in Algiers told me that every
day his charwoman, a local Mohammedan, used to say to his wife as she looked
at their children, 'They're so good-looking. What a pity it is!' When asked to
explain, she would say, 'Well, when they're good-looking, it's sad to see them die.'
    Would Malherbe's condolences still be thought suitable today?
    'A rose, she lived as long as ever lives the rose:
    She spanned the morning hours.'
he said. To the primitive Algerian woman his words would have seemed apt
enough.
2 It is the same with the clergy. Sooner or later in any conversation, they will
begin to cry up their 'youth organisations'.

great importance in the choice of the doge. There was something exceptional and almost sacred about it. Moreover, if an old man had made a success of his life, he was worth knowing. He had accumulated a fund of experience. In all previous stages of civilisation, the function of the written word was restricted in the extreme. Tradition was kept alive by the old—they were living history-books. And as there were not many of them, their presence was not nearly so irksome as it is today.

Things are quite different now. In the first place, there are large numbers of old people. You see them everywhere. And it has become evident that old age is not a physiological state to which the Lord has given more notable graces than to the other phases of life: the old are often self-centred and abominably indifferent to everything except their own personal comfort.

They have come to constitute a special section of the electorate, with demands of its own.[1] And how perfect they are in that respect! They are content with so little, provided they get it at once, for the idea of disaster in the distant future leaves them cold. But they are a dead weight. We are only too conscious of the burden they impose.

Any grown man will willingly work for a child's benefit, but he will not be so enthusiastic about working to help an old person. And no one can say that the old make it easy for the young to help them.

If any book needs rewriting, it is the *De Senectute*. Someone ought to tell us how we can teach elderly people to accept old age and adapt themselves to it. The problem is one for the Church, too, to consider. It is time that a form of asceticism were devised for the old, with due regard to the physical, psychological and social conditions peculiar to their circumstances.

Throughout the world, people have recently begun to show concern for social security, old-age pensions are everywhere a subject of discussion. Since the beginning of the century, the average length of human life has increased from thirty-three years to sixty. Thus, on an average, a boy of twenty would formerly have had ten years before him to do what he liked with. He had not much future to make provision for; he could

---

1 This is true even in the international sphere. The United Nations Organisation has been asked to make a declaration of the rights of the old.

be enterprising. A boy of the same age now has forty years in front of him and he becomes cautious. In every country in the world, people are strangely agitated by a sort of fear of wasting this additional span of life. They are becoming miserly about their gains. The average gambler would rather stake a fortune than risk a shilling.

In a way, everybody is 'ageing' (though not in the biological sense of the term) : we all have to think of tomorrow and the day after. Life may have been short in former times, but at least you could say, 'Let it be good while it lasts'. Today, you have to manage your life for thirty or forty years, ensuring professional success and providing for your family the while. That takes some of the zest out of living and weakens the spirit of adventure. It explains why the European peoples, though once great colonisers and adventurers, now bicker in their parliaments over bills on old-age pensions.

Lastly, the revolution in population has had a further obvious consequence; one that we might express in mathematical terms by saying that parallel to the increase in density of population and the development of urban centres, there has also been considerable increase in the number of human contacts within every individual's reach. This last factor has been increasing at a faster rate than the density of population.

To my mind, the situation is of considerable significance from many points of view. It seems to me that we all now see many more people, and many more different kinds of people, than we should have done if we had been born a hundred years ago, let alone two hundred, three hundred or two thousand.

I am not forgetting that it was in the middle ages that Marco Polo went on his travels, and I am sure that none of us will ever have the experience of men that he had. But all the same, it is becoming more and more usual for ever larger numbers of people to be in touch with an increasingly wide variety of other people. The increase in human contacts is, to my mind, a significant phenomenon and one that may well explain quite a number of others.

I will not develop the point at the moment, as I intend to treat it at greater length in my concluding section. It seems to me to be partly responsible for another phenomenon, which is leading to a kind of civilisation much more closely-knit than before, viz. the emergence of a new class-consciousness, a new awareness of the collective. I think this point is more important than the others and one we must return to later.

2. I do not propose to spend long on the second topic, the industrial revolution. So much has been said about it already that there is nothing left to add.

All I want to do is to draw attention to two or three small points. First, the industrial civilisation of the last hundred and fifty years has so evolved on the technical side that it has multiplied those activities called by economists secondary and tertiary.[1] Psychologically, all those forms of activity have something in common: they all (things like office-work, for example, and commercial jobs) are occupations which bring men into touch only with other men. In other words, increasing numbers of people today have only human contacts in their lives.

I use the expression 'human contact' as the opposite of 'contact with things'. Whatever anyone may say, the fact that the two kinds of contact are different does mean that a different kind of adaptation is required in each case. Adapting oneself to things is very different from adapting oneself to people, a life devoted to the one kind of adaptation is very different from a life devoted to the other.

There is another side to this transformation. We are living, and more and more people are coming to live, entirely divorced from contact with what in literature is called 'nature' (though I would not like to say exactly what 'nature' means). A reflection of this fact or, if you like, the other side of it, is to be found in the extensive cult of activities which, though really forms of play, are pursued as substitutes for something else. As we all know, it was a literary commonplace in the seventeenth century that nature made you think of 'frightful solitude'; but today, the city-dweller is only too glad to immerse himself in nature from time to time. And the office-worker, the man concerned with secondary or tertiary activities, plays games because by that means he can engage in physical activity, which he no longer has, or never has had, in his daily life.

1 See Fourastie's books, especially *Le Mythe du XXe siècle* (Presses Universitaires de France).

The two factors present in the situation—loss of contact with things and a considerable drop in physical effort of every kind —are two distinct phenomena and should not be confused with each other. This is worth at least passing notice.

But the third feature in this evolution is the one I want to stress most. Rather than state it in abstract terms, I prefer to appeal to our common experience of life in the concrete: I will try and describe a typical day in our own lives and compare it with a day in the life of a 'primitive'.

The first thing I did when I woke this morning was to look at my watch to see the time. I then switched on the electric light. As I felt I had had enough sleep, I turned on the wireless and listened to the news. I lit the gas to boil the kettle for breakfast and heat the bath-water. I put my clothes on, and very commonplace clothes they are: many of my readers probably have the same kind. Every single thing I touched during these operations had the same two characteristics—it had been made by human agency and it was entirely beyond my comprehension.

The suit I am wearing is a complete mystery to me. I should be quite incapable of carrying out any single process involved in its making. I do not even know what it is made of. I know that the cloth is mainly woollen, but all the wool suggests to me is an object-lesson at school: my teachers told me that there were such things as sheep, and so on. And of course, when my wireless set is out of order, all I can do is to keep my hands off it, because if I cannot make it go again by the simple method of giving it a bang, I am at the end of my resources.

Up to the present, I have been considering my material surroundings, but I might just as well have taken the human environment I live in. In a later chapter we are reminded that when people want to cross the Atlantic, they find the preparations for the voyage much more tiresome than the voyage itself. In my case, half my time every day is spent in an office, where I am one of the powers that be. I am thus, generally speaking, on the right side of the fence, but as a consumer I am on the wrong side. It was a fearful business, for example, when I had to get a new identity-card. I had to have a birth-certificate and I applied for one to the town where I was born. An illiterate clerk misspelt my name and I did not notice the mistake. So there I was with a false identity-card, which was of no use to me, and I could not manage to get a proper one. A minister might give evidence for me, the President himself might swear in my favour, but their depositions would not be sufficient to prove that my real name is the right one. And I had all that trouble even though I pulled all possible strings to prevail on the deputy head of the department concerned.

Thus I know what it is to come up against the authorities, in spite of being one of them myself. The red-tape disease is not confined to France.[1] As a prisoner of war, I had to deal with the German authorities; in North Africa I have had dealings with the English civil service and the American. I found them all exactly the same. And it seems that in Russia things are worse.

In conclusion, then, the civilised man is surrounded all day long by things he cannot fathom at all, and yet, as they were made by men they ought not to be such a mystery to him. Primitive people, on the other hand, know the whole history of the things they live among, with the exception of a few which have only recently been imported. They know the history of the fibre cloth their clothes are made of, they know where their food comes from. The social structure of the tribe they live in is a simple one; they know what it is, they were born into it. They have no need to be taught the laws against breaches of which 'ignorance is no excuse'.[2]

It may be objected that in fact primitive people no more understand their world than the civilised understand theirs. The social structure of the tribe is just as incomprehensible to a primitive mind as the mass of regimentation and legislation in the European countries is to us.

If primitive people ever asked themselves questions, they would become aware of the difficulty. But as their world is a familiar one, they do not mind if they fail to understand it. The logicians are not wrong in thinking that familiarity is a substitute for understanding, but from the psychological point of view it is understanding that is a substitute for familiarity.

Thus, primitive people do not understand their world, but

1 That this is so is evident from Georghiu's book, *La vingt-cinquième heure*.
2 The adage is one of the many instances of the survival of parts of the primitive social structure in our present way of living.

then, they do not realise that it presents any problem. Even if they did, they would have only one kind of solution to offer. If some catastrophe occurs, they account for it by saying that the gods made it happen because they wanted to do them harm. If they feel an urge to strike their neighbour in the face, they say it is because he has been disrespectful. The explanation is always of the same type.

We, on the other hand, know that there is no mystery about a wireless set. When I was told how the wireless works, I thought I understood. I ought to have understood. As far as intellectual capacities go, I am capable of understanding—more or less at any rate. There is no mystery; it just is that I do not know how the thing works. It makes me feel that I am good for nothing. I feel that at every turn. My only excuse is that I cannot know everything.

I am inclined to think that this attitude on the part of civilised people or people today (since 'civilised' is not too good a term) to their everyday surroundings is responsible for the contrast often drawn between the natural and the artificial, between things that come from nature and things made by art.

Personally, I do not much care for the antithesis. I think I can see the difference, philosophically speaking, between natural and supernatural, but I cannot see the difference between natural and artificial. An artificial product is one made by men, but as the means used in its making belong to nature, there is continuity all the way.

But the mere fact that the antithesis has come into such common use shows that there is something we do not understand—something the man of today does not understand—in the artificial or, if you prefer the term, the abstract character of modern life.

To my mind, the element of artificiality explains two kinds of neurotic reaction often met with today.

The first of these is the rebellion against artificiality implicit in the practice of magic. The man of today still trusts in magic —to an extent which could be shown statistically if all fakirs, astrologers and fortune-tellers, whose profession is one of the most satisfactory there are from the financial point of view, could be forced to make accurate income-tax returns. The

horoscopes and the columns of astrological advice in the lesser
weeklies have a very wide circle of readers. Doctors constantly
come up against the attitude in their patients. That point I will
return to later.

The other reaction, a more commonplace one, is simply to
give in and obey. 'They know more about it than I do.' It is not
so often met with as trust in magic—it requires intellectual
humility. But you do sometimes find a patient saying to his
doctor, 'I have faith in you, doctor. I know nothing about it.
You are the doctor, not I.' The attitude is not, however, very
common.

3. As I said above, the last section is concerned with the
gradual disappearance of illiteracy.

It is beyond question that if the information possessed by any
given individual[1] now is compared with the information the
same individual would have possessed a hundred and fifty years
ago, a considerable increase will be noticeable. At one time, this
was called the advance of enlightenment. And as a matter of
fact, I very nearly confused it myself with one of the questions
discussed in an earlier chapter—the awakening of individualism,
the new awareness of the individual which came into being at
the dawn of the renaissance.

It seems to me that the two phenomena are independent but
that they react one upon the other. And having thought the
matter over, I have come to the conclusion that I do not much
care for the expression, 'awakening of a new consciousness of
the value of the individual', which is sometimes used to denote
the main characteristic of the present age. The first reason why
I am not in favour of it is that to talk of a new consciousness in
terms like that gives the impression that the acquisition of it is a

1 It will not, perhaps, be out of place to draw attention in this brief note to another
point, obvious though it is and universally admitted: 'individual' does not denote
the male citizen alone. If there has been a considerable increase in knowledge
in men's case, there has been an ever greater increase in women's. The last
century gave women a recognised place in the intellectual world for the first
time. The consequences are incalculable. Has it ever been considered what their
implications are for religion? Until the last century, women were treated as
minors and it was assumed that they were ignorant, which they were. They were
also treated as minors and assumed to be ignorant where their spiritual life was
concerned. The time has surely come to treat them as well-informed and
independent, like men, and teach them to regard the Church as their guardian
and acquire freedom in Christ and come to know God personally.

single solemn event—one fine day, a man sees the light and realises that he is an individual and that he is worth something.

But what actually happens, as far as I can see, both in the history of individuals and in the history of civilisations, is that there are awakenings of consciousness, in the plural, successive awakenings—I prefer that expression to the one used by Brunschvicq as the title of his book, *Le progrès de la conscience*. I would rather speak of awakenings of consciousness, in the plural, than talk about the awakening of consciousness or the advance of consciousness. The latter phrase implies a continuous process, whereas in fact the phenomenon is, I think, discontinuous.

As we all know, there is always an obstacle in the way of this increase of knowledge and these successive awakenings of consciousness. The obstacle is nearly always the absence of inter-human contacts. In other words, increase in awareness occurs in the form of mental experience, which comes long before experience of the real. The point deserves stress. It is undeniable that one of the characteristics of the man of today is that he acquires mental experience of a considerable number of things long before he comes into contact with the things themselves. Long before we ever saw a Chinaman or a Negro, we knew that such people as Chinamen and Negroes existed. Long before we ever saw an iceberg or a desert—if indeed we have seen one, for it may be that we never shall—we knew that there were such things as icebergs and deserts. Before we actually went up in an aeroplane, we knew what it was like from our mental experience of it.

Between the man of today, then, and contact with things is a buffer of acquired information. How is that information acquired? In most instances, and especially in the case of people who never reach an advanced standard in education, people who stay at the elementary level, the striking thing one notices is that what they learn at school teaches them nothing. All the mental experience they acquire comes by an involuntary process of education, by 'osmosis', through human contacts.

For that reason, as political parties, governments and all who have to do with propaganda very well know, no official propaganda, however intelligent it may be, can stand up to the sort of propaganda that passes from mouth to mouth. When you repeat a slogan to someone to see what he will say, if the person you repeat it to has a certain amount of confidence in you, even if he has already read the slogan, he reacts as though you were the source of his information, because what he reads or hears on the wireless is not real to him, whereas what you tell him by word of mouth in the Underground is as real as anything can be.

That is one of the ways in which ideas and propaganda filter through. The phenomenon is extremely striking. A certain number of official lines of propaganda in the western countries run counter to it.[1]

People cannot be got at straight away. To my mind, they are never got at at all, except through what other people tell them.

Another side to the phenomena we are considering is that we have become conscious of a very large number of things which our forebears were not conscious of at all. It seems to me that insufficient stress is laid upon the importance and variety of the things we now do consciously, whereas formerly people did them without thinking. There are examples even in the biological order.

We all know, because it is a thing the ethnologists have been much amused by, that there are certain small tribes which have not yet discovered the link between procreation and the sexual act. It is not only ethnologists, either, who find that amusing; any twentieth-century European will smile when he hears of it. It strikes us as really astonishing.

A quite large number of inferences must necessarily have been made, it seems to me, and a considerable amount of biological information acquired and slowly clarified before the discovery was arrived at that procreation is connected with the sexual act. If it comes to that, how long ago did we moderns start thinking about procreation? After all, the necessary inferences might have been made long before in fact they were. For long, procreation was a function nobody thought about; people began thinking about it only in the last century.

Another biological function of fundamental importance is

1 In reality, they do so only for a time, because, after all, propaganda transmitted from mouth to mouth is generally unconscious, or at any rate involuntary and therefore is gradually modified by the surrounding atmosphere. Thus, in ten or twenty years, successive relays of official propaganda may change the surrounding atmosphere.

nutrition. That too has come to the forefront of our consciousness in recent years to an amazing extent. In some countries, I
believe, where the popularisation of scientific theories has gone
further than it has here, it is years since anyone ate potatoes or
meat: what they all eat now is sixty grammes of animal protein
or four hundred calories.

In France, people have come to think about their diet in consequence of the shortage of food. They now eat proteins and
vitamins. The old ideas about food have been exploded and
new ones are taking their place. In France, as in China, so they
tell me—I speak from hearsay—eating and drinking had their
own traditions, which were part and parcel of the national
civilisation. There were hosts of little recipes, all lovingly kept
secret. The thing was typical of those practical kinds of knowledge which are transmitted, with all their fine shades, from one
generation to another and yet are never codified. But in the
space of a few years, eating and drinking became functions to
be carried out with the utmost deliberation, things subject to
supervision and criticism by science.

Then there is another thing we used not to be conscious of
but now are—the examples are not all good but I will mention
them all even so—and that is the fact that we belong to groups.

Three years ago I lost my old godmother. She was eighty-five
when she died. She was a very good Catholic, but I remember
one occasion in my youth when she shocked me very much. I
was at the grammar school at the time and I was something of
an intellectual. Her Catholicism was the kind you find in
Ardeche, a region that still exudes the atmosphere of the Wars
of Religion. She told me about another woman from the same
district who forty years before—it was an old story—had renounced protestantism and become a Catholic. My godmother
was very indignant with her for doing so. We argued the point.
I was about twelve years old. There was a sharp argument on
the theological score. 'It's outrageous', I said. 'You are a Catholic; you think that salvation is to be found only in the Catholic
Church. The girl was quite right to become a Catholic.' 'No',
she replied, 'people shouldn't change the religion they were
brought up in.' And eventually she said, 'It's just as if I were to
become a protestant. How could I? What do I know about it?'

I think that is a very good story. You must not suppose that I tell it with a view to casting doubts on my old godmother's saintliness. I am sure God has forgiven her her theological error. I mention the incident to show how infinitely more conscious we have become of the fact that we belong to a political party, a Church, a nation. We have come almost to choose those groups deliberately.

A phenomenon that caused much surprise during the last world war (though a casual glance through Thucydides, Plutarch or de Retz would have furnished precedents galore), was that in every country the frontier receded to the interior.

Not long ago, I heard of a psychologist, an opponent of psychoanalysis and (or perhaps because) a Communist, who came out with this little quip. 'Where will psychoanalysis poke its nose in next?' he asked. 'It seems that in America there are people who have themselves psychoanalysed to account for their political opinions.' The example he chose is a striking one. Modesty apart (for he would not have said, 'What do *I* know about it?' but would have tried to demonstrate the dialectical materialism and the entirely rational nature of his belief), the psychologist's attitude is not very different from my old godmother's.

Nevertheless, we are becoming just as conscious of our membership of social groups as we are of the functions of nutrition and procreation.

But it is time we concluded,[1] or rather summarised, this parallel between life in the world of the primitive and life in the world the man of today lives in. The man of today sees things much more clearly or at any rate is in a much better position to see them so; and, of course, this is accompanied by very heavy

1 This chapter is more in need of amplification than any of the others. Thus, it would be impossible to overstress the importance of the phenomenon of the proletariate, of division of labour in the factory or of the hurried, hallucinating rhythm of life today. Dr Zilboorg comments as follows on one of the essential features of modern life: lack of solitude. 'One thing in the chapter surprises me', he says, 'and that is that absence of solitude is a typical thing about modern civilisation. When people wake in the morning, instead of greeting the day with a reflection on this topic or that, they turn on the wireless: they cannot bear to be alone for a moment. I would not like to say what is responsible for this craving—the question is a complicated one. But the result has a direct bearing on the problem before us. The psychological consequence clearly is that people do not want to be by themselves; they are afraid of having silence in their lives.'

affective pressure, since all increase in consciousness brings an increase in the power of choice as well.

Escape from this affective pressure or reduction of the burden it imposes may be sought by flight in one of two directions.

The first form that flight from the problem may take is a sort of longing for a more childlike kind of behaviour. It is found in many quarters, from movements like scouting (which, of course, is worthy of all respect) down to *The Two Sources of Morality and Religion*, at the end of which the hope is expressed that we may one day return to a form of society in which the technical will not count for so much. The French are well acquainted with this state of mind, because they have lived through a period when the theme of the state's official progaganda was inspired by it.

I will not dwell on this 'retrogressive' type of solution; I will devote more attention to the 'progressive' type (and the word 'progressive' I take in no very good sense).

The suggested remedy is that we should deliberately plunge into the social, become absorbed in other people, choose out a group and join it. That, it seems to me, is a solution we are all in danger of adopting. Personally, I can see no greater peril.

Like others of my age, when I did my philosophy, I read a great deal of Durkheim. Now that I look back, it seems rather comical that poor Durkheim should have been so distressed because society was then so frightfully individualistic and should have hoped for a State in which individuals would be integral parts of the one whole. If he could be reborn from his ashes, he would see what such states are like. The judge who conducted the Kravchenko trial must have smiled a little as he reread his uncle's books, for all states are tending to go that way.

Individualism is much criticised these days. That in itself is significant. When an age is individualistic, it neither criticises nor defends individualism; it just *is* individualistic. The problem is not now one of integration, but one of disintegration.

It cannot be denied that since the appearance of the Communist Party, a comparatively recent event, as it dates only from Lenin, and since the advent of nationalism a hundred and fifty years ago, we have had groups which offer to take all responsibility from us if we will weakly consent to abdicate in their favour. The totalitarian character of the group today is the real danger of tomorrow. (For once, I am taking sides.) The danger is a serious one, because this is a case where the remedy comes from the thing that caused the disease—if you can call individualism a disease.

In all the revolutionary changes that have made the man of today what he is, there is one dominant feature: increase in human and social contacts. Ought we to use this to the full and sink ourselves in the collective? That, assuredly, is the great temptation assailing the majority of people today. It is certainly very pleasant to know what one ought to do and what writers one ought to read and like. It is very pleasant for the mind—the mind tired of choosing—to say one day that Tito is a great man and the next that he is a consummate fool. The number of people today who are looking for this voluptuous repose of the intellect can be counted by the million. And the danger is increased by the fact that since there is a stout buffer of mental experience between us and things, as I said above, we are always on that very slippery slope that leads to hasty rationalisation.[1]

Facile rationalisation is, to my mind, an intellectual danger to which we are perpetually exposed, and that to a much greater extent now than formerly.

Can these considerations possibly provide any practical hints that may be of use to lawyers, doctors, priests and others who in one field or another have to direct or advise people today? I will try and show, by way of conclusion, that they can.

First, it is of the utmost importance that the person who comes for advice should have his rationalisations brought into the light; but, at the same time, an honest attempt should be made to satisfy his desire to understand. When people ask us for an explanation, we must try and make them see what type of explanation we cannot give them and why, and show them what type we can give them and why. It is not too easy to do, because

---

1 An example of the effects of hasty rationalisation may be found in the charlatan's technique, which consists of giving the ignorant patient a scientific explanation of his complaint and making him 'familiar' with something which in fact he could not understand unless he had studied medicine for years. Charlatans on the Stock Exchange and in industry proceed in the same way (with diagrams, explanations of physical and chemical processes, etc.)

there are times when you are forced to tell people that they do not know enough to follow you any further. The odd thing is that they take it much better than you would think. We must also avoid what I call pious lies—truths so couched as to bear indefinite repetition in just that form. They are very dangerous, to my mind, because they change into slogans. They may not be dangerous to the people you tell them to in the first place, but they will be very dangerous to the people those people repeat them to. If you tell pious lies, they will fall back on your own head.

At the same time, the consultant must at all costs dispel any prestige that may attach to him as a sort of magician. We must never consent to be magicians. It is sometimes difficult not to, but I think it is essential to try. It may even be advisable as a personal precaution.

If instead of regarding the question from the angle of the relationship between 'director' and directed, doctor and patient, lawyer and client, we consider it from the point of view of the individual's relationship to society, two points will claim our attention. The first is the power of the individual, a factor which has not received its due stress. The individual still has some power, as can be seen on a sociological scale in the fact that the countries occupied by the conquerors in the last world-war sabotaged the conquerors' work, to a great extent, not so much by isolated acts of heroism as by a kind of ill-feeling all round. G. Rougeron's *La Guerre future*, a book that rewards the reader with a certain amount of amusement, tells a story taken from the Travels of Marco Polo. In a certain town in the lands of the Great Moghul, one of the guards—there were ten of them to a population of ten thousand—said to one of the inhabitants, 'I don't like the look of you. Come here and I'll cut off your head.' The man knelt down and took up a convenient position for being beheaded. The guard then realised that he had forgotten his sabre. 'Stay where you are', he said, 'while I go and fetch it.' And the victim waited patiently.

That story is symbolical. It shows that although the individual may think himself powerless, he nevertheless has more power than he supposes, even where collective bodies are concerned.

We need not wonder overmuch at what happened under the

N

Great Moghul: the same kind of thing happens today as well.[1]

The second point is a moral one. What we must do is to try and make people see that no collective body can relieve them of their personal responsibilities. The problem is one that has been much discussed of late east of the Rhine.

---

[1] Books by recent writers on concentration-camps (Daniel Rousser and Kogon) raise the very difficult question of passivity in the face of deportation, torture and execution. That is modern enough. An example between Marco Polo's day and ours can be found in Merimée's observations on the subject (in the *Chronique du règne de Charles IX*), in connection with the non-resistance of the protestants at the time of the massacre of St Bartholomew.

Chapter XII

ANTHROPOLOGICAL FACTORS CONDITIONING ACTS OF PENANCE

By D. DUBARLE, o.p.

I. 1. The problem. 2. Main avenues to be explored: (*a*) the psycho-physiological correlation and its evolution; (*b*) cultural changes. II. Psycho-biological problems: 1. The organo-vegetative side of the recent changes in the western races. 2. The neuropsychic side: (*a*) general; (*b*) a particular case: sensitivity to pain. 3. Application of findings to the problem of the act of penance: (*a*) curbing the appetites; (*b*) devices for causing bodily discomfort. 4. Things to be done. III. Cultural changes and the problems raised by them. 1. Changes in the sentiments; possible perversions of penance: (*a*) connection between pain and the satisfaction of sensual or amatory tendencies; (*b*) connection between pain [and the craving prompted by anxiety. 2. Growth of a sense of human dignity and its bearing on penitential practices. IV. Conclusion.

I

IT is impossible to live a really Christian life to the full without bringing into play the virtue known as penance. The constitutive elements of that virtue have long been the subject of theological investigation. The means by which it can be put into practice have been discussed with great care and attention by the theologians of the spiritual life, and the instruction they provide us with is of the highest value. Other chapters explain in some detail the religious and ascetic foundations on which the virtue rests. There is thus no need to consider it at any length at the moment. It will be enough if we remind ourselves of the ultimate motive behind the Christian use of penance—in the last resort, the aim is to join in the divine act of atonement made on the Cross and, as St Paul says (Col. 1: 24), in this

mortal frame to help pay off the debt which the afflictions of
Christ still leave to be paid. We may also note that the traditional system of penance is a complex, extensive thing. It will
be seen to revolve round two poles. The first of these is the
sacrament, which for all practical purposes we may leave out
of account in the investigations we are about to undertake. The
other is the centre of such devices for inflicting pain as are meant
either to atone for sins already committed or to mortify evil
tendencies. This penitential system has been developing among
Christians for centuries. It forms an organic whole, which tends
to regulate the religious practice of all the faithful to a greater
or lesser extent and always enters into the spiritual training of
those whose aim is to lead the perfect life.

It would seem, however, that at the present day something has
gone slightly wrong with the relationship between this traditional system and the general run of men, whom it is meant to
help on towards holiness. The problem that forms our starting-
point in this chapter is confined within fairly narrow limits. The
traditional teaching about the spiritual life recommends certain
practices which it calls 'penitential'—things like fasting, the discipline, curtailment of sleep, the wearing of hair-shirts or, at
another level, the use of self-imposed humiliations, acts of passive obedience and so on. These practices are considered as
means of sanctification, though of course discrimination and
restraint are always advised in the use of them. It appears, however, that today some of them are apt to provide opportunities
for a kind of satisfaction quite foreign to holiness and in fact
opposed to holiness, even when the people using them are
seeking holiness through them. Errors of judgment on the point
are attaining such proportions that it may be wondered whether
the classical rules about moderation really get to grips with the
problem. It may perhaps be advisable to subject the facts to a
more detailed analysis instead of interpreting them without
more ado in the light of what is regarded as an already water-
tight theory. The matter is a weighty one, to my mind, and one
I should like to help in clarifying.

But in actual fact, the problem is wider than this rather
limited field might imply. The taste for penance is said to be
declining among Christians and it is becoming difficult to make

people realise its importance, even those who as priests or religious aim at giving themselves to God. A certain disinclination to envisage the Christian life as a life of penance is discernible in many quarters, and there is still less inclination to make systematic use of the classical penitential practices. This has led to accusations of spiritual tepidity: present-day Christians are sometimes reproached with considerable severity for failing to realise the meaning of the Cross. Certainly, such complaints are to a large extent justified. But we must ask ourselves whether the blame for the deterioration in the Christian spirit can be laid exclusively on what is commonly called the naturalism of the surroundings. There is another thing that ought probably to be taken into account as well: in many cases there is every sign that Christians are extremely uncomfortable at the thought of resorting to certain practices, even though a whole line of tradition is there to recommend them.

The reasons for this feeling of discomfort are spiritual. People are reluctant to resort to these practices because in many instances the result they produce is equivocal. That is the case, for instance, with certain bodily penances, which sometimes take on a colouring that is at least ambiguous, if not frankly suspect. Reluctance to adopt the traditional practices also springs from the fact that in many other cases they now seem somewhat pointless and ineffective. There are stereotyped mortifications which now do not mortify anything at all; they no longer make any impression, except as funny little bits of theatrical business, and their effects are transitory. Such things are to be found among the customs in use in the noviciates of certain religious institutes. There may also be disinclination to use the traditional practices because often enough they are considered to endanger spiritual qualities of real value, which it would be shocking to see blunted or even destroyed by an attempt to carry out an ill-conceived programme of mortification. Humiliation, mortification of self-esteem and the curbing of the will by obedience ought not to diminish the sense of personal dignity, stun the active faculties or lead to passivity and infantilism.

These reactions are crude and often little more than instinctive, but behind them can be discerned a perfectly legitimate desire for a kind of penance that people will see is real and effective, a thing that will be as worthy of their efforts by human standards as it is balanced by Christian standards. If many people at present hesitate to adopt the traditional Christian system of penance, the reason is that it strikes them as not quite answering the needs of those who today are seeking perfection and a life inspired by the Cross.

If the inadequacy is real enough, there are nevertheless signs that it has not always been what it is today. In so far as we can judge of history, we can say that in the past, the classical Christian system of penance seems to have fulfilled its function very well: its intimate connection with theology kept it clear about its true aims, and the use the various schools of spirituality made of it gave it the support it needed. Hence it seems to follow that if what is now required is not just a sort of reawakening to the meaning of Christianity but a readjustment in the factual sphere as well, the reason is that there has been a global change in men themselves since the time when penitential practices acquired their present form, a change considerable enough to require the Christian virtue of penance to begin operations, as it were, in a new way. Is it altogether presumptuous to suppose that if that virtue would keep its balance, it must henceforth take account of the characteristic ways in which human beings are conditioned at the present stage of civilisation, since we are reaching a point where it is becoming essential to take such things into consideration? We are not, perhaps, altogether in a position to give a positive answer to that question. But it would seem advisable at least to raise the question and, if possible, to examine its main facets. The chief object of the present chapter is thus to ascertain the principal human factors giving rise to the need for adjustment. I must beg the reader's indulgence if the following pages contain more question-marks than answers or certainties. They are intended simply as a preface to more competent studies, which are the proper medium for elucidating the many points I shall leave vague and for reaching conclusions in the many instances where I can only suspend judgment.

2. To clarify the problem, it will be well to start with a brief analysis. If we leave the sacrament of penance out of the picture, we shall say that practising penance actively means imposing

some moral or physical hardship on oneself—a fast or a humiliation, for example—and this in view of the attainment of certain
ends, such as atoning for a sin of pride or curbing a sensual
appetite. It goes without saying that the hardship alone,
materially considered, is not sufficient to constitute an act of
penance. To realise that that is so, one need only think of the
unbalanced people who practise flagellation for reasons the
reverse of virtuous.

Acts of penance, like all acts of virtue in their several degrees,
thus involve on the one hand the intervention of a group of
spiritual factors—intentions, motives and so forth—which determines the species of the acts in the moral order, and on the
other hand the formation, as it were, of a sort of quasi-material
substratum, without which the virtue could not be put into
operation at all.

But it is important to observe that in the case of penance,
more than in any other, this substratum is itself a thing of considerable complexity, both where externals are concerned and
from the psychological point of view. With regard to externals,
penance and mortification make use of definite, concrete,
material practices, which can quite well be described and
studied in strict conformity with the objective rules followed in
psychology and sociology. With regard to psychology, these
practices ultimately produce a certain effect on the psychic
activity, feelings and emotions of the people who use them; they
have certain repercussions on character, personality and so on.
All this forms part of the material at the disposal of the spiritual
factors which determine the species of the act.

Hence, between the network of spiritual factors that determine the species of the virtuous act on the one hand and the
objective practices by means of which the virtue is actually put
into operation on the other, the network of psychic determina-
tions resulting from those practices and forming the inner content of the material available for the spirit to work on comes in
all the time as a sort of intermediary.[1] The two relationships

1 It may be observed that in the various factors here involved, we have practically
the same categories as those comprised in St Paul's famous trichotomy of body,
soul and spirit—σῶμα, ψυχή, πνεῦμα. The act is not composed of two elements
only, its matter and the principles that determine its species; it has, as it were,
three layers, one above the other. The 'somatic' layer is constituted by states of

will provide us with guiding threads and show us the sort of analysis to aim at.

(a) To begin with, it is obvious that when the virtue of penance produces an act, it cannot just choose any psychic element at random and function through that; it must choose something that will cause hardship. Nothing pleasant, nothing that satisfies instinctive tendencies, even if the things concerned are perfectly good in themselves, can be an instrument of mortification or a means of doing penance. And even the choice of things that do cause hardship cannot be left to chance: the disagreeable effects of the things so chosen must be compatible with the rest of the moral life, in keeping with the motives behind the act and conducive to the ends which are to be attained by means of them. Otherwise, as time goes on, the will is bound to be deflected from the intention of doing penance and the act is doomed to produce a result quite different from the sort of thing the virtue ought to lead to. This principle indirectly governs the choice of the material expedients meant to produce such reactions at the psychic level as will conduce to the end envisaged by the virtue.

That there should be connecting-links between these expedients and psychic reactions is due in the last resort to the fact that man is by nature psychobiological. The effects produced by material expedients at the psychic level can be ascertained from experience, which shows, for instance, what are the effects of fasting and lack of sleep, or again, what results follow the practice of humiliation, either at once or in the distant future. It is for experience to show how far the relationships between psychological factors and psychic ones are invariable. When they settled the final form of the traditional penitential practices, the masters of the spiritual life tacitly assumed that a considerable number of psychophysiological relationships were reasonably constant. It remains to be seen whether those relationships are

consciousness conditioned by the somatic or, to use more general terms, considered as passive or swayed by a conglomeration of factors originally determined by the passions. The 'pneumatic' layer is the one where the spirit can take the initiative and produce acts that are fully human. That is the ground for the distinction between 'psychic' and 'pneumatic' operation in the moral life. It also opens up a greater possibility of understanding the concrete incidents of the moral life, which the analysis of human acts into two factors only does not enable one to arrive at.

still exactly the same in our case as they were in the days of those to whom we owe the definitive shaping of the traditional practices. The question is of the utmost importance and it affords scope for research on quite a number of points.

In the course of the last few hundred years, the relationship between certain influences on the body considered as stimuli provoking psychic activity, and the psychic resultant of those influences, seems to have undergone modification. A greater refinement of feeling, it is said, is noticeable in the civilised races. It may be that where the affections are concerned, too, the reactions of a civilised person today to some of the more or less routine situations in life will again be rather different. To take an example from outside the sphere of penance, it may be questioned whether the various feelings aroused by sexual love are quite the same now as they were a thousand years ago. Of course, cultural factors come in here. But it cannot be said for certain that they are the only ones involved; the organic, neurological and constitutional sides of the relationship between the psychic and the biological ought perhaps to be investigated as well. In any case, it is becoming impossible to rule out the supposition that even at this level a certain development has taken place in the things about which experience is required to pronounce judgment.

(b) Again, the relationships between free spiritual activity and determined psychic activity, in the sense in which we are now taking the term, are at bottom fairly complex. The type of spiritual activity chosen and the course of its development depend all the time on whether the material available at the psychic level is malleable or whether it makes demands of its own. Conversely, everything that happens at the spiritual level reacts on the constitution of the psyche as a whole and helps to shape its functional pattern. Thus, the general tone of an individual's tendencies is to a large extent the result not simply of his antecedent experiences materially considered but also of the underlying significance attributed to those experiences. When the significance thus attached to an experience becomes explicit, it tends to act on the psyche as a fixing-agent and to determine subsequent selection. Hence the importance and the polarising character of all events likely to sink deep into the consciousness.

This interlocking of influences is responsible for the appearance of different activity-patterns in the life of the spirit. If psychic activity is fed from the contributions unceasingly brought in by the senses, it also matures, so to say, under the influence of the spiritual functions which it allows to emerge within the human consciousness. And in so far as it matures, it enables the spiritual functions themselves to operate with more autonomy and greater wealth of means. This is true of every individual spirit, throughout a process of internal development stretching from childhood to manhood. Human activity thus takes a different turn according to the stage it happens to have reached, and the practice of the virtues can be seen to follow a more or less different pattern at each stage. When spiritual writers have been at all wide-awake, they have not failed to notice this. In particular, they have pointed out that it was only to be expected that penance and the practice of asceticism should take on a different colouring according to the extent of individual progress in the spiritual life.

But it would seem that today the problems presented by this spiritual transformation in men would be better stated in a much wider context. Much more sharply than in the past, the realisation is forced upon us that there are processes which cannot be reduced to the simple facts of individual development. Collective factors come into the picture, things to do with environment, the nation and even the whole of mankind, things responsible, for instance, for the moral tone of a generation.

And more than that, among these phenomena characteristic of the collective aspect of man, signs of development are discernible, which show that in the course of successive generations the human race undergoes a kind of evolution, both where the psychic constitution itself is concerned and with regard to the spiritual functions of the consciousness. Hence it happens that at different periods the civilised portion of mankind has different resources available, one might almost say, for the principles of spiritual existence and moral activity to draw upon. Those in search of an example need only cast their minds back to the end of the middle ages, when the theme of a man's love for a woman and her love for him first attained popularity. Hence, again, the general characteristics of the mature outlook likewise appears as a result of the maturing of psychic activity under the influence of the cultural environment.

It may be, for example, that for us in these days, fulness of spiritual maturity ought to imply something different from what it meant in the middle ages, before the great convulsion of the renaissance. That does not, of course, mean that there has been any essential change in the principles of the spiritual life since that period, nor does it necessarily imply that there has been any improvement in morality or religion either. But we instinctively feel that to be genuinely mature today, a man's spiritual life must be shaped after new models. We need a different kind of lucidity in the inner life. We must secure autonomy in our personal outlook, make our own position clear to other people and take proper notice of theirs; but all this in new ways. And we need new moral reactions to the psycho-biological material our existence provides us with.

Despite its very general character, this sort of approach is far from being without significance for the quite circumscribed problem of determining the place of penance in the spiritual life. If mankind has undergone a certain change in the cultural sphere, so that new elements have been introduced into some of the social factors affecting the psychic constitution and into some of the channels through which the principles of the spiritual life take effect, the question arises of adjusting the virtue to keep pace with this evolution. In these days, certain means of mortifying the senses may be more dangerous and more likely to serve dubious ends than was the case some centuries ago. And certain devices for diminishing self-esteem, certain methods of curbing the will, may now in some cases impair or even destroy spiritual potentialities, though formerly, perhaps, they would never have given cause for anxiety on that score.

The outlines of two processes of development thus begin to be discernible. One of them is taking place in the biological sphere and it calls for a re-examination of the question as to whether the use of certain concrete practices is in keeping with the object of the virtue of penance. The other is taking place in the cultural sphere and it calls for at least partial reconsideration of the question as to what are the specific objects of the virtue and of the system according to which its actions are produced.

Hence, the most we can set out to do is to ascertain, first in the one case and then in the other, such points as may give a useful direction to our thoughts when we aim at stating the question of Christian penance in terms adapted to the present day.

II

LET me repeat once more that we really know very little about the questions before us. In the present state of our knowledge, nothing is more difficult than to say with any degree of certainty what are the characteristics of such changes as may have occurred in the western races during the last thousand years with regard to bodily constitution, psychology, temperament, character and the determination of psychic activity. Still, we may perhaps hazard one or two hypotheses which seem to be not altogether devoid of probability.

1 (a) From the *somatic* point of view, it seems that the civilised peoples of the west, particularly in urban centres, have tended to show a certain increase in size and that the type of stature known as 'longilinear' has increased in frequency among them. The body of the man of today reveals a fairly systematic departure from the set of proportions comprised in the classical Greek 'canon of beauty' and also from the canon established at the renaissance, both of these deriving from a build that was more thickset than slender.

(b) It also seems that where *organic development* is concerned, full maturity tends to be reached at a later age. It has long been known that the Nordic peoples and others who live in cold climates reach puberty later than the peoples of the south and those who live in warm climates. The climatic factor is certainly not the only one involved. Several enquiries have been conducted into the apparent delay in puberty noticed in undernourished adolescents during the war and the results have recently been published. Some of these studies question whether the transitory phenomenon does not give the clue to another, more fundamental one beneath it, a process stretching over centuries, a sort of drift of the civilised races towards a later puberty.[1]

1 It would perhaps be better to speak of slower development in puberty rather than of the appearance of the initial phenomena at a distinctly later age, since

(*c*) It is also possible to risk an estimate of the direction taken by the change in so far as it has affected *temperaments*. As far as one can judge, the sanguine temperament predominated to a greater extent a few hundred years ago than it does today, and if there has been any change in this respect in the civilised peoples of the west, it would seem to have taken the form of an increase in the proportion of nervous temperaments.

There is doubtless some truth in the complaints of the novice-masters of the principal orders, who lament the constant increase in the number of recruits with temperaments unsuited to the usages laid down by the existing Rules for the religious state. More and more often the rhythm and conditions of eating, sleeping, work and social intercourse prove to be ill-adapted to the organism, which is worn out by the observance instead of being helped by it to develop the qualities necessary for sustaining a really spiritual life with a feeling of well-being. This is probably a sign that temperaments really are evolving more towards the lymphatic or the nervous.

2 (*a*) It seems clear that all this is accompanied by a certain number of neuro-psychic concomitants, one at least of which is of prime importance to the matter we are concerned with at the moment. It looks as though the organic and organo-vegetative changes of which I have just put forward a partial estimate have led to fairly considerable modifications in certain psychic factors. It is not very likely that 'exteroceptive' sense-activity, as it is called—the activity of the more perfect senses: sight and hearing, for instance—has been much modified by these changes. But it does seem that there have been appreciable repercussions on the lower forms of sense-activity—reaction to tactile sensations of all kinds, sensitivity to pain and even coenaesthetic or 'proprioceptive' sense-activity.

In other words, as the human organism evolves, the nervous system tends more and more to turn the biological contacts effected through it into means of determining sense-activity. Conscious contacts increase in number and intensity and psychic connections are formed, sorted out and given permanent shape,

the secondary characteristics, especially the psychic fixations accompanying adult sexual equipment, do not appear until a fair length of time has elapsed from the beginning of organic puberty. Hence, the intermediate phase is longer for the adolescent in modern civilisation.

whereas formerly all this was buried in the biological substratum of the consciousness and never became explicit. We are becoming familiar with the practice of taking psychoanalytical soundings of this region. If such things are now possible, it is not just because we have worked out the right technique for that kind of exploration. There is probably another reason, too, which is that in the civilised races the ground to be explored has begun to fall within the psychic sphere properly so called and to form part of the field of consciousness. We shall not, perhaps, be far wrong about the direction the bio-psychic changes in man are taking as a whole is we suppose that there is a tendency for the senses to be better informed about events in the organo-vegetative sphere, a tendency, that is, for the individual to become more aware of what is happening to him in the biological order because he feels it more.

(b) This will enable us to understand, among other things, the changes that have taken place during the last few centuries in one very important quality, sensitivity to pain. Of course, the situation is difficult to size up and we must be on our guard against generalising. Yet it does seem that the degree of sensitivity to pain may vary widely from one population-group to another. What some groups find tolerable others may not be able to bear at all. It is generally agreed that the western peoples reach the limits of their endurance sooner than the peoples of the east. It is also fairly extensively held that there is some difference in this respect between urban districts, where there is a certain refinement in the living conditions, and country districts or others where life is rougher.

But the reasons for these differences cannot be reduced, as far as one can see, to mere differences in geographical conditions. Surgeons are now often found to question whether some change has not taken place in men in the course of the last hundred and fifty years; they doubt whether people today could dispense with anaesthetics or analgetics in various cases normally treated by surgeons in former times without their aid. It would seem that organic injuries now have more power to stimulate the parts of the nervous system which are responsible for pain in the psychic sphere.

There is a tendency, then, for the pain produced by organic

lesions and disturbances of organic equilibrium to become more intense. But there is another factor involved, too, though not so dramatically. It has been known since Plato's time that there is a connection between organic discomfort and organic pleasure, in some circumstances at least. There are things that produce somewhat ambiguous effects on the body. They may be a source of pain but they also cause a certain amount of pleasure. The connection between the two things is quite independent of the mind and may show itself in an infinite number of ways. But as time has gone on, the process of interaction seems to have become more involved. There are more things now, apparently, that may bridge the gap between pleasure and pain, things more subtle and more general in character than previously, at any rate at a certain level. Modern psychologists have often had occasion to point out that the import of certain sense-stimuli—a slight electric shock or the sensation of hunger in the early stages, to take two of the thousand and one possible examples— is not always clear from the beginning. Such stimuli are at first ambivalent, some elements in them being vaguely pleasant, others vaguely unpleasant.

Roughly speaking, where pain of moderate intensity is concerned, it seems that the nervous system has tended to develop a network of relationships with the organo-neurological substrata underlying pleasure, especially with the group of factors behind the pleasures known as sexual. Thus, there appear to be at least two main elements involved in the change that has come over sensitivity to pain. On the one hand, reactions to organic injury are more violent, but on the other, wherever the suffering is only slight, ability to provide the pain-reaction to organic injury with a context of more or less veiled pleasure is greater. Pleasure and pain are two different branches, as it were, of the same proprioceptive sense-activity. The evolution we are undergoing in the neuro-psychic sphere is tending to put us into touch with them, not just at the stage where they have separated into two distinct branches, but much lower down, at the point where they are still growing together as one on the same biopsychic stem. This will be enough to show something of the hitherto unknown complexity involved and to indicate the extent to which, at this stage of human development, the affections may

step in and give motives a twist, more or less from the time
when psychic activity begins. The factor is no doubt of importance for understanding the workings of sexual activity and, with
regard to the matter we are concerned with at present, it sheds
a certain amount of light on a process which seems to have been
reinforced to a considerable degree in the course of the last few
hundred years of human development, viz. the eroticisation of
pain.

3. If we now proceed to a more detailed consideration of the
penitential practices in traditional use among Catholics, we may
say that from our present point of view they fall into three
classes. Some, such as fasting, abstinence, continence and curtailment of sleep aim at keeping quasi-instinctive human appetites in check. In other cases, the object is to cause discomfort by
means of devices like the discipline and the hair-shirt, which
mortify the body. In other cases again, discomfort is produced
by moral means—things like humiliations, passive obedience
and so on.

For the time being, we may leave aside the third class of
penances, which owe their disagreeable character to the
influence exerted in the psychic field by things very different in
kind from the basic sense-reactions, things like mental representations and sentiments, i.e. things with more of the cerebral
element in them and in a sense conditioned more by cultural
factors than by bio-psychological ones. The other two classes,
however, are distinctly relevant to the point we are now
considering.

(a) Obviously, we cannot abandon the principle that the
quasi-instinctive natural appetites need restraining, simply because we appear to have discovered that somatic, organo-vegetative and idiosyncratic factors are subject to change. We must,
however, try to decide what forms and means of restraint are
appropriate to the excessive tendencies actually found at the
moment. We must also see to it that they are compatible with
fundamental balance of character, for Christians have never
advocated that asceticism should be used to upset that. If the
late-maturing, predominantly nervous type of temperament
tends to occur more often now among Christians in the west, it
is clear that on the whole fasting and curtailment of sleep will

not in the long run be so conducive to the end asceticism is meant to serve, even though in the short run they will still be very effective as means of producing acute discomfort for religious motives. It is much more likely that they will ultimately disturb the balance of the vegetative system and eliminate certain general conditions which human beings require if they are to act virtuously. And because maturity of character is attained at an increasingly later age, it becomes particularly important in this connection to distinguish the sort of penance and asceticism within the reach of the adult from the kind the adolescent may safely practise. The quality of the training given in the early stages of the religious life would probably improve considerably as a result.

By way of illustration, I may perhaps be allowed to describe a series of experiments recently carried out in the U.S.A. in connection with the moral and psychological effects of malnutrition. A group of volunteers, all men of the highest character, were for six months put on a fasting diet of 1,600 calories a day instead of the 3,000, more or less, required for the daily ration necessary to keep a man going normally. The result showed anything but moral improvement. The men eventually became quarrelsome; they began to steal, first from one another and then from other people; they lost all initiative and would not exert themselves unless they were told to; it was noticed that they developed a dislike for their surroundings and even for the other sex; they hated men who were better fed than they were themselves. The conditions created in the experiment were obviously in excess of those usually obtaining in the fasts undertaken for penitential purposes by Christians. All the same, the experiment surely does show that if penance is carried very far in this field, the results it yields will rarely be of the best from all points of view. The same could doubtless be said of excessive curtailment of sleep. And again—at any rate if we consider the matter in the light of merely natural morality and leave out of account the special value of virginity in the religious context—we ought perhaps to venture a similar question about the value of strict continence as a means of penance.

(b) In most cases, the pain caused by such things as the

o

discipline and the hair-shirt, however severe it may be, does not indicate the presence of any serious lesion in the organism itself. Hence, physical pain of this sort is more likely to be surreptitiously streaked or tinged to some extent by the desire for pleasure and thus to become a rather doubtful influence on psychic activity.

We will deal later with the other factors that may be operative in associating this kind of physical pain with pleasure. But the question to ask at the moment is whether, as civilisation becomes more refined, even the way the nervous system conditions the use to which psychic activity puts sensation does not tend to disturb the motivation of certain acts of penance right from the start. As well as causing a particular kind of pain, deliberately chosen for some moral or religious reason, the use of instruments of penance may occasion the actualisation of other psychic potentialities and thus provide a much less respectable kind of satisfaction. That is the weak point of those practices. As soon as psychic activity ceases to have the requisite degree of straightforwardness and simplicity or a reasonable amount of the stability that comes of healthy development, the imposition of that kind of suffering on the body opens the door to dishonesty and morbidity. The moment the use of the discipline and kindred devices begins to be an indirect occasion for pleasure-seeking (for general neurological reasons—the explanation is fundamentally quite simple), it ceases to have much value as a means of penance. Even if it does not become in the main a sort of covert compensation for the repression of certain kinds of activity in other quarters or a disguised substitute for such activity—which is what does seem to happen in some cases—it will be accompanied by an aura of affective disturbance which will be highly prejudicial to any real progress in the spiritual life.

4. That concludes our rough, tentative outline of a selection of the facts and their possible implications for Christians where penance is concerned. A glance at these few data clearly shows that two things are urgently necessary.

The first need is for a systematically objective enquiry into the facts mentioned. There is doubtless not much hope that we shall be able to reconstruct with any degree of certitude

the different types of psycho-biological conditioning to which
men have been subject in the past. We have not enough
information from which to judge, and the little we have is too
much open to misinterpretation. But we could surely do better
with regard to the present. There are facts about which it seems
essential that we should acquire fairly detailed information.
These could probably be examined by methods of research
similar to those now sometimes used in investigating sexual
behaviour, as, for instance, in the series of studies known as
the 'Kinsey Report'. Moreover, the results of these studies
seem even at this stage to provide material for one or two
preliminary suggestions. They show that where the fundamental tendencies of the human animal are concerned,
psycho-biological types differ considerably. An even more
important thing to realise is that among behaviour-patterns
in this sphere, the difference between the extremes is very
strongly marked. This may perhaps be more characteristic of
men in tolerably civilised conditions than of people living in
rougher conditions, but little is actually known about it for
certain. Whatever the truth may prove to be, the fact itself
is a warning that extreme caution is needed over generalising
about means of penance and mortification. There can be no
common rules; no one device can be thought to fit every
need, even if it is applied in a group with all its members
working for the same ends, as is the case with a religious insti-
tute or noviciate.

The other need is to take into account to a greater extent
than hitherto (with due regard to the kind of surroundings the
individual comes from) the increased importance, complexity
and duration of the transitional element in the adolescent
attitude. It is hard to tell whether the biological factor really
has varied to any extent as far as the rhythm of growth from
childhood to maturity is concerned, but the psychic factor in
that growth does seem to have varied considerably. To put
the matter succinctly, it appears that in civilised countries
adolescence now lasts longer and is more of an embarrassment.
Hence, where the bulk of moral and religious training is given
during the adolescent stage of mental development—as in
practice it generally is in the case of people embarking on the

religious life or preparing for the priesthood—it may perhaps be advisable to revise the syllabus and introduce certain elements at different points. But we must not pursue this line of thought or we shall be going beyond our terms of reference.

III

IF consideration of the last few hundred years gives us grounds for suspecting that the civilised races have undergone a certain change in the bio-psychic sphere, it reveals much clearer evidence of cultural change, the main features of which are fairly easy to define. Several of the changes which have thus occurred in men are of great importance for their bearing on the question of what is at present possible and what essential in the exercise of the virtue of penance. While not pretending to give a complete list or go into the question at all thoroughly, we may nevertheless outline some of the chief factors and say how or to what extent they make it advisable to reconsider certain customary approaches to penance and asceticism.

1. To take the matter by the side of it which, materially speaking, is closest to us, the first of the outstanding events that have taken place within modern civilised society seems to be the thorough reshaping of the connecting links between various things which are physically or morally painful and the play of certain sentiments. Hence the formation of new complexes, which may entirely alter the affective and moral values commonly attached to certain actions. It would seem that henceforth there will be two major possibilities to be reckoned with where these connecting links are concerned. There is the possibility that a whole system of connecting links may be set up in the psychic sphere between the suffering or infliction of pain and the satisfaction of sensual or amatory tendencies. There is also the possibility—it may be more recent in origin but it is more disturbing, even so—that pain may be brought into the psychic structures produced by the various forms of anxiety. We may think it deplorable, but the existence of such connecting links at the conscious level, openly admitted, described and sometimes extolled, is a fact, and one that we cannot banish from

civilised society all of a sudden. It is also a phenomenon which
for some decades has been becoming a matter of general knowledge, at any rate on the theoretical side. The fact that it is now
notorious puts many penitential practices almost automatically
into a context where the right interpretation of the facts is
extremely dubious.

(a) It is a truly astonishing thing that ever since classical
times the significance people have attached to the infliction and
acceptance of pain should have varied to such an extent, through
its connection with a wide variety of areas in the sentimental
sphere. Three of these sentiments seem to have had special importance: the way men have felt about justice, their attitude to
religion and their feelings about things to do with love.

To take the matter in its religious bearings, it seems that when
suffering entered into the ancient cults, it very rarely acquired a
religious value independently of either a certain idea of justice
towards the god who, the devotees thought, was angry and
would accept human suffering in atonement, or of some sort of
erotic complex, the stimulation of which might be reinforced (or
camouflaged) by resort to pain. It is well known that as the old
religions degenerated in the Mediterranean world, there came a
tendency to transfer the connection between suffering and justice to a secular basis. As the Christian religion gained a hold, it
consented to endow suffering with a religious value once more,
but it showed a constant and, so to say, relentless determination
to eliminate from the genuinely religious sphere all trace of
erotic practices and all interference by factors of that kind. Suffering may have a religious value if it springs from the idea of
making atonement to God; it is certainly not worth anything
at all if it stimulates orgiastic ecstasy, as in the Dionysaic
cults.

In the ancient world, the connection between the various
erotic complexes and the manipulation of pain received relatively little expression in the cultural sphere. The Romans of
the imperial era certainly knew of it and speculated about it,
but the context in which they did so was almost entirely secular,
even when it was decked with a few conventional scraps of
religious practice. Awareness of the connection can be seen
unmistakably emerging here and there in literature; in some of

Martial's epigrams it occurs in the pure state.[1] But two things—
the disappearance of the refined civilisation of the period under
the waves of the barbarian invasions, which brought a biological influx of a much coarser kind, and the growth of a Christian
civilisation—weakened its force and curbed its influence. For a
short time in the ancient world it was a thing that men were
explicitly aware of; then it practically disappeared. The infliction of certain kinds of pain on the body may still, perhaps, have
had something vaguely disturbing about it; but for centuries the
disturbing note was so muffled and so unproductive of avowedly
erotic reactions that in practice the problem was almost entirely
neglected until the end of the medieval period.

The reappearance of the connection as an established
phenomenon in secular culture seems characteristic of the end
of the middle ages. There is indisputable evidence of it in a certain section of renaissance literature and still more in a certain
class of work produced in the sixteenth century. From that time
onwards, the more educated members of the civilised western
races have explicitly recognised that such a thing is possible and
have possessed more or less detailed knowledge of the ways in
which it can be produced. This is true of some individuals; it
does not yet apply to absolutely everyone. Not only is human
psychic activity becoming more prone to establish the connection and to eroticise some at least of the pains men suffer and
inflict upon themselves, but human means of expression are
coming to be devoted to it more fully and deliberately, from
pornographic books or articles and suggestive pictures to the
semi-philosophical essays which are now beginning to appear,
things coldly scientific in tone and corresponding to prototypes
dating from the end of the eighteenth century. It is perhaps
characteristic of our times that all this is now practically a
matter of common knowledge, so that the problem has at last
become unavoidable.

Of course, I do not at all mean that the erotic consequences
of pain are in fact to be found, in the concrete, in every civilised
man today. Anyone who thought that they were would be mak-

---

1 The specifically erotic character of pain was most clearly realised in the case of
flagellation, presumably for reasons very like those which make the practice
so very common in sado-masochistic intercourse as practiced or described
today, at the present level of civilisation.

ing a very big mistake. It is highly probable that the majority of people are still untouched by any such conditioning; at any rate, they do not seem to possess it in the form of that strong, imperious urge which is evident in the workings of open sadism and masochism. The cultural changes in which we are caught up are far from having made us all perverts. But it seems that although the erotic sequel to pain occurs in this form in only a relatively small number of individuals, it has nevertheless become more of a proximate possibility for all of us and one against which we must be on our guard. This is true for everyone of us as regards our present conduct and also as regards the adventure of our spiritual development. You never can tell whether a past experience, which had nothing sadistic or masochistic about it at the time, may not one day be repeated for motives plainly of that kind.

Attention must also be drawn to another point. As we have said, the recognition of the ties that bind the pursuit of certain kinds of suffering to the satisfaction of erotic tendencies is now an influential factor in our cultural system. It does not, however, stand alone. It accompanies (and no doubt causes) the subjection of sexual activity to a general process of cerebralisation, a phenomenon that seems to be a consequence of the increase of refinement in culture. Realisation of this fact may perhaps provide the key to certain features characteristic of sexual behaviour among the more cultivated classes in countries where modern civilisation has taken root.[1] At any rate, it is unquestionable that in many cases the cerebralisation of sex facilitates the impregnation of certain human practices with a whole world of sexual implications, scarcely conscious in some instances but in the last resort still capable of furnishing the real motives for conduct.

This needs to be borne in mind particularly in connection with the operation of such human relationships as tend to produce in the psychological sphere conditions akin to those found where there is pain of body. Receiving or inflicting a humiliation or what is commonly called a blow to one's self-esteem,

1 A certain number of these features are picked out and analysed in Kinsey's 'Sexual Behaviour of the Human Male'. Kinsey seems to have established objectively that there are important differences in the general tone of sexual behaviour at different cultural levels.

submitting to another person's orders in the spiritual sphere or giving such orders to somebody else more or less systematically oneself—things like that are rather liable, with some persons at any rate, to be permeated by an atmosphere of latent sex, a subtle, indefinable thing perhaps, but one that bring with it the heady seductiveness which a faint suggestion of sexual pleasure has for certain temperaments. The prominence now given in literature to sadism and masochism has made us all familiar with the extremes of this kind of sexual satisfaction. We cannot go so far as to lump everything together indiscriminately under the heading of those extreme forms of behaviour, but it does seem that something of the sort will henceforth be inescapable. The kind of effort required of those in training for the spiritual life leads to the formation of human relationships, as does the state of spiritual dependence that normally accompanies the attempt to live a more deeply religious life. The span of knowledge in civilised individuals today being what it is, such relationships are often in danger of producing consequences of a fundamentally sexual nature, even if they are unconscious or quasi-unconscious. These consequences are all the more real in that they may constitute a sort of outlet for tendencies repressed at other points, on their own specific ground.

In particular, we must have the courage to admit that the turn our civilisation is taking may gradually foster the development of something like sentimental motives in spiritual direction. When there is too much of the human element in spiritual direction, it is often rather dubious and anything but religious in character. The thing is perhaps inevitable, if you take it as an unconscious factor in these human relationships, which in turn are probably necessary themselves. But it ought as far as possible to be recognised and consciously mastered as morality requires. Otherwise, it will bear out the opinion which regards such relationships merely as hypocritical means of bringing into play tendencies that are not at all concerned to promote moral progress.

In mentioning these different points, I do not mean to suggest any particular conclusion. I simply want to point out that the civilisation in which we live is tending to facilitate the introduction of new values into the practice of penance, things quite different from the ends hitherto envisaged. When these changed values are consciously grasped and accepted, they do nothing to make penance virtuous—rather the reverse. At best, they steer it towards a doubtful goal, an end incompatible with the Christian ideal of sanctity.

(b) It is perhaps one of the distinctive features of modern civilisation that it has quasi-specifically determined what might be called the 'psychological sphere of anxiety'. It is by no means certain that before modern western civilisation came into being, anything more than the rudiments of the feeling we call *anxiety* were known or, in the affective sphere, anything more than the factors preparing its way. To judge from the explicit evidence of literature, it would seem that anxiety hardened into a specific psychological state at a relatively recent date. One might perhaps be tempted to reduce it to the passion that has for so long been known as fear. It does contain a good number of the features found in fear, but in the modern sense of the word, anxiety is not at all equivalent to fear, although it presupposes the presence of well-developed fear-complexes. In actual fact, it belongs to another level. It presupposes, first of all, that the mind has become conscious of a more fundamental layer of reality than the one reached in ordinary fear; it has a quasi-ontological bearing. That is why we automatically call it a feeling rather than a passion. It also includes a sort of deliberate fostering of certain states of mind, either openly, with the consent of the will or, if need be, in an underhand way, the mind meanwhile camouflaging its real intentions. The result is that it tends to colour all mental activity more or less from the roots: people may feel a sort of need for anxiety and tend to construct around themselves a network of motivation conducive to the satisfaction of that need.

At a certain level, anxiety may be the natural reaction of a mind aware of its problems and faced with certain facts. But it does not seem that the effects are always happy when the whole of a person's existence is permeated by this feeling. In any case, it is undeniable that behaviour determined by anxiety or, more precisely, by the craving for anxiety, is not for that reason morally justifiable—far from it.

However that may be, it can be established that anxiety

develops more or less automatically along two lines. On the one hand, it leads people to take great interest in the sort of situation that calls for extremes of behaviour, the kind of circumstances that harmonise with the psychological drama. On the other hand, it tempts them to build up a world of terror as an external and quasi-sacramental substitute for the internal world of anxiety. As a natural consequence, great importance is attached to everything endowed with the power of causing hardship. Such things are chosen as instruments for anxiety to wield and stress may be laid for preference on the more theatrical ways of using them.

There is no need for us to psychoanalyse modern society in this respect. But we must at least note that from whichever point of view penitential practices are considered, whether in connection with the propensity to enact a psychological drama or with respect to the temptation to construct a world of terror, they may come to have a quasi-instinctive attraction for the anxious. When people are tormented by the feeling of anxiety, they are inclined to resort to penance almost without thinking, or even to plan it systematically, because they want to feel in the physical sphere something of the dramatic extremity which is always to the fore in their minds. They may also be led to inflict penitential practices on others, if they can, as a more or less effective means of bringing the world of terror or part of it into being, and as a way of expressing the sort of doubt that people brought into a world like that feel to be weighing on them. There was doubtless something of both these points in the Jansenist complex.

But there is no need to go so far back for an example or to choose so notorious a case. It is indisputable that in some instances whole religious communities and noviciates have literally been victimised because the religious who had been chosen as superiors or novice-masters on account of their reputation for austerity proved to be suffering from anxiety-complexes. It is by no means certain that from the spiritual point of view all went well in every respect with the people concerned.

It may be, too, that we ought not *a priori* to exclude every form of the feeling of anxiety from the religious sphere. If there are legitimate forms of anxiety, penitential practices cannot be styled unacceptable simply because they are subordinated to such varieties of the feeling. But it does not seem nearly so certain that a general disposition to be anxious about everything —a vague state of feeling and one sometimes bound up with various kinds of tension in the sexual sphere—is morally sound, spiritually fruitful or justifiable on Christian premises.

Developments in human culture, then, are leading to a situation in which it is becoming possible to produce an atmosphere of anxiety more and more systematically; in some cases, they even give rise to the collective diffusion of that atmosphere. They thus cannot fail to raise serious problems for the Christian theology of penance.

2. Up to the present, we have touched only on such points in the transformation occurring in man as belong to the more material aspects of cultural change. We ought perhaps to say at least a few words about a rather different aspect of the problems raised for Christians with respect to penance in consequence of that change.

It seems that for some centuries there has been a tendency for members of the civilised races, when they reach a certain natural maturity of mind, to acquire a type of self-consciousness hardly known in former ages. Where man's relationship to nature is concerned, this increase in mental clarity has been turned to account in science: thanks to technical enterprise, man's control over the things below him has entered on an entirely new phase. Where human relationships are concerned, the manifestation of opinion and the maintenance of personal autonomy with respect to other persons have come to be accepted as ideals, as is suggested, for instance, by the terms 'toleration' and 'equality'. In many ways, men have come to regard themselves as more autonomous and creative and more in the nature of brothers to other men, in theory at least, than was generally the case before in fact. This has been accompanied, it is true, by an attack of anti-religious feeling, as witness the present forms of unbelief and irreligion. But in spite of all the unfortunate consequences of this attack and of the sinful state of man separated from God, it still remains true that the majority of the gains made in the human sphere represent a genuine advance in the adult character of man's spiritual outlook.

We know, too, that pride and excess of self-esteem are vices as old as man himself. The Christian tradition in the matter of penance has always made a great point of devising means to atone for them, mortify them and keep them under strict control. The Christian life should be a humble life; there is no room in it for any jibbing at humiliation. Christians should not be self-centred or refuse, if occasion arises, to follow the counsel to renounce their own desires altogether and for religious motives practise obedience. If a certain state of mind today is big with new temptations to pride and self-assertion even against God— and we shall not be wrong in thinking that such is the case— Christian asceticism must make special provision for it. Here, then, is a sphere where penance is called for. The practices which naturally occur to the mind in connection with it are those that inflict pain through humiliation and self-denial.

And yet, a serious problem arises in connection with the use of such practices. The ultimate aim is to bring Christian souls to their full flowering in the plenitude of spiritual life or at any rate in such plenitude as their capacities allow. The conditions in which some at least seem called to achieve the full flowering of religious life require the soul to make the utmost possible use of the more adult qualities of mind—i.e., it must genuinely attain its majority, in the concrete sense attaching to the word today. It remains to be seen whether a new technique of spiritual guidance ought not to be worked out in view of this end—in view of its real nature—and whether such a technique (though of course necessarily welcoming the deliberate pursuit of humility and the practice of self-denial and of obedience for religious motives) will be compatible with the use of any and every device supposed to be good for mortifying pride, self-esteem or the spirit of independence. The devices employed must not at one and the same time destroy both the thing that really needs mortifying and the possibility of achieving the end which they are meant to help the soul to attain.

It will be said that the danger is purely chimerical. Unfortunately, that is not so, especially in the case of people normally bound to try and live the spiritual life as adults, to the degree to which such a thing is possible at present. The problem of finding forms of asceticism suited to present needs is thus closely connected with the problem of devising a new form of spiritual training, one capable of arousing a religious response without producing a quasi-infantilising effect in the human sphere as such. For the moment, I will confine myself to observing that a detailed analysis of the transformation men's conscious ideals have undergone in the last few centuries would be extremely useful for the theology of the spiritual life as well.

IV

For the most part, I have been stressing the various factors which necessitate reconsideration of the penitential practices in traditional use among Christians, in so far as they are *active* expressions either of penance properly so called or of the will to asceticism. Let me repeat once more that I am not proposing the total exclusion of active penance or asceticism from every sphere of Christian life in consequence of the difficulties I have just raised. All I suggest is that we should be prepared to make certain adjustments to the traditional expedients. If the proceeding is to be of any use, a much more detailed enquiry will be needed into the extent to which the observations here collected together are valid. What is needed at present is not the elimination of penance and asceticism, but a change—perhaps —in their incidence.

Whatever the solution may be in the case of active penance, we may note in conclusion that the Christian practice of penance has two other aspects, which are probably more fundamental. The first of these is the ability to take the ordinary circumstances of life, with the pain and mortification that issue from them automatically, in a *spirit of penance*. It was not my intention to examine the result that sometimes follows the deliberate and even spectacular performance of certain acts of penance, viz. that in the end they become a means of flight from a more radical attitude, a harder kind of penance, which without help from any artificial contrivance, goes right to the roots of the thing that is still keeping the soul apart from God. Attention needs drawing once more to the value of this kind of penance, which gets at the essentials and has nothing to fear from hypocrisy, since it is seen, perhaps, by no one save by him 'who sees what is done in secret'. (Matt. 6: 4.)

A return to the sacramental side of penance, with a deeper understanding of its potentialities, is probably still more desirable. I have said nothing about it in the course of this chapter. But I must observe before I close that frequentation of the sacrament shelters the Christian virtues of penance from many of the dangers to which it is exposed when it resorts to penitential practices of a more external kind. Taking it in that way would no doubt permit of much easier solutions of the problems now being raised by the changes occurring in men in this civilisation of ours.

Of course, there are things in sacramental confession which probably need new life infusing into them; for too many people they have become reduced to an empty, meaningless formula. But if properly reinstated, the human act required by the sacrament of penance could become the basis of a spiritual practice particularly well adapted to some of the major circumstances in the development at present taking place in the human field of consciousness.

The act possesses a special virtue, which of its very nature more or less compensates for the lack of balance in the modern attitude to God. By reason of the clearsightedness and the human gesture of communication it requires, it has unique possibilities of obviating the danger of fresh spiritual disturbances, an eventuality which the present potentialities of the human psychic equipment seem to portend. The rediscovery of a more vital meaning in the sacrament that some of us receive so often—together with more attention to the liturgical side and wider scope for the human element—would surely be the right starting-point in the quest for that balance which it is so desirable that the virtue of penance should attain.

CHAPTER XIII

SUBJECTIVE PAIN AND OBJECTIVE PAIN

By Dr P. CHAUCHARD

MORTIFICATION means seeking the disagreeable, looking for pain. It will thus not be out of place if we glance for a moment at the organic substructures of the sensation of pain and see what physiology has to say about the question.

Among the innumerable sensory messages received by the brain, there is a special class which give rise to the sensation of pain. The sensation always brings the affections into play and is always unpleasant. It is not felt in normal conditions; it is an alarm-signal. It occurs in special circumstances, either when there is excessive stimulation from without or when one of the internal organs, though ordinarily insensible, reveals a pathological sensibility conditioned by some sort of functional disorder.

Pain thus has its purpose in the nervous system. Its function appears to be pre-eminently a protective one. As Combemale says, whether it is normal or pathological, it enters into nature's plan. To regard pain from this angle as an element in the harmonious pattern of the human organism is legitimate enough, but there are doctors with great compassion for the sick who consider the idea scandalous. Leriche, for instance, cannot bring himself to regard pain as the 'mere working of a defensive sixth sense'; to his mind, that would be 'monstrous'. He refuses to accept the 'strange metaphysical notion that pain is a gift from the gods, a salutary warning. . . . Pain is neither redemptive nor a warning. It is only a disordered physiological condition.' The reaction is a monstrosity, a discord entirely devoid of purpose.

The two contrasting points of view will both seem justifiable if they are referred to the two contrasting kinds of pain. When I think of the burning sensation I feel if I take up an object that is too hot to hold, I am grateful for the pain because it prevents an irreducible lesion, and I pity the poor man with syringomyelia because he cannot feel it. But when I think of the iron band that sometimes presses on my aching brow and stops me from sleeping or working, I feel that the vasomotor disorders or the variations in the tensions of the cephalorachidian liquid which may have caused the migraine could very well have refrained from manifesting their presence.

There is thus a tendency to regard the two types of pain as opposites. The first kind may be called objective, since it provides information about the hurtfulness of external actions and its cause is well known. This kind of pain, the pain we experience every day, is also the easiest to study in the laboratory, for like all sensory stimulations it can be easily produced and graduated. The other kind of pain is internal and arises for no apparent reason: in general, the cause escapes us. Pain of this type is subjective and is not perceived by the people round us; we have to make its presence known. It is a sign of illness. It is much more difficult to study scientifically. It is persistent and often unbearable and we have to resort to medicine to get rid of it.

Physiologists ought, it is true, to pay more attention to the pain that goes with illness; they have sometimes shown too strong a tendency to confine their researches to cutaneous pain, as it can be made the subject of experiment. But in actual fact, the two kinds of pain are one. Pain is objective in so far as it depends on an external or internal disturbance affecting the receptors, the nerves or the centres of the part of the nervous system concerned with pain. It is unthinkable that a harmonious organism should be capable of suffering in the one case but not in the other. Is not illness, to use Combemale's phrase, the result of complex physiological reactions, which are using normal mechanisms to withstand continued aggression from causes either without or within? 'If it is true that illness often confers on pain an affective character of a fairly lasting kind, it is not that this is attributable to any particular essence but rather that the tissues from which the process starts or those in which it becomes amenable to mental interpretation happen to be in functionally abnormal conditions.'

But in so far as it is a sensation or state of consciousness, pain is particularly subjective. The pain resulting from a given cause will differ from person to person and even in the same will vary according to the state he happens to be in; it may be anything from extreme hypalgesia to the most terrible hyperalgesia. As Leriche says, pain is something people create for themselves; it is their personal interpretation of the facts.

I

Detailed study of cutaneous sensibility and the variations it undergoes in different experimental and pathological conditions shows that there are certain spots the excitation of which produces sensations of touch, while others in similar circumstances cause feelings of heat and cold and prickly sensations. The sensation which informs us that an object is pointed and capable of piercing the integument is due to the mechanical excitation of the free nerve-endings in the skin. These are probably the specific receptors for the feeling of pain (pricking sensation). When the surface of the object exerting the pressure is more extensive, mechanical compression of the cutaneous nerves produces another type of pain, the feeling of being *pinched*. Lastly, certain physical influences (an excessively cold or excessively hot temperature) and certain chemical influences, both external and internal in origin, may produce a chemical excitation of the nerves, perhaps by a discharge of histamine, and so give rise to a sensation of burning and often to an antecedent itching. Different nerve-fibres are responsible for the mild pricking sensation and the much more violent sensations of being pinched and burned. Tactile impulses are conducted at high speed by thick fibres and pain-impulses of the pricking type at a slower speed by medium fibres, while pain-impulses of the pinching type and to a still greater extent those of the burning type travel very slowly along fine fibres, which in many cases are also unmyelinated. There is nothing to distinguish these latter fibres from the sympathetic nerve-fibres, and surgical experiments (Leriche's) show that some

P

of the pain-fibres do in fact reach the centres by a very round-about route *via* the sympathetic system: the happy effects of sympathectomy are not entirely confined to the correction of vasomotor disturbances by the cutting of the centrifugal sympathetic fibres.

The existence of specific receptors cannot, however, be admitted where internal pain is concerned. It is rather to be supposed that in this case all the nerve-formations are sensitive to excessively strong stimuli, whether of a mechanical kind, like traction and the effects of tension or of the chemical variety. The pain-messages in this instance are very pronounced sensory messages which, instead of remaining in the unconscious field of the sympathetic system, manage to secure transmission to the central pathways of pain. Very often the brain cannot decipher these messages of internal origin. It attributes them to the corresponding cutaneous zone, the one from which it is in the habit of receiving messages at the same level in the medulla. This cutaneous pain from internal diseases is very useful in diagnosis. It is more, too, than a mere report: the skin really does suffer, reflexively. Application of an anaes-thetic to the skin will sooth the internal pain.

Cutaneous sensibility to pain is only one kind, then, of sensibility to pain, but it comes to be the most important because in all individuals, quite apart from any pathological cause, pain is so often manifested in that region. It thus becomes a real pain-sense; it specialises in pain for utilitarian purposes and is the nucleus to which other pains are afterwards attached.

Pain usually arises from the excitation of the sensory endings but it may also be produced by irritation of the conducting fibres at any point in their course. The irritation may come from the most diverse of causes, is sometimes latent and can be produced by the slightest vasomotor disturbance upsetting cellular nutrition. There are two contrasting types of pain in the nerves as well as at the periphery. The first type, the one found in ordinary facial neuralgia and in tabetic disorders, consists of sharp pains shooting out from a definite spot in the tract of one of the cerebrospinal nerves. It comes on in fits provoked by excitation of the corresponding cutaneous zone, is accompanied by little in the way of disturbance in the vasomotor or trophic sympathetic reflexes and is soothed by interruption of the nervous conduction. The other type of of pain is just as intense but more agonising. It is dull, diffuse and hard to locate. It burns and smarts. It is continuous and is reinforced by paraxysms, which always entail vasomotors and trophic disorders, and as these in turn help to increase the pain, a vicious circle is set up. Pain of this kind is accompanied by considerable affective modifications; it can change the character and make life impossible. Operations on the sympathetic system are the only things that cause any improvement. The pain felt in the stumps of amputated limbs, and sometimes referred to as the absent limbs, is of this kind, and so are the distressing sensations of a burning type produced in causalgia: an apparently trifling lesion may cause unbearable suffering, as Leriche has shown from observation of a large number of cases. It is this type of pain which makes him refuse to admit that suffering can ever serve a useful purpose.

The peripheral nervous system affecting pain has a central apparatus corresponding to it, a bundle of conducting fibres entering the lateral cord of the medulla towards the thalamus, the great centre where pain-impulses, like all other sensory impulses, are co-ordinated before a final relay-station conducts them to the cerebral cortex, which is the seat of the sensation of pain. There have been important controversies about the respective parts played in the genesis of these sensation by the basal cerebral centres and those in the cerebral cortex. Some think that the cortex is responsible only for the objective sensation of cutaneous pain definitely localised in the body, and that the dull, intense, diffusely localised type of pain is of purely thalamic origin. According to them, the cortex normally exercises a restraining influence, its disappearance in pathological conditions being at the root of the frightful pain felt in the thalamic syndrome. Lhermitte's contention that conscious sensation is always cortical is perhaps more probable. Whereas in the case of definitely localised pain the message arrives at the cerebral neuron, which is specially made for receiving and interpreting it, in the case of dull pain the reception is mainly thalamic and the thing perceived by the cortex as diffusely localised pain is a violent disturbance in the thalamus. Thus, cutaneous sensibility to pain is the only kind that is directly related to the cerebral cortex. 'When the thalamus is disorganised by a lesion', Lhermitte writes, 'integration and consequently transformation of the afferent excitations at the thalamus ceases. The result is that they reach the cerebral cortex without having been worked on and adapted. The cerebral cortex is thus thrown into a commotion by stimuli, currents and waves to which it is not accustomed and it expresses its agitation as pain.'

The importance of the thalamic pain-centres cannot be too strongly emphasised, as it is there, at the unconscious level, thanks to the propinquity of the centres co-ordinating the autonomic motor processes and the centres regulating the equilibrium of the sympathetic system and the functioning of the endocrine glands (especially the hypophysis), that the reflexive diversion of the pain-messages takes place which gives rise to the whole gamut of the objective organic symptomatology of pain, just as diversion towards the cerebral cortex produces conscious sensation. I will not dwell on all the signs of pain (mimicry, tears, visceral signs, secretion of adrenaline, etc.) which indicate that pain disturbs the whole functioning of the organism. These organic disorders have repercussions on cerebral and psychic activity, both of which have been disturbed already by the sensation of pain. In addition, there is the influence exerted by pain on such centres regulating cerebral activity as are localised in this region at the base of the brain, viz., the sleep centres and the waking centre, which are responsible for fainting, and the centres regulating character. Even at the elementary levels, the pain-messages provoke local reflex responses, particularly vasomotor ones. We have already seen how important these reactions are. They are originally meant as correctives, but when they do not take effect they aggravate the disorder.

It is at the thalamic level that pain is integrated into the individual's autonomic instinctive activity and into the elementary affective orientation of that activity: the thalamus is the reflex centre of the emotions.

Most emotions can be produced by any kind of sensory stimulus. Pain and the perception of the disagreeable are the only ones that also have specific receptors, the stimulation of which has always an affective tinge.

In the case of pleasure, the question of the existence of specific receptors, the stimulation of which always has an affectively pleasant tinge, arises in a much more limited form —it occurs in connection with the excitation of the sexual zones; but the specific element is to be found rather in the cerebral interpretation of ordinary tactile messages.

The part the cerebral cortex has to play is not simply to create the sensation of pain and to interpret it; it fulfils an inhibitory function too, which makes self-mastery possible and so enables the individual not to react to pain. But it also increases the causes of pain to an infinite extent, by reason of a conditioning process which enables moral as well as physical pain to appear. The difference between this function of the superior affective forces and the ordinary emotional reflex is enormous, even allowing for the conscious sensation that accompanies the reflex.

Thus, however regrettable the frightful pains found in pathological conditions may be, physiology shows the importance—the necessity, even—of pain for the normal functioning of the human organism; it allays the instinctive feelings of revolt against pain.

II

Why, as Leriche asks, do we not all suffer to the same extent? The reason is that the sensation of pain and the interpretation the brain gives of it depend on the state of the cerebral neuron. If the cerebral neurons are hypersensible, the reaction will be intensified; if they are hyposensible, on the inhibitory side, the reaction will be weaker. Such modifications in cerebral excitability can be seen both in the course of the ordinary physiological functioning of the brain and in various pathological states.

Pain increases with attention and fear; it diminishes when the patient turns his mind from it. A sharp contraction of the jaws, or a deliberate clenching of the fist, will be sufficient to raise the threshold of pain; hence the real utility of those practices. A soldier does not feel his wound so much while he is still on the go. A horse can be operated on without an anaesthetic if it is munching its hay.

It is even possible to reverse reactions to pain by such means. Pavlov made his animals associate a good meal with burning and in the end he obtained a pleasure response to the burning on its own. While not expecting to find too close a parallel to this in human psychology, we can nevertheless see from it what an extensive change a merely physiological modification in the functioning of the brain may make in the attitude to pain.

When modifications in internal conditions have repercussions on the cerebral cortex, they have the same effect: the feeling of pain is less in cases of anoxic stupefaction and it also leaves the patient indifferent. In the course of endocrine affections, there may be a disturbance of the sensibility as a result of modifications in the calcium or the sugar present in the blood. In certain kinds of rheumatism, parathyroid-ectomy has the spectacular effect of removing pain instantaneously.

As the internal chemistry of every individual, and of the same individual at different times, has its own peculiar characteristics, especially with regard to organo-vegetative equilibrium and the rate of hormonal secretion, it will be seen that pain is an essentially subjective thing and that what one person can bear another will find unbearable.

To this must be added the influence of character: the melancholic find everything painful. Education plays a prominent part: people accustomed to seeking relief from every pain they feel—and that is becoming more and more the case today now that such advances have been made in the use of analgesics in therapeutics—come to be incapable of enduring as much as other people. Those who attribute redemptive power to suffering are better placed than those who rebel against it as useless or accept it resignedly.

As late as the Empire period, in the time of Dupuytren and Larrey, the conditions in which operations were carried out were terrible: the patient was fully conscious and was held down by force. No one could bear an operation like that today. 'After years of close attention to the problem of avoiding pain', Leriche says, 'our capacity for feeling pain has become much more subtle and extensive than it was before. Aspirin tablets and anaesthetics have done more to make us afraid of pain than any hypothetical loss of moral energy.' For many people today, learning to bear a moderate degree of pain without taking medicine and to conform to the requirements of hygiene in the matter of sleep instead of taking hypnotics would be an excellent mortification.

Pathology provides us with extreme cases of variation in sensibility to pain. They are interesting to know, because they show how amazing the physiological resources of the human organism are—resources which proper training of the will might perhaps enable us to tap.

Hysterical anaesthesia is of this kind. In a given zone, the patient is insensible to pain-stimuli which would otherwise be unbearable, but the boundaries of the zone once crossed, pain is immediately perceived. The cerebral inhibition involved is a curiously localised thing. Hysterical patients also suffer, on the other hand, from agonising pains, which appear to indicate the presence of organic lesions, although in fact they are hallucinations caused by some form of cerebral disorder. There is often a great difference between pain that is produced deliberately and pain that is felt involuntarily. A man suffering from dementia will sit on a red-hot iron plate or inflict frightful mutilations on himself without feeling anything at all, because the obsession by which he is actuated inhibits all pain, but he will react violently if he is nipped or pricked. The hypnotic insensibility which has been utilised in surgical operations may also be mentioned. A hyperexcitable centre transforms all the excitations it receives into pain. Mere contact will be painful. Sometimes, as in the facial neuralgia described by Baudoin, the charging of the centre seems to go on silently as a result of peripheral excitation, and when the charge is sufficient, the slightest additional excitation brings on an attack.

A curious example of hallucinatory pain is provided by the case of people who, after losing a limb by amputation, feel terrible pains, sometimes of a causalgic nature, in the missing member. The mechanism determining the phenomenon is complex. It is in part peripheral and dependent on excitations arising at the level of the cicatrication neurinoma, excitations which may be eliminated by sympathectomy if it succeeds in producing a cure; but it is also attributable to disturbance of the cerebral processes affecting the mental image of the body. Lhermitte says that an injection of calcium made so as to avoid touching the neurinoma may soothe the pain by acting on the cerebral neurons.

In addition to therapeutic devices aiming at interrupting the conduction of the pain-messages by the use of local anaesthetics or by cutting the nerves, viz. by sympathectomics eliminating both the sympathetic conduction of pain and the vasomotor repercussions which increase it, most analgetic devices aim at diminishing the sensibility of the pain-centres, especially in the cerebral cortex, either by chemical means or by restoring normal psychic activity.[1] Here again, individual susceptibility to therapeutic treatment varies considerably. Some people react to only one type of medicament; operations often have unexpected results.

We are no longer defenceless against pain, but we cannot apply just any therapeutic treatment at random; we have first to examine the alarm-signal, so as to try and discover the cause of the pain and see what remedy to apply. We must also beware of using antalgic medicines more than they are strictly necessary in each individual case, so as to avoid sensibilisation and to prevent people from becoming accustomed to them. It is much easier today to advise people to accept suffering, because in view of the means we now have for relieving pain, acceptance of it really can become a matter for the will to decide on. The great advantage we derive from civilisation should be used for our development and not to deprive us of virility.

To sum up, the modest contribution of neurophysiology to the problem of the voluntary acceptance of suffering is first to show that however painful it may be, suffering is still a reasonable and useful feature in the human organism, a sign of the solidarity of the universe and a thing not altogether independent of free will. In the second place, it stresses the fact that both reactions to pain and the amount of pain that can be borne

---

[1] Surgical isolation of the prefrontal lobe (*lobotomy*) may make pain bearable by making the psychological interpretation of it an impossibility.

without upsetting the organism vary greatly from one individual to another and from one time to another: no fixed rules can be laid down beforehand and codified.

CHAPTER XIV

PSYCHIATRIC CONSIDERATIONS OF THE ASCETIC IDEAL

By Dr GREGORY ZILBOORG, M.D., D.SC.

THE very use of the terms designating the fields of abnormal human behaviour and abnormal mentation raises a question: why should psychopathology impose itself, even intrude itself, into the field of purely religious experiences? And what can it teach the faithful about faith and self-denial which the faithful do not learn through direct religious experience? These are not idle or purely formal questions. They are questions which must be answered not only for the sake of the faithful, but for the sake of the scientific psychopathologist as well.

The first answer that suggests itself is both obvious and practical. It is important to be able to differentiate abnormal from normal mental states. It is important, therefore, for the faithful as well as for the psychiatrist, to differentiate between the refusal to accept food on the part of a pathologically depressed individual and the fasting done as penance. It is important to note the difference between the reflections of the faithful layman or priest about his unworthiness while he carefully examines and re-examines his relations to God, and that state of ruminative, obsessive, self-tormenting doubt which is known at times as scrupulosity and which is a manifestation of a depressive, obsessional state. Such differential diagnosis is important, of course; psychiatry here has a utilitarian, pragmatic value, as much as medicine would have in differentiating hypertension and a state of being ashamed—although both make a man's face red.

However, the purely utilitarian value of psychopathology is not the only one that could interest those dealing with religious problems; it is not even the most important one. The issues are much more complex and more profound. And both psychopathology and religion have common concerns. These concerns are not easy to enumerate but they will become clarified, we hope, as we proceed; suffice it to say that these concerns are numerous and important. In a general way one may state that that which goes on in the human mind, both from the point of view of content as well as form, has been learned empirically mostly through psychopathology. What appears normal is not usually seen by the psychopathologist, or anyone else for that matter; it is through the deviations from the normal functions that medicine (and this does include medical psychology, of course) learns a great deal; it can then reconstruct the concepts of the normal which it is never able to observe directly, but by which it is always guided in the evaluation of human functions.

Psychopathology enriched immensely our knowledge of the human mind, particularly since the discoveries of the dynamics of the psychic apparatus, which is mostly unconscious. But unfortunately, psychopathology, and especially psychoanalytic psychopathology, developed an undue partiality for the abnormal and became inclined to consider as neurotic-pathological, every mental phenomenon which seemed to utilise the same psychological mechanisms as the neuroses. *Now, it is not true that everything that follows the laws of chemistry as we observe them in organic disease is pathological.* The laws of chemistry are the same in organic disease as in health, and health and disease do not differ from one another in this respect. The difference between health and disease lies in the arrangement in the constellations of the by-products and their combinations, which the human individual is at times unable to tolerate biologically and which at times threaten his life. The fact, then, that the same laws of physics, chemistry and psychology are found in disease, physical and psychological, does not make health and religion a disease when we discover in their human manifestations and unconscious dynamics the same laws of physics, chemistry and psychology. The fact that many, if not all, human instincts play an active role in our religious experiences does not make religion an instinct. 'It is wrong to speak of an instinct of religion or an instinct of worship. Religious behaviour has an instinctive basis, but is not itself a primary instinct. Were it so, we should be able to trace its counterpart in the lower forms of animal life, where it would be even more clearly defined than in man.'[1]

Since we have mentioned instincts, we might state now that a great many of our instinctual wishes, i.e., either the instinctual tensions themselves or the goals to which they aspire, are frequently repressed; they remain outside the field of consciousness, in a primitive state of primitive impulses and primitive goals. They would do neither harm nor good and would be of no interest (scientific or spiritual) to anyone were it not for the fact that in their repressed state they retain all the psychological energy which they possessed originally; under certain circumstances, these psychological energies attach themselves to some of the higher and therefore less disturbing functions of our lives and thus 'break through' to expression. In other words, these repressed impulses remain constantly dynamic; when they seem most static, they are actually in search of an outlet. They are always, therefore, either 'almost' kinetic or fully kinetic—and are actually never static. It is this that must be considered as Freud's greatest discovery.

In view of the above, it will be clear if we join with a writer who said: 'Symbols capture repressed tendencies because the unconscious seizes upon the symbols to get displaced outlet for repression. Religion thus draws the forbidden impulses to strengthen belief or action which consciously was intended to have a different character.'[2] This would lead one to agree with another statement by the same writer: 'A life of self-sacrifice, for example, may be the expression of a free and highly developed personality; on the other hand, it may be the outcome of a strongly repressed masochism—a tendency or impulse to seek suffering because of the unconscious pleasure which is derived from it, and which is neurotic. . . .'[3]

Perhaps because of the admixture of neurotic trends in the religious practices of many people, perhaps also because deeply religious states frequently seem to fail to bring happiness to

1 R. S. Lee: *Freud and Christianity*; London, 1948, p. 44.
2 *Ibid.*, p. 91.
3 *Ibid.*, p. 55.

man, so many among the psychoanalytic psychologists began to consider religion itself as a neurosis, or a pathological illusion. Perhaps, therefore, I may be permitted to quote once more from R. S. Lee, who said, 'We should not look for life to be made easy for us. Some people are disheartened when in genuine sincerity they have made some active profession of faith, been converted or confirmed, and find that they still have to struggle against temptations to do evil. Such people have a mistaken idea of what true Christianity offers. It offers the grace and power that come from communion with God to reach heights of living, of self-realisation, and so of happiness, that are impossible without them. But the heights cannot be reached without struggle. To suppose that conversion will make us good in the sense that we shall not have to struggle against sin any more is to indulge in a form of the womb[1] fantasy, for it looks for a spiritual life of security and bliss that comes without our putting forth effort. The Christian cannot hope to find life easier than Christ found it, and the Gospels bear witness to the fact that all that he did cost him great effort.'[2]

To religious people and particularly to priests the above is, of course, self-evident. It bears repetition, however, in so far as there is danger because of this very self-evidence, of a tendency both on the part of the psychopathologist and the religious to misunderstand one another rather completely. Present-day psychology, the one enlightened by the findings of psychoanalysis, not infrequently mistakes religion as a restrictive moral discipline which stands up in arms to combat man's instinctual life. Since psychoanalysis recognised the cardinal importance of sexuality in human psychology and behaviour, any serious attempt systematically to restrict the expression of the basic human instincts is considered wrong and even pathogenic, and therefore, overtly or covertly, psychoanalysis seems to have found itself opposed to religion. On the other hand, psychoanalysis appeared to the uninitiated to be based almost solely on principles of hedonism and, it would follow, of unrestricted sexuality; religion, therefore, found it necessary to turn away from psychoanalysis, because in the eyes of religion it was a

1 Intra-uterine.
2 LEE, *op. cit.*, p. 105.

newer agency of unbridled hedonism which could not be
accepted as a guiding principle of life.

Anyone who takes pains to try to solve this conflict, which
seems at times hopelessly insoluble, is at once struck by the fact
that the problem is really not as difficult as it appears, that the
misunderstanding is not justified by the empirical, clinical findings of psychoanalysis, nor is it justified by the demand which a
true and healthy religious attitude makes on a person.

It is true that psychoanalysis, like any medicobiological discipline, is based on the mechanistic principle of a utilitarian or,
if you wish, hedonistic teleology and determinism. This is as it
really should be, because a science always works within a closed
system, and this restriction represents both the advantages as
well as the limitations of any science. But despite these limitations psychoanalysis has made a great contribution to the
labours of those who are in search of a true philosophy of life.
Psychoanalysis itself, like physics or mathematics, permits of a
number of generalisations and syntheses; but not a single one of
these scientific disciplines, nor all these disciplines taken together, can be made into a philosophy of life. It is the mass of
empirical data which these disciplines offer to philosophy and
religion which represents their true contribution to philosophy
and religion. In this respect, despite its desultory excursions into
materialistic philosophy and even anti-religious intellectualism,
psychoanalysis has made a major contribution to the greater
understanding of religious life. This again is as it should be,
because no true empirical findings of facts in human nature can
contradict the fundamental religious truths; what is more, the
more correct and the more fundamental these facts are, the
more they are found to support rather than to contradict the
religious truths dealing with the destiny of man. The confusion
and mutual suspicion and distrust that surround the relationship of psychoanalysis and religion are due to many causes;
without considering any of these causes in particular, we may
say that they would all fall under the heading of reciprocal
ignorance resulting in most cases in an active opposition to learn
something about one another.

Nothing, therefore, could be more welcome than the work of
this study group, which is both an auspicious undertaking and

an enlightened effort to understand and to produce a synthesis rather than to disregard and to reject various particulars.

Let us clear up one misunderstanding which stands in the way of dealing with our main topic.

The hedonistic trend, the pleasure principle, on which psychoanalysis is supposed to be based, was discarded by psychoanalysis itself over twenty years ago when Freud wrote his *Beyond the Pleasure Principle*. And in one of his earliest writings, *Studies of Hysteria*, Freud concluded one of his essays by saying: And if our patients ask us whether they will be happy after they are psychoanalysed, we should answer, 'We will try to relieve you of your symptoms, and this will leave you with the unhappiness common to mankind.' As you see, Freud did not exclude unhappiness, suffering, from health. You may be psychologically healthy, and yet have to struggle with many forces within and outside of yourself, and suffer the pain of the struggle, and *live* the suffering as an integral part of your life. It is not true, therefore, that every suffering within the supposedly normal person is a neurotic symptom. It is still less true that every suffering when it is constant and perhaps a direct result of the given activity chosen is masochism—as so many would mistakenly insist. Suffering is masochism only when it is a perversion, when it leads directly to sexual gratification or when it is a singular substitute for it. This type of suffering is deeply neurotic from the point of view of psychoanalysis, and this type of suffering was specifically recognised by the Church as not leading to sainthood, and as being unworthy of the attitude of Benedict XIV toward this problem.

What kind of 'unhappiness common to mankind' did Freud have in mind? Freud's conception of a normal person was very briefly this: a person who in his growth and development from childhood reaches *genital* adulthood. By 'genital' Freud meant not the physiological-sexual maturity which is commonly known as genital, but that state of psychological development in which the various infantile, partial, hedonistic ('sexual' in the Freudian sense) impulses become synthesised in such a way that the sensual-egocentric (infantile-sexual) drives become adult-altruistic and the infantile, exclusive love for the object outside one's self (father and/or mother, and/or sister or brother) becomes love for other people. The earlier infantile impulses are all characterised not only by an egocentric, narcissistic sensuality, but by a sort of utilitarian, mercenary love bestowed on others only if and when one gets something for it. This utilitarian love is also an unsteady love, which becomes hate rather easily at the first experience of frustration; it is a mixed, ambivalent love in which anxiety and anger, aggressiveness, fear and cowering passivity are all combined in unequal proportions and in a state of considerable lability.

All these states and processes are unconscious, of course, and their psychological representations are unconscious. The *behaviour* of the individual is subject to direct observation, but the unconscious can be uncovered only by special psychoanalytic techniques. The adult, object-libidinous state is also unconscious. And, of course, it never reaches its absolute completion; the weight of the infantile drives and of the various stages of adolescence, with all their unconscious constellations and charges of psychological energies, is carried over in varying degrees into the adult, object-libidinous stage. If too many of these early burdens are carried over, either the object-libidinous stage is never reached or its proper function is interfered with, and then we deal with neuroses of varying severities. But if the primacy of the object-libidinous state is established, the adult ego lives a normal life, and within the frame of this normal life, the adult has to struggle to live with or overcome some of the leftovers of socially modified, infantile drives. This struggle is apparently what Freud had in mind when he spoke of 'the unhappiness common to mankind'. In other words, 'normality' or 'adulthood' is not a state which can be attained once and for all, and once attained, basked in without any difficulties or concerns. At its very best it is something which must be maintained, sustained, held on to, to avoid regressions to earlier levels, to avoid too much anxiety, to avoid being thrown into too much psychological passivity which thwarts initiative and original thought and independent activity, to avoid the mobilisation of too much unconscious hostility which robs one of the object-libidinous, altruistic, paternal and fraternal attitude toward one's equals. Such unconscious hostility makes a man live on the forces which give him a sense of power over others. This sense of power may be expressed in many ways: through the acquisition of unnecessary wealth, through a sense of megalomania which thwarts a man's rational choice to exercise his will in the direction of object-libidinous interest and instead evokes in him the captious, impulsive, yet persevering, all-powerful egocentricity which gives the illusion of great will-power.

This is as far as Freud went in his psychological findings with regard to man's place in the world and in the society in which he lives. Freud's Eros is an Eros which painfully grows from the state of purely biological urges and whims of the infant to the altruistic, creative synthesis of adulthood. Neither Freud nor the Freudian analysts went any further, not because they did not consider it important, nor because they considered it difficult (although some of them did), but because this is the natural limit of psychoanalysis. Its sphere is man's relationship to Eros from the crib to complex social life, and the vicissitudes of Eros from the relative simplicity of childhood to the synthesised complexity of adulthood. Caritas and Agape have remained outside the field of psychological analysis; it is to be hoped that Caritas and Agape, their psychological dynamics and place in the life of man, will be the subject of study of future psychoanalysts. Certain it is that in order to study Caritas and Agape, one will have to learn to observe them and then study their phenomenology as well as their dynamics. Heretofore the Freudian adult logos and adult Eros seemed to be the limits of psychoanalytic studies and Caritas and Agape were left to the religious as purely unscientific. This attitude, while it estranged analysis from religion and from true religious psychology, was nevertheless a good thing, because Caritas and Agape are intimately interwoven with the problem of values, and a science which preoccupies itself with highly evaluative problems, particularly such a young science as psychoanalytic psychology, is apt to get lost in confusion between the psychological phenomena as they are and the moral values they either represent or flout.

That is why the deeper religious problems have hardly ever been touched by psychoanalysis. In its whole literature we find, for instance, only one article on asceticism, which was published a quarter of a century ago. As could be expected, the author did

Q

not understand the problem very well; to him asceticism meant
primarily self-denial of sexual pleasure, and he saw in it a particular form of search for power, overlooking the fact that the
ascetic in his self-denial of genital eroticism also denies himself
the will to be rich as well as the will to have power.

However, the cardinal psychological problem with which
one is confronted in the consideration of the ascetic ideal and the
striving to fulfil it is not so much which psychological mechanisms are involved in the formation of this ideal and which in its
exercise. As has been said, mechanisms *per se* do not yield much
information as to true psychological characteristics; it is the
total constellation of man's primary instincts which matters. It
is obvious that I do not feel qualified to subject asceticism to a
proper psychoanalytic examination. Neither my personal
experience nor the neurotic experiences of those religious persons who have come to me for medico-psychological help suffice.
They do not suffice for the formation of a definitive formulation,
but they do permit me to attempt to formulate a few preliminary conclusions, some tentative thoughts on the subject.

A few years ago, while studying the psychological dynamics
of current social prejudice, I made a list of things the prejudiced
say against those who are the subject of their prejudice. This
list proved both surprising and, for a moment, disconcerting
and revealing. I was interested in what the anti-Catholic has to
say about the Church and its priests, what the anti-Semite says
about the Jews, the Southerner in the United States about the
Negro, the capitalist about the labourite, and the labourite
about the capitalist, the communist about the capitalistic
bourgeois, and the capitalistic bourgeois about the communist.

Whatever was said, it all could be summarised as follows: the
prejudiced usually accuses the group against which he is
prejudiced of being rather keen intellectually, but ill-willed,
perverse, well-organised, power-seeking. He accuses it of being
a closed group whose members stand together to acquire all
riches and power at the expense of others and to keep them for
themselves in order to enjoy life 'fully', that is, to enjoy the full
sensual gamut of one's instinctual urges. The members of the
group are accused, in short, of sexual incontinence and promis-
cuity, of accumulating worldly riches, and of seeking to estab-

lish and keep their power over others. What struck me in all this is the essential psychological uniformity with which blind prejudice would accuse a monastic order and the communist regime of exactly the same things—a drive for sexuality, riches and power.

But what impressed me even more was the unique characteristics of monastic vows, which demand chastity instead of unrestricted sexuality, poverty instead of riches, and obedience instead of power. As one thinks of it all, one is impressed with the depth of intuition which the Christian ascetic ideal displays (you will permit me, of course, to speak here only in psychological terms). I was led to the conclusion that prejudiced people always project on to others those things which they themselves are unconsciously tempted to have and to be and to which they do not dare to confess within themselves. I was led to the further conclusion that the ascetic ideal is inwardly cognizant of this fact, and that it demands conscious and deliberate renunciation of those drives, which renunciation various non-ascetic individuals and groups factually accept. Ultimately, however, they project these drives on to others who are the victims of their prejudices.

I was led to one further conclusion which I did not state at the time I published my paper on 'The Psychopathology of Social Prejudice', namely: Only the struggle of various partial sexualities for expression, only the incomplete synthesis of Eros in the adult makes prejudice (hate) possible and makes possible the contingent projections of the pseudo-socialised, pseudo-sublimated erotic drives, such as drives for power (in its form of extreme sadism), drives for worldly possessions (in its form of extreme lecherous avarice) and orgiastic restlessness which becomes sensual depravity. All three of these drives or groups of drives came to their tragic and catastrophic expression in the Nazi philosophy and practice, which was acquisitive, sadistic and sensual to the point of reducing the male and female humans to machines for the mass production of future German guardians of Nazi-exclusivism.

As I said above, in the so-called normal life of normal civilisations, these crassest drives of man are usually projected on to others by the aberrations of prejudices and this is more or less a normal phenomenon. Therefore, as long as we stop and do not go beyond the limits of formal normalcy established by psychoanalysis, it is really impossible to visualise a greater and deeper ideal. It is impossible, not because psychoanalysis does not recognise one, but because the business of psychoanalysis is to investigate the human psychic apparatus and to establish the psychobiological level which it must reach to be healthy—and that is all. However, psychoanalysis does demonstrate that there is no health without the transformation of our sexual instincts into the constellation of an altruistic ego; therefore, in the final analysis, psychoanalysis points not only to that which is healthy but to that which is good. As I said before, it stops at the culmination of erotic adulthood. The whole concept of Eros in Freud is Platonic in origin, and it is nothing against Freud if we find that his Hellenic Eros coincides with the psychobiological unit that is man but does not cover the formation of those masses of trends which we might call ego ideals and which, while rooted in Eros, do in our utopian and religious actions transgress beyond the confines set by Eros. Fr M. C. D'Arcy, s.j., quoting Simmel, says: 'The Hellenic Eros is a will-to-have, even when it is used in the nobler sense of the desire to have the loved person as an object for ideal instruction, ethical training and education in culture. It is for this reason that love for the Greeks is a middle-state between having and not having, and consequently must die when its aim is attained.'[1]

We cannot go here into the details of differentiation between Eros and Caritas and Agape, and we shall have to limit ourselves to the more or less dogmatic statement that Caritas and Agape are not states that can be fully reached without one's having reached a sufficiently high level of psycho-biological erotic organisation. If we were to limit ourselves to the purely phenomenological and formal aspects of human behaviour, we might fall into a pit of truly miserable errors. For instance, a very anxious, neurotically frightened person who unconsciously runs away from genitality might become impotent. Pragmatically his lack of exercise of his genital functions may be looked upon as being the same as that of the one who is abstinent on moral, religious grounds, but I need not tell this gathering or

[1] M. C. D'ARCY, *The Mind and the Heart of Love*; New York, 1947, p. 61.

any gathering of psychoanalysis how vast a difference there is in psychological content and dynamics between abstinence and impotence. The neurotically impotent is a passive individual unable to love, unable to achieve erotic adulthood; the abstinent individual must first achieve erotic adulthood to be able to abstain from the exercise of its demands. The healthy sexuality which psychoanalysts have in mind is not the sexuality which must constantly express itself, but the one which is capable of expressing itself fully if one permits it to do so. There is no question of conscious will in a case of impotence. The same and similar differences can be found between shy, neurotic passivity and inability to be independent, and that powerful self-control which enters into the practice of conscious obedience. The same and similar differences can be found in the aspirations to be rich and in the self-conscious acceptance of the ideal of poverty.

As in the case of 'the unhappiness common to mankind', man does not necessarily become happy, free from suffering, through the mere acceptance of the ascetic ideal of chastity, poverty, and obedience. Acceptance of the ideal carries with it the need for a constant struggle with those genital and pregenital forces (I am continuing to use the Freudian terminology) into which our personality breaks up, or to which our personality is drawn, or which come up within us as unwelcome irritants as soon as we voluntarily and deliberately suppress one of our major instinctual drives. There is always, therefore, a certain amount of suffering present, as Regamey pointed out when he said, 'The absence of suffering from the practice of poverty proves that detachment has not gone far enough.' (Mgr Ancel.)[1] There is not only suffering but discomfort, that state of a sense of privation which Freud found to be present in our daily civilised life. 'In the whole context in which religious poverty is to be found, and which governs it, there will be room for an appearance of excessive unreasonableness. We might even say, with Father Chevrier, that there can be no true religious poverty without inconvenience, discomfort, suffering and a certain "ill-being".' The fundamental struggle between that which man is psycho-biologically and psycho-socially, and that which

1 P. R. REGAMEY, *La Pauvreté religieuse*. Supplement, *La Vie Spirituelle*. Paris, 1948, p. 380.

man aspires to be by accepting Agape as an Ego ideal, is very simply and very beautifully stated by Regamey when he quotes Fr Chevrier and says: 'He who has the spirit of poverty always has too much and tends always to be cutting down. He who has the spirit of the world never has enough, is never content and always wants something more.'[1]

In this simple description more than merely one of the principles of the ascetic ideal is stated; the root of the psychological problem is exposed to our view most poignantly. One cannot repeat too often that the ascetic ideal of poverty does not represent the absence of the acquisitive instinct, nor its atrophy, nor a neurotic overcompensation covering its hypertrophy; it represents, rather, a conscious rejection of a 'healthy' acquisitive instinct and a refusal to obey its demands. What this rejection might entail we will mention presently. In the meantime, let us bear in mind that there were people whose intuition was so great that they perceived and took into account a number of data which were later yielded by laborious psychoanalysis—all this without perhaps being even acquainted with Freud's writings.

I would want to cite one of these men as a particularly good example. I have in mind Fr Yves de Montcheuil, who said about the ascetic ideal: 'It is not a question of conforming to a particular pattern or of making oneself wise or holy, but of surrendering all one's forces to charity.'[2] In other words, the ascetic ideal is not a narcissistic, egocentric ideal, not a form of neurosis which springs from one's anxious, neurotic inability to accept life; rather, it is an object-libidinous ideal coming from other sources which have not yet been sufficiently studied. It is important, however, to say again that the neurotic denial of life has nothing to do with it. Fr Montcheuil has stated this with unique psychological acumen when he said, as if foreseeing the objections of some sensual, hedonistic psychologists: 'Christian asceticism springs not from a conviction that the world is evil; it is not inspired by contempt for life and joy. One must deliberately reject asceticism of this kind—gloomy, sullen, distrustful and suspicious—for it is no more than a caricature of Christian asceticism.'[3] This growing up to life and acceptance

1 *Ibid.*, p. 379.
2 YVES DE MONTCHEUIL, *La Vie Spirituelle*, Paris, 2nd edition, p. 142.
3 *Ibid.*

of the ascetic ideals, despite the acceptance of all that is good in this life, is a complicated process, because 'the notion of asceticism carries with it the idea of a practice which has an irksome and onerous character, of something deliberate and methodical'.[1] This testimony of some one who himself espoused the ascetic ideal with profound devotion and success is serious and ample testimony of great psychological value. For the problem with which scientific psychoanalytic psychology is confronted here is quite complex and perhaps even baffling. But let us look again at Fr Montcheuil before we attempt a tentative, final formulation. We know what it is to be in the throes of human actualities despite one's complete abandon to Caritas, · for he tells us: 'Charity having come upon us meets with obstacles to its expression in our lives. There is in us an involuntary love of evil, and consequently an aversion to good, which does not disappear simply by virtue of receiving grace. There are in us baser desires which seek satisfaction at the expense of loftier ones. There are egoistic tendencies which impel us to help ourselves rather than our neighbour, and which make us pass him by in order to subject him to our designs. There is a tendency towards amusement which hinders the concentration necessary for prayer. There is the fury that carries us away, and the idleness that ties us down—one could go on listing them for a long time.'[2] It would be difficult, if not impossible, to summarise the whole mass of instinctual struggles which Fr Montcheuil so completely enumerated. He uses evaluative terms, of course, because he looks upon all the enumerated difficulties as tendencies toward that which is bad. But if we examine these tendencies regardless of their moral value or immorality and look upon them as various instinctual drives which are common to man in his individual and social life, we cannot help but be impressed with the extraordinary insight of Fr Montcheuil into the actual psychological processes which make up the energy of human behaviour.

As we have said, it so happens that in the scheme of the drives which make up man's life and living in relation to his own corporal self and to his environment, no important or sufficiently

1 *Ibid.*, p. 136.
2 *Ibid.*, p. 137.

intense drive can be consciously suppressed or unconsciously repressed without this drive breaking down into its more primitive infantile components and either producing psychogenic symptoms or offering some other outlet for the repressed or suppressed drives. The outlet on such occasion will be of an inferior, more infantile nature; therefore, the whole process is considered to be first a breaking-down of a synthesised drive into its component parts and, second, a regression to the level of these components, to an earlier, infantile level. Thus, a repression of genitality would produce a regression to a sadistic level, which socially might express itself in the form of an intensified drive for power or an intensified avariciousness, which in turn would lead to that dubious ideal of accumulating a great amount of money as soon as possible so as to be able to retire as young as possible and thus be able 'to enjoy life', to do nothing, like a foetus living at the expense of its mother's metabolism—an ideal of highly socialised parasitism.

It is, therefore, particularly noteworthy that the ascetic ideal of Caritas gives us corporeal genitality and, as if knowing (or because of knowing) the danger, it cuts off also the paths to which such a suppressed genitality might go—power and riches. What the obscure psychological processes are by means of which psychological genitality in the highest sense of the word is preserved, thus making human beings function in a manner both serene and healthy, is a question which even modern psychology, with all its exploratory capacity to enter the deeper layer of the unconscious, is as yet unable to answer scientifically. Perhaps it never will be able to do more: like biology, which knows so much about life and its attributes and manifestations and is yet unable to say what life is.

Chapter XV

OBSTACLES TO THE REALISATION OF THE ASCETIC IDEAL

By N. MAILLOUX, o.p.

TO cure oneself of one's faults is the most difficult thing in the world. It is always disconcerting to see how they persist in spoiling the beauty of lives which in other respects are as disciplined and brave as could be wished. A scholar or an artist may fill his days with hard, unremitting toil and yet will never, perhaps, succeed in repressing the impulse of vanity, ridiculous though he plainly sees it to be. An administrator may be capable of dealing with the most diverse matters, yet time after time he will have to reproach himself with lack of promptitude in the despatch of urgent business. The man who gives his services in the cause of charity will find, in spite of his devotion and disinterestedness, that he is constantly brushing aside a passing feeling of disgust as he sets himself against the small-mindedness that mars even the most worthwhile undertakings. The devout layman makes the sacrifice of rising early every morning to go to Mass, but the few minutes he spends in church he cannot keep free from distraction.

And we cannot leave the sphere of the conscious without pointing out another class of failings, to which people are apt to give the appearance of virtue, the better to avoid the necessity of correcting them. The faint-hearted do their best to hide their fear of even the most reasonable risks by making perpetual appeals for caution. The timid, passive underling at once sees in obedience a convenient excuse for prolonging the complicity that pays him so well. Economy provides the miser with an excellent pretext for depriving his dependants of necessities. The claims of justice become more exacting when they offer an opportunity for vengeance on an enemy or the removal of a dreaded rival. And only too often, enthusiasm for the common good and its defence has served as a cloak for the activities of ambitious go-getters. In these cases, the indulgence is not explicable, as it was in the others, by fear of intense, sustained effort. But although these deviations are far from assuming the proportions of open vice—although they display themselves to the modest extent which is all that respectable persons will allow—they yet bear all the signs, it must be admitted, of conniving at the satisfaction of tendencies bent on securing full acceptance for themselves. Recovery is not to be had simply by shaking off listlessness and setting about things with greater determination: from the outset we must be prepared to encounter long, stubborn resistance.

A mere glance thus shows something of the deformity in so many human lives that are generally regarded as balanced and fruitful. In spite of ourselves, we are struck by the spectacle of a mind and will capable of vigorous self-assertion in some directions but quickly caving in or even ceasing to function at all the moment they turn in others. At first sight, we find it difficult to understand how such opposite qualities can exist side by side in so many of the people we esteem and love. How can evident childishness go with a high degree of maturity, weakness bordering on prostration with an energy that surmounts the most formidable obstacles, hesitation and the inconsistency that follows it with clear-sightedness and firm determination, pettiness that is almost common with a certain nobility of mind and character?

The apparent contradiction is always a source of surprise and disappointment; and yet we know very well that the only lives that are not self-contradictory are lives that have reached a degree of perfection bearing the stamp of heroism—the lives of the saints. But the deformity we are so quick to notice in other people and so ready to believe almost non-existent in ourselves calls for an explanation. Those psychologists who confine themselves within the limits of the strictly descriptive method have one ready to offer: the attitudes and traits that make up the personality are mere bundles, they say, of specifically distinct characteristics, acquired and developed independently of one another and in a manner far from uniform. But psychologists who take up a dynamic standpoint refuse to be imposed upon by the diversity of the phenomena: they try to probe beneath the surface and see how in spite of appearances the individual preserves his functional unity. Thus it is that in the border-land between reason and sense-activity they discover two zones, a peaceful one devoid of conflict and a more or less troubled one in which conflict is the rule. In the first zone, the forces functioning side by side are so arranged as to avoid any break in continuity and the links between the two sets of forces are securely kept in position. The sway of stability, order and real creativeness extends as far as the limits of this zone. In the other zone, however, things wear a very different look. There, reason and sense-activity face each other rather like two armies, each bent on invading territory to which the other denies it access. The pattern formed by the forces along the dividing-line changes all the time: a rapid advance may be made at one point but a forced retreat will be noted at another, and elsewhere again firm resistance may be reduced to the mere marking of time. In these cases, the prevalent pattern is marked by stiffness and inconsistency; almost the only thing accomplished is defence. But it is important to realise that on both sides a certain degree of functional and dynamic unity is preserved throughout, in spite of the varying fortunes of the fray. Yet unless the ultimate outcome is either the triumph of reason or a thorough breakdown of sense-activity or the psychic apparatus, this unity must inevitably rest on a compromise. The kind of organisation I am thinking of is the sort kept up by structures dependent on neurosis or character. In spite of their relative utility, such forms of organisation to a large extent withdraw the psychic apparatus from the influence of the reason and prevent it from serving to the full as the natural instrument the reason needs.

These few considerations are enough to show something of the close connection between spiritual progress and the psychological structures governing the use of the dynamic activity within the individual. In other words, the moralist is of necessity interested in what psychology has to say about the nature, origin and independence of those structures. He must learn to distinguish clearly the extent of the influence which free will can exert on conduct in any given case and to appraise the troublesome consequences of its absence. Where the dynamic activity is concerned, he must also ascertain the precise range open to every course of behaviour—whether it be pursued firmly, unsteadily or with total want of resolution—according to the structure resorted to in times of difficulty. Those are the main points I propose to look at here, in the hope of promoting a more concrete understanding of the moral life and of drawing attention to the things that paralyse development in the most ordinary, normal conditions.

When we have occasion to live continuously for some little time with the same people, we sooner or later come to discern in them three different types of behaviour, which assume modalities sharply enough defined to warrant us in assigning them to three sources: personality, character, and neurosis. We have begun to explore all three, though not with the same degree of precision in each case. Though fully recognising the very great importance of the metaphysical implications involved, we yet need not dwell on them at the moment; we may from the outset adopt the viewpoint of the natural sciences.

When a metaphysician tackles the problem of the human person and its characteristic properties, he is hardly concerned at all, at bottom, with the particular conditions in which the human person may develop, the pitch of maturity it may reach or the extent to which it may achieve a stable balance. In his eyes, the child is as much a human person as the adult, the man of unstable equilibrium as much as the man who makes full use of the means at his disposal, the lunatic as much as the man of sound mind: they all possess the same essential characteristics and are all endowed with the same natural privileges.

The psychologist, however, will at once be struck by the fact that Peter has more personality than Paul and that Paul is of a more unbending character than Peter or that he shows all the signs of being neurotic, perhaps chronically so. What the psychologist studies is the functioning of a particular kind of dynamic activity; he tries to see how it works and to gain some idea of its effectiveness. His first concern is to trace the factors determining present conduct either overtly or covertly. But he does not stop there, for the section he thus obtains is too superficial to enable him to foresee what direction the life of the individual under observation will probably take. If he is to do that, he must make an accurate assessment of the opposing forces and see how they are distributed in the individual's internal mechanism. As there is only a limited quantity of energy available, some knowledge of the strength of the charges now being accumulated for release in a given direction is essential to the prediction of future reactions. And if the psychologist wants to give a full explanation of the behaviour he is observing, and particularly if he undertakes to modify its course, he will have to reconstruct the whole process of which that behaviour is the culmination.

I will give an example to make my meaning clear. A jealous attitude will have a quite different import according as it is merely a rather exaggerated reaction to a provoking situation or the fruit of a projection or a means of self-defence against latent homosexual impulses. Will confronting it with the facts be sufficient to dispel it, or must it be regarded as a prelude to unfaithfulness or paranoid dementia? Is it chiefly determined by fixation at an earlier stage or by a momentary regression? All these questions call for solution by the investigator of concrete cases.

But before beginning this analysis, it is essential to determine from exactly what sources the given behaviour springs. From a superficial examination, it may seem identical in all who practise it; but if we observe it attentively as it becomes more manifest, we shall soon notice considerable differences, dependent on different modalities of dynamic expression and incapable of being reduced one to another.

To acquire a basis for comparison, we will start with the normal and first study the case of the man whose personality has attained its full development, i.e. the man in whom the dynamic attributes of the person—reason and free will—have gained a firm hold over the psychic apparatus. In such a man constant effort, well thought out, has made possible the organisation and consolidation of dynamic patterns corresponding to his many functional potentialities in the way of art, science and virtue, and these give additional perfection and vigour to his natural dynamic activity. Let us stop for a moment and watch a man like that at work in some field of his own choice.

He may be taking part in a tennis tournament and finding

himself in the grip of a formidable opponent, or he may be at the wheel of a car and suddenly have to negotiate a dangerous corner. We can be sure that in both cases he will promptly and with ease take whatever action the situation requires, even though this is probably the first time it has been demanded of him. His great clarity of mind enables him to see the situation as it really is, with all the factors involved, and to solve the problem it presents. Moreover, even if his emotion is intense enough to rob him of his calm, he knows all the time that it is sustaining his activity and not enfeebling it.

The situation is very much the same when he exercises his calling as a thinker. He at once grapples with every difficulty as it occurs and goes on formulating fresh hypotheses until he reaches the ultimate solution. When he has a temptation to avoid or an act of virtue to perform, he behaves unhesitatingly like an ascetic, for whom the more perfect choice, the one excluding all compromise with evil, is the only one possible.

In short, it is easy to foresee the line of conduct he will follow: the course he will take is the one his reason prescribes and his will freely chooses. His autonomy is complete, because nothing in him is outside the scope of consciousness and choice. His psychic apparatus offers him no resistance and plays its part as *instrumental cause* as perfectly as nature intended. With the adaptability of the perfect tool, it subordinates its own ends to those of the agent using it, so much so that it merges its own dynamic movement in the agent's and helps him to achieve the most ambitious of aims. We must hasten to add that because the psychic apparatus fulfils this function it is not therefore to all intents and purposes enslaved, as people so often seem to imply. There is no slavery about it and nothing that leads to paralysis or annihilation; in fact, the contrary is the case. Fulfilment of this function is a step up for the psychic apparatus, a source of emancipation and the means of imparting to its working a touch of reason and freedom.

Let us see now what happens when the principal part in the determination of action is played by character. We must not in this case expect to find superior dynamic activity perfecting the natural dynamic units, so that whenever they are wanted they can be brought into play without the use of force and will remain braced for an effort of adaptation, creation or invention which, for the power concerned, will represent the height of its capacities. Instead of that, we at once come upon fixed, unyielding character traits, which always direct activity into the same unvarying channels. With regard to reality, any new or unexpected situation is likely to have a more or less completely incapacitating effect. It will be the same if the affections awake and begin to express themselves with greater spirit than usual or if ideas coming into the mind call for action that has not been foreseen. Far from discovering the appropriate solution, the one that circumstances demand, a man will then fall back on the tricks he already knows or resort to merely conventional expedients; he will refuse to grapple with such elements of the situation as are not thoroughly familiar to him, because they demand that he should make certain changes in the way he normally behaves. If an emotion threatens to assume somewhat more ample proportions than usual or to steer him in a direction where he has never penetrated, he will at once damp it down and keep it severely in check. He may suffer the outline of the new plan of action to be filled in without offering any opposition, but only if there is no question of putting the plan into effect at once. In short, whether it takes the form of sublimation or whether it shows itself as escape or as reaction-formation, a character trait is always more of a defence mechanism than a judicious device for utilising the available means of action to good advantage. That is the justification of the comparison which likens character itself to a suit of protective armour, its few openings being just as lacking in flexibility as the surrounding steel and allowing the accumulated stock of available energy to express itself only in one determined way and on a limited scale.

From a strictly psychological point of view, the attitudes resulting from such modes of functioning may represent a reasonably happy or momentarily satisfying adaptation. But anyone who looks at the situation from the point of view of the values involved will find it difficult not to conclude—very often at any rate—that there are real defects in it, or defects camouflaged as good qualities, as is shown by the examples given at the beginning of this chapter. Again, a lengthy process of rationalisation will have made such attitudes more or less syntonic to the ego: they will have managed to become an integral part of the ego without arousing any real anxiety. It will thus be seen what clear thinking, honesty and determination will be needed to unmask them and get the better of them.

We cannot stop to deal with the case of those whose behaviour depends on some neurotic structure, for the very good reason that genuine asceticism is out of the question for them until they are cured. A man with a limp cannot train for racing, neither can a neurotic train in real earnest for virtue. As they are both in a very weak state, the most that can be expected of them is that they should just manage to go on without falling, that their conscious wills should not to any extent connive at impulses which they are powerless to keep in check.

We may sum up the situation in a few words if we remember that in these cases, both dynamic activity with its adaptability and effectiveness and the rigid paralysing character trait are replaced by the symptom. In other words, there is a compromise and the thing repressed breaks out again and invades the territory of the ego, which is powerless to turn it to account or even to divert it into a by-pass so as to prevent it from unduly disturbing the working of the whole. Thus confused and swamped, the ego will evidently feel the full weight of anxiety as it realises that it is in the grip of impulses coming from without and unacceptable to it. With the very inadequate means of defence which as yet are all that it has at its disposal, it will strive to limit the extent of the disaster and protect the zones more immediately exposed to danger.

But what is the source of the great difficulty that so much slows down the upward drive towards human perfection, even though the aspirations of all our spiritual energies go out towards that perfection and it is in the last resort a requirement of our nature, the fulfilment which is its due? What unconscious resistance at once thwarts the desire for asceticism which is felt with such intensity in early adolescence, i.e. at the time when human freedom begins to try and assert itself with some degree of consistency, and afterwards accentuates the indifference, distaste or dismay which lead to the continual postponement of the attempt to realise the ideal dimly apprehended and accepted by the mind? For centuries those whose business is the care of souls have been waiting for an answer to that question. Depth-psychology ought to be able to give them it.

Like the psychologist, the moralist is well aware that man is born free in the same sense in which he is born reasonable, i.e. that he is born with an aptitude for reasoning and an aptitude for free activity but that these will attain their full development, will produce acts that are fully rational, fully free and properly adapted to individual circumstances only when they have undergone a long process of cultivation. Of course, a dynamic inclination is discernible in the will from the very beginning, a natural tendency towards the good in general, a tendency which is at the root of all obligation. But where particular goods are concerned, we are in a state of complete indetermination or ambivalence, or more precisely, we are full of disturbing potentialities: which is at the root of anxiety. That is why we need to seek enlightenment from a branch of psychology capable of informing us about the functional aspects of our freedom at the stage when it is still on the way to self-achievement, still engaged, so to say, in self-creation. We need that as well as the light that moral philosophy and theology can shed, with their more precise and certain illumination of the normative points in the expression of freedom. Both will help us to understand how, with the means available at the various stages of development, we gradually manage to break down the original indetermination.

At the beginning, obviously, the reason is not yet in a position to provide flexible categories for the whole field of thought, divisions which the full rigour of logic, far from making hard and fast, will eventually endow with the greatest possible elasticity. If determination is to be achieved at all in such circumstances, it must be based on imitation or identification, i.e. on the reproduction of norms embodied in the conduct of others; and because they are concrete, those norms will inevitably be fixed, rigid and lacking in adaptability. But all the same, by using them as models, we step out of our original state of indeterminateness with regard to good and evil; and since being free is equivalent to following after the good wherever it leads the way, we may regard ourselves as being at least *materially* free from that time onwards.

R

But we soon come to realise that the good we can achieve in our lives is susceptible of accomplishment in many different ways and that our potentialities of personal development will scarcely allow us to remain set in forms of moral goodness borrowed from other people. In short, before long we reach a point where we must become aware of our own capacity for scaling the heights and resolve to give it full play. In other words, if we want to be *formally* free, we must break down a further form of indeterminateness, the one that stands between us and moral autonomy. And when we have achieved self-determination, we shall have to consolidate it by bravely persevering in the practice of asceticism.

The transition, then, from mere training to asceticism properly so-called presupposes that a step of the greatest importance has been taken, one of those that men have the greatest difficulty in facing; it implies that freedom has been accepted to the full. Our persistent aversion from asceticism and the tendency we have to defer to a very distant future the selfless, unqualified effort it involves simply cloak our reluctance to take stock of our position and hide the anxiety the very thought inspires. It was with great difficulty that we escaped in the first instance from the pressure of the unforeseen and from the chaos in which we were left by the ambivalence of our impulses. We did so with the aid of psychological structures which made the expression of our impulses take certain necessary forms and left no room for the unexpected. Is it surprising that we should feel strongly disinclined for the risk of abandoning the security we derive from acting along the well-known lines, even if we realise that our behaviour is stereotyped and exclusive to an exaggerated degree? Need we wonder at our unwillingness to embark on a fresh adventure? Inevitably, as we contemplate the self-determination that is the characteristic note of freedom, a disquieting vista opens before us and we begin to see ourselves caught again in sheer potentiality. We cannot escape from it unless at every turn we choose what we will do, and choose with a clear head and a resolute will; but these we cannot be sure of possessing while for want of time consistent dynamic orientation is as yet unformed or unstable.

We see, then, what the unconscious motive is that leads us to postpone the correction of our habitual failings with a stubbornness little short of invincible. We shall thus find ourselves in agreement with Dr Juliette Boutonnier when she writes that 'anxiety is the emotion caused by freedom, but only *in the sense that it betokens the coming of freedom and not because it implies the exercise of freedom.* Observation seems to show that when a man has made up his mind and begun to act freely, he ceases to be anxious. The time when he feels anxious is *before* he achieves this free activity, the time when, as we have said, he runs the risk of losing what he already possesses and has not yet obtained what he wants. Kierkegaard was well aware of that, and if he stressed the part played by freedom in the formation of anxiety, he also stated with some emphasis that what caused anxiety was the *capacity* for freedom and not freedom itself. There is a kind of anxiety that comes from the *prospect* of freedom, but there is also a kind of anxiety that is produced by the *prospect* of necessity. 'Anxiety is not an appurtenance of necessity, but neither is it an accessory of freedom.' It lies between necessity and freedom, in that middle region which, as it is the sphere of the possible and the undetermined, is also the condition both of neurosis and of free activity, for neither of these would be comprehensible were it not for the fundamental indeterminateness of the human instincts.'[1]

That is enough to show that our weaknesses of character are as deeply rooted in us as our fear of anxiety. Moreover, unlike symptoms, weaknesses of character are bolstered up by rationalisations, which enable them to preserve some appearance of continuity with the structure of the personality, the framework of which is by this time more or less in place, and therefore they are not very likely to give rise to apprehension or to the feeling that all is not well. In short, the symptom may have its uses but it is also a nuisance, and that is enough to make people want to be rid of it, even if the process will probably involve another encounter with anxiety. Faults of character, however, serve a useful purpose and they generally have the advantage that they appear in the guise of rational and effective means of resisting unwanted impulses. They limit the expression of the affective life and make it rigid, but the perception of this is vague and

1 *L'Angoisse*, Paris, Presses Universitaires de France, 1945, p. 295.

superficial and the temptation of consenting to them for good
and all is one that we are hardly disinclined to resist. The will
has very little hold upon them, for the simple reason that it
depends essentially on their elimination for the proper exercise
of its own powers of self-determination. In other words, it seems
inaccurate to say that we really do correct our faults, for to do
that we should have to give an entirely new shape to a character-
structure fashioned in earliest childhood and incapable even of
analysis. Moreover, experience is there to show that sooner or
later they reappear even in people who fight against them with
the utmost determination and devote the bulk of their forces in
the ascetic field to inhibiting the manifestations of them. There
will be victory—though in the most relative of senses—only to
the extent to which through continual development the personality gains ground from the character and deprives it of its
usefulness. In so far as the psyche obtains emancipation—i.e. in
so far as it comes to share in the life of reason and freedom—it
ceases to need the assistance of automatic mechanisms.

So much for the natural order. Speaking as Christians, we
shall be able to say that to be free is not just to respond to the
attractiveness of the good; it means responding to the love of
God as well and to that alone. When the boundary is reached,
when the time comes for transcending the self-determination
achieved through reason and freedom, there will again be
anxiety, because there will again be indeterminateness. The
anxiety that then supervenes has been compared to the darkness
of night and the experience of the mystics shows how deep and
keen it is. A man can obtain release from this further anxiety
only by identifying his will with the will of God, God's freedom
being more precisely determined than ours—in the active sense
of the term—because it is surer of accomplishing its aim and is
more incapable of evil. Yet the identification of a human will
with God's will is a thing that depends on God's good pleasure.
Hence, to the anxiety flowing from the risk is added the uncertainty belonging to a period of waiting. But here psychology can
only stutter and stammer; it had best keep silent about these
things.

To end with, we must see exactly what attitudes men take up
towards the ascetic ideal, not in the realm of speculative con-

viction but in real life. For this purpose we shall rely on the plain results of clinical experience, even though they may somewhat disconcert the over-optimistic charity of the confessor, the spiritual director and the educator, all of whom are apt to place extensive trust in the good intentions of the will and the power of enlightenment to prevail on the mind: they will not readily admit that they are powerless to pierce the armour which they hope one day to break through.

First, a word about the neurotic. The neurotic is a man for whom in the concrete the ascetic ideal can have no meaning. As his conduct is to a large extent governed by necessity, he does not feel that he is free. He is forever lamenting that he does what he does, yet he realises more or less clearly that he has no control at all over his actions. Think, for example, of the extreme case of scruples. The fear of responsibility discernible in the scrupulous shows unmistakably the extent of their desire for reassurance as to their inability to act otherwise than in fact they do. They spend their time protesting that they did not intend things to happen as they did, that their consent was not given to the acts they somehow performed, that their behaviour has something of the reflex about it. They are so afraid of being responsible for evil that the desire to become capable of doing good never takes root in them and they avoid freedom and its risks at all costs. A gnawing sense of inferiority leads them to deny and even destroy the real potentialities they possess, so as not to have to develop them; they shut themselves up in their own passivity and become less and less capable of action.

Those whose behaviour is governed by the automatic reactions their characters prescribe for them do not, however, go as far as that. They feel free with regard to good and evil and in the main they accept their responsibilities. But in comparison with those who have achieved real freedom, they stand as people who have obtained their knowledge from text-books do to men of real learning, who think for themselves and make discoveries on their own. Their freedom is always rather limited and is confined to the bare essentials. Its influence scarcely extends at all to the fine shades which are imposed on human activity by changing circumstances and contribute to the finishing and perfecting of the moral life. We thus have people who in the moral sphere are content to perform actions only half under the agency of freedom; their actions still have about them all the vagueness and unadaptability of the conventional rite or the formality. At best, these people will generally manage to do the right thing, but they will hardly ever do it in the right spirit. They are morally uncouth and the art of inventing a really virtuous form of conduct in which freedom may assert itself to the full—i.e. the art of prudence—is as much beyond them as the art of carving a Moses is beyond the mass-producers of dummy figures for shop-windows.

Lastly, experience provides us with another inference which deserves record—viz. the man whose behaviour is governed by freedom, the man who, as we often say, has a strong personality, is the only one who accepts full responsibility for his actions. If an imperfection in his conduct is pointed out to him, however small it may be, he will not seriously try to excuse it. Just as no one can be always learning and making fresh discoveries unless he realises his mistakes and frankly acknowledges them, so no one can become really free and capable of taking the sort of decision that will make his life a great one unless he realises his faults and bravely admits them to be such. That is the point where depth-psychology can join hands with moral philosophy and moral theology. Depth-psychology is in a position to help people to the clarity of vision and the generosity that will bring them to the threshold of freedom; the moral sciences can give them precise directions about the use to which their freedom should be put and the lines along which they may develop. But when all is said and done, psychologist and moralist alike must realise their limitations whenever they are confronted with a human person and its destined lot. They will perhaps fulfil their respective tasks the better if they remember that it does not depend on them whether a man accepts or refuses the risk attendant on freedom pure and simple, freedom whole and entire, freedom informed by charity.

It seems to me that no one will be able to pass successfully through these critical stages unless he succeeds in integrating the dynamic functioning of his aggressive faculties—in so far as it is opposed to the passivity mentioned above—into the dynamic pattern contrived by love. I thus subscribe wholeheartedly to this further conclusion of Juliette Boutonnier's: 'Freedom, then', she writes, 'is at once the principle of anxiety and the remedy for it. It could be said that if freedom in small quantities causes anxiety, freedom in large quantities cures anxiety. There is an anxious kind of anxiety, the anxiety of the man to whom freedom seems a mere source of catastrophe; but there is also the radiant anxiety of the man who has heard the call to life and has responded with all his being. That fluttering uncertainty with the thread of joy in it I hesitate, really, to call anxiety; and yet there is no other suitable word for it, unless the word hope could be re-endowed with the forgotten meaning to which it owes its inclusion among the theological virtues. It may be that when a man discovers his appointed place in the scheme of things and gives it lasting expression in a particular vocation, he ceases to feel anxiety; but for my part, I think there will always be a corner in the human soul for anxiety—only it will be a non-anxious kind of anxiety, and for that reason no one will think of mentioning it.'[1]

Faced with such facts gathered from empirical observation, a disciple of St Thomas cannot but stress some of the points where the two disciplines meet. This does not imply a trivial, superficial pretence of agreement; it confirms the accuracy of data which are of the utmost importance for the thorough understanding of individual development.

St Thomas often stresses the fact that men are haunted by anxiety to the extent to which their acts escape deliberate determination by their wills acting as their reason directs. He sees, too, that the necessity of acquiring habitus, i.e. of ensuring the full development of freedom in the sphere of its use or exercise, rests on the necessity of escaping from an original state of indeterminateness. He even sees in hope, which sends us in pursuit of the *bonum arduum*, the highest manifestation of human aggressive powers as used in the service of love. And we have only to think of his analysis of what he calls the certitude of hope to see what is meant by the 'non-anxious anxiety' or, to use the more expressive term, the 'radiant anxiety' of the man who has 'discovered his place in the scheme of things and given it lasting expression in a particular vocation': we see that it consists in his

1 *Op. cit.*, p. 301.

striving with all his strength for the good he loves and desires. It is, in short, the anxiety of the man who is aware of the means at his disposal, knows them to be adequate for the end he has in view and is sure of reaching his goal if he uses them to the full, and yet, concurrently with that, feels all the time that he may give way and make mistakes.

Chapter XVI

TENTATIVE CONCLUSIONS

By P. M. ALLEGRE, o.p.

T HE title is deliberately cautious so as to prevent the reader from being led astray by any possibly pretentious implication in the term 'conclusion'. Although the foregoing chapters firmly maintain what they hold to be established truths, they find it necessary to make quite a number of distinctions where innovations are concerned. This fact, as also the intention of the writers themselves, stands in the way of premature inference in a field where the work done has been essentially in the nature of research and no more. Thus the most that can be asked of the present chapter is that it should give an outline-synthesis of the positive elements emerging from the previous chapters. I will therefore confine myself to synthetising for the benefit of the average reader the essential requirements which Catholics should bear in mind when they take the liberty of asking questions about the nature and purpose of asceticism and particularly about the necessity of adapting it to modern needs. To ensure a certain amount of clarity it will be sufficient if we keep to the plan of the book itself. We shall thus be led on the one hand to bring out the characteristics discernible in all forms of asceticism, whatever they may be, and on the other, as man has developed in the course of history, to show in what direction asceticism ought to turn at present if it is to remain Christian without ceasing to be human.

On the first question, the one about the constitutive elements found in all forms of Catholic asceticism alike, the factual and theological statements given in this book and worked out in the light of faith, history and reason are as precise as they are categorical. In view of their teaching, there can be no ground for questioning the justification of renunciation in Christianity. Not only that, but we can also see from it that Christian renunciation is what it is by reason of two invariable and inseparable factors in it. The first of these factors is the realisation that asceticism is a necessary means to holiness but that it is nothing more than a means. This second statement, which is so important for the balance of any spiritual life, depends on the fact that through an absolutely gratuitous intervention on God's part, man has been given friendship with God in and through Christ, a friendship beginning in time but not reaching its full flowering in the vision of God until history is over. This supernatural promotion of man to the vocation of being God's adopted son means that he ought not to want simply to shape his own life like the wise among the pagans. It also means that both our call to friendship with God and the response we make to it all through our lives can have no principle but charity at their beginning and their term. Charity alone can be man's end now that his nature has been made like God's. As the end of humanity is that towards which all free activity should be directed, the end of the Christian life appears as the ever-increasing ascendancy of Christ over us, a progressively closer assimilation to him whose being, life and movement we receive by nature and by grace.

As faith presents us with this vision of man's destiny in the concrete and as by definition asceticism is renunciation, it is clear that asceticism can never be the end of mankind or of Christianity. The end of mankind and Christianity is not refusal but unreasoned acceptance or conscious deliberate seeking, and in so far as it is not yet present, it is matter for hope.

Asceticism is thus of its very nature a relative thing. That is the first conclusion brought to our minds by the theological considerations in the first part of this book. We thus see one of the palpable errors which we must avoid, although many ascetics have succumbed to it in the course of history—asceticism is worthless unless it is placed at the service of the love of God, which is the source and object of our perfection. That does not mean that we should therefore fall into another error, one more dangerous to Christians today than the first one, and all the more specious in that it claims, on the pretext that the primacy must go to love, that asceticism is only optional or that it has had its day.

The merit of this study of asceticism from the doctrinal point
of view is that it reminds us, if we need reminding, that asceticism
is still necessary; and not only that, but that as Christians
we must see it as marked with the sign of the Cross, in conformity with the mystery of our redemption by Christ, the merits
of which are applied to us in baptism so as to shape us in the
likeness of his being and set us in the path he trod. Little thought
is needed to see that there is no ground for surprise at this statement; it is implicit in the very idea of Christian humanism,
which is humanism on the Cross. Because God calls men to
share his divine life through grace and the infused virtues, he
does not therefore destroy the laws of human nature. We remain
incarnate spirits, and as far as our natural equipment is concerned, we start richer in possibilities for the future than in
actual achievement. This is true both of the soul and of the body.
It explains why man, having intelligence and freedom, is called
upon to achieve his full stature himself, by directing his conscious activity to the end of his being with God's help and the
aid of the supernatural light that filters through his conscience.
But this inward growth is not obtained without difficulty, either
because the conscience is hampered in its judgments by the
more or less anarchical particularism of the desires and passions,
or because man's nature itself is labouring under a hereditary
taint and wounded by original sin, which, though brought to
light by faith, is not eliminated, at any rate where its after-
effects are concerned, by baptism. These truths are at the base
of all forms of Catholic humanism. When the theologians remind us of them they show us two different dimensions. One
appears to be the antithesis of the other but both have a bearing
on the question, as they each throw light on the duties of man
and the necessity for asceticism in all who would follow Christ.
The fact that grace does not destroy nature but makes use of it,
as the mind makes use of the body, shows that humanism in the
moral sphere means the introduction of a spiritual order into
the natural activities of the mind and body. It is therefore
radically different from the more or less platonist conception of
humanism according to which man becomes perfect in so far as
he is freed from dependence on matter. It is equally distinct
from the humanism of the stoics, for insensibility is at least an

integral part of that, if not the ideal. There is an inward continuity between nature and grace, and the whole is subordinated now to a supernatural end, not to a natural one. It can thus sometimes justify renunciation of a kind which the human conscience would not sanction if it had not to reckon with sin and faith.

If this condensed summary is a faithful epitome of the earlier part of the book—a point which can easily be ascertained—the reader will see for himself that a form of asceticism in close correlation with friendship is necessary on three grounds, now that a crucified God has defined it once and for all as a new form of wisdom by giving us an example of it himself and appealing to us to follow it. The first reason for its necessity is to be found in the dialectic of the life of virtue itself. As the virtuous life is based on charity and the act of virtue is simply the subordination of a given means to a supernatural end, it follows that the preference thus implied essentially involves the renunciation of other ties. In this context, to talk about renouncing evil or giving up a relative good if the conscience considers it incompatible with perfection, is to admit that in a sense virtue and asceticism are inseparable. As Valery says with such insight, 'Man is born many; he dies one'.

The second reason for the necessity of asceticism is simply a material or technical prerequisite for the application of the principles just mentioned. The specific function of conscience in the Christian is to bring all free acts under the control of the reason acting at the prompting of charity and in the light shed by faith. As the exercise of this function is thwarted by the selfish desires of the senses and other faculties, it is not surprising that those who are determined to follow Christ should be led to fight against them. The best way to weaken these hotbeds of anarchy is to strike deliberately at the source from which they derive their fuel, viz. everything capable of disturbing self-control either in bodily matters or in spiritual. Measures taken against food, sleep and pleasures thus transform asceticism into a preventive treatment as well as a cure.

Whatever the specific differences between the various states of life may be, it is on these lines that the ultimate explanation of the conduct of those under the vows of religion must be sought. This is the reason for their deliberate sacrifice of the use of certain natural goods, this is why they have given up the right to dispose of their freedom, to procreate and to possess private property. The third reason for Christian asceticism is to be found in that thing which Jew and gentile alike find so mad and scandalous—the Cross. Love presupposes or creates equality. That being so, it is not surprising that those who upset the calculations of human prudence by the response they make to the appeal of God's redeeming love should find a spiritual balance in a closer identification with him who was crucified on Calvary. Catholic asceticism occupies a position midway between two errors: the belief that salvation, i.e. sanctity, is compatible with the laws of the world, and the supposition that perfection varies in direct proportion to the degree in which the human element is eliminated. The history of religion, the story of the saints whose lives can most easily be imitated, bears out the contention that Christian humanism is a balanced thing, with love for its motive-force and end. However, love is a function of generosity, which is a personal quality, since it depends on the free dispositions of divine love; it is perhaps advisable not to look to sociology or ignorance alone for the ultimate explanation of the defiance of prudence discernible in certain forms of sanctity. God is free to call whom he will to what he will, and the imprudence of the saints may be the form of prudence prescribed for them by this transcendent liberty of his.

Now that we have reached the end of this review of the essential data, asceticism stands before us as something still necessary but related to virtue and first and foremost an instrument of love. We also see that the degree of austerity may vary according to personal and social considerations—asceticism as practised by religious is not the same as the asceticism of the laity—and *a fortiori* according to the methods used. The history of Christian asceticism is there to show that there have been variations in spirit and method in the past, and thus that there may legitimately be more in the future. The type of asceticism practised in the patristic age was quite different from the kind followed in the middle ages and at the renaissance. In so far as it is permissible to impose a shape of one's own on a living thing, asceticism seems to have assumed three different forms in succession, according to differences in forms of spirituality and human needs. Thus from being eschatological in the earliest times it became concerned chiefly with the body in the middle ages, and after the sixteenth century it was transformed into a kind of psychological or even cerebral technique. It may be, however, that it was not sufficiently realised in the past that there is as much difference between the various states of life as there is between different forms of the spiritual life itself. The aim the writers of this book set before themselves was to question the wisdom of too literal an application of the common stock of ascetic devices inherited by the religious orders. All of these were probably due to the same intellectual and moral influences —pessimism and contempt for or mistrust of the flesh—or else they sprang from a common ignorance of the impossibility of changing human nature as it is in the concrete. The second group of chapters aims at clearing the ground for a discussion of this problem.

They begin by studying the evidence which shows that a considerable sociological change has been produced by the mere fact that an urban civilisation with a rhythm depending on technical production has been substituted for the old rural civilisation whose rhythm was biological. Among other upheavals which this transformation has brought in its wake is the introduction of a more gregarious way of living, since it is now easier to get to know people and to know greater numbers. Another feature of this development is that through the progress recently made in science we have acquired a deeper knowledge of the subjective world, both in the physiological sphere and in connection with the relations between biology and the psychology of the unconscious and of the conscious—in other words, we now know more about the human person. A third feature very often found today is that this revelation of the life of the ego coincides with an incessant shower of provocation from a host of external stimuli and so leads to the development of pseudo-personalities. These prevent people from getting at their true selves and bring the disturbance in balance up from the physical plane to the moral one.

The man of today is a creature divorced from his own nature.

More and more his body is losing its roots in the earth, his faith its anchorage in God, his mind its hold on being, his conscience its grasp of ultimate values. He may not be at the mercy of his instincts, but he is more and more influenced by environment, class and party. Though this all-pervading materialism is not directly linked with progress in the technical sphere by a causal relationship, it nevertheless favours the development of a form of existence from which periods like night and the weekly day of rest, which nature has provided for refuelling purposes, are missing, and the city is transformed into an autonomous machine, so that as time goes on people will find it more and more difficult to pull themselves together and think for themselves.

This realisation of the revolution that has taken place in our time in the conditions of human life provides food for thought if it is applied to the problem of Christian asceticism. It is impossible to overlook the results which the maintenance of the usual ascetic techniques, both psychological and physical, seems to lead to, now that the centre of gravity has changed both as regards the needs people feel and as regards their capacities.

It will be enough if I mention a few of the signs. The old forms of asceticism were invented with a view to damping the exuberant manifestation of biological tendencies and so reviving the energies of the spirit, which in the rather brutish conditions of rural civilisation were to some extent languishing. Whereas it would seem that for many of our contemporaries the problem is more to know how to cope with over-wrought feelings and satisfy the need they feel for a less superficial existence. That means that anything that involves cutting down food, sleep, etc., does not conduce to this end but favours the unhealthy and unbalanced condition. It is only prudent, too, to ask how far certain methods of humiliation and even certain forms of command are ideal for obtaining obedience in such cases. Showing that one understands the value of the individual or even stressing the role of liberty—things very different from the old educational system, in which the pupil was always kept well in hand and the institutional and objective side was what counted most—is the best way to win confidence and secure the assent of the will.

It may be questioned whether the custom of subjecting all sorts of people to the same ascetic treatment, whatever their age or sex, on the ground that it is the Rule of the Order, is really wise or in keeping with the irreducible originality of the individual vocation.

The moral flabbiness of the day raises more than one problem in connection with the vows. A notable difficulty is that moral maturity now comes later than physical and has been very ill served by the gradual elimination of all effort and pain.

The reader may rest assured that these reservations do not aim at proving that asceticism and the practice of it are undesirable or useless. As we saw above, the necessity of asceticism follows from the very nature of man's end after the fall, and the practice of it is postulated for the same reasons. The essential thing to do is to find a kind of asceticism in harmony with the needs of Christians today, adapted to the novel phenomena just mentioned. The proper method and means in asceticism cannot be imposed from above; they will be discovered by taking account of the requirements of faith and human nature on the one hand and of the data provided by history on the other. Otherwise the result will be catastrophe or the sort of hypocrisy that professes to observe a Rule and in fact does not.

It is for religious communities to try out the new methods in so far as they are in harmony with the Church, who has the last word on the question. It must be remembered that in this sphere, as in spirituality and theology, progress cannot go counter to Tradition. But Tradition is not to be identified with any of the particular traditions of which it is composed. These particular traditions stand to the real thing as habit does to virtue or routine to life.

It now remains to suggest the spirit in which asceticism should be envisaged and the lines on which it should be applied.

The great difficulty confronting our times is not that the developments mentioned above are in danger of making pain and suffering unbearable and thus of making asceticism unacceptable. Doctors have shown that the opposite is the truth: pain can be good and suffering wholesome, and they should be accepted all the more readily now that science is capable of eliminating them, because they foster manliness. Neither is the difficulty that as progress in the technical sphere has increased man's power tenfold it has taken away the need for renunciation. Now more than ever, as the preceding chapters show so clearly, do the essential requirements of the spiritual life demand that the ego, which has gone astray after 'diversions' in Pascal's sense of the word, should be brought back under control. No, the difficulty lies in the fact that the practice of virtue—the positive side of asceticism and *a fortiori* of the various forms of ascetic discipline inspired by it—postulates a world that is human in its ideals and structures, a world, that is to say, very different from this world of ours in which man tends to become spiritually a plaything and professionally an automaton. The capacities of asceticism, like the capacities of the moral life, are coming to be conditioned more and more by the historical situation man finds himself in, so much so that they are partly determined by it. The inference is that Christians in touch with the world will be able to meet the demands for suffering made on them by their ideal of religious perfection only in so far as an attempt is made to remodel civilisation and make it fit man's needs, so that it does not run counter to his biological rhythms, his spiritual character or the call he receives through faith and his own conscience to pass beyond his natural limits to something higher.

If these preliminaries are accepted as showing the scope of the question, it would seem in the light of what we have said (at any rate where the essentials of asceticism are concerned, the elements affecting all Christians, both clerical and lay) that effort could most profitably be directed first and foremost to all that positively promotes perfection. This being so, what we must put first is not respect for methods in themselves, even if they are traditional, but the acquisition of physical and psychological balance, which is normally the essential condition for moral health. The salvation of nature's incurable failures may safely be left to God, but asceticism should not be exposed to the danger of producing them: nothing sound can be built on a rotten foundation. Inevitably, when this is the immediate end in view, it will bring an individual note into the use of ascetic techniques. But that is only preliminary to the main thing. Taking into account the needs of men today, the best way to cultivate the spirit of renunciation which the gospels declare to be essential, seems to be to make religion more and more personal, to put more and more thought into it and to persevere in the attempt to subject the whole of the inner life to firm discipline. As the things most unfavourable to the inner life are the insistent presence of an environment tending all the time towards materialism in thought and action, the cult of the self, failure to distinguish between sincerity and truth, fickleness of character and hypersensitiveness of the nerves, these are the points against which the ascetic campaign should be directed. As the world is threatened by herd-instinct and the pursuit of action for action's sake, these must be countered by the building of individual worlds of recollection and silence so as to allow of thought and prayer, for, as Lacordaire says, silence is the homeland of the strong. Material practices should be increased or not according to their ability to conduce to this end, unless it is quite evident that there is a vocation to the victim-life—a matter, however, about which experience and psychiatry show that only too often there is more illusion than mysticism—for prudence ought always to reign supreme, in the asceticism that is obligatory just as much as in the optional kind. Christian humanism ought to make its first aim the establishment of the reign of the spirit over the whole of life, in order to ensure the reign of divine Love. Asceticism cannot take as its goal either insensibility or the extinction of biological factors which have a real value of their own. In its technical application it ought to be like a medical treatment, either preventative or curative as the case may be and resorted to only in so far as it is essential to health, i.e. to holiness. That no doubt means that except where God steps in and calls someone to be a co-redeemer with him, renunciation will never cease to be necessary until this earthly life is over, but also that if it is to fulfil its function it must keep all its relativity and therefore be adaptable to the needs of human beings as they vary in time and space. The purpose of Calvary was not the death of Christ but his resurrection, and the purpose of asceticism is not to annihilate life but to increase it, to further the life of grace and the life of rational nature as well. In God's plan, hope goes with fidelity to the law of love, love on the Cross, which is the light and measure of all sanctity.